D0152582

Bill

06/11/08

BORROWED SOLDIERS
AMERICANS UNDER BRITISH COMMAND, 1918

With much appreciation for your interest in the First World War.

Mitchell A. Yockelson

Foreword by John S. D. Eisenhower

University of Oklahoma Press : Norman

Library of Congress Cataloging-in-Publication Data

Yockelson, Mitchell A., 1962–
   Borrowed soldiers : Americans under British command, 1918 / Mitchell A.
Yockelson ; foreword by John S.D. Eisenhower.
      p.   cm. — (Campaigns and commanders ; v. 17)
   Includes bibliographical references and index.
   ISBN-13: 978-0-8061-3919-7 (hbk. : alk. paper)
   1. United States. Army. Corps, 2nd. 2. Great Britain. Army. Army, 4th.
3. World War, 1914–1918—Regimental histories—United States. 4. World
War, 1914–1918—Campaigns—France. 5. World War, 1914–1918—Cam-
paigns—Belgium. I. Title.
   D570.274th .Y63 2008
   940.4'1273—dc22
                                                                2007037264

Borrowed Soldiers: Americans under British Command, 1918 is Volume 17
in the Campaigns and Commanders series.

The paper in this book meets the guidelines for permanence and durability
of the Committee on Production Guidelines for Book Longevity of the
Council on Library Resources, Inc. ∞

Copyright © 2008 by Mitchell A. Yockelson. Published by the University
of Oklahoma Press, Norman, Publishing Division of the University. Manu-
factured in the U.S.A.

All rights reserved. No part of this publication may be reproduced, stored in
a retrieval system, or transmitted, in any form or by any means, electronic,
mechanical, photocopying, recording, or otherwise—except as permitted
under Section 107 or 108 of the United States Copyright Act—without the
prior permission of the University of Oklahoma Press.

1 2 3 4 5 6 7 8 9 10

CONTENTS

ILLUSTRATIONS

Maps

FOREWORD

JOHN S. D. EISENHOWER

Some years ago, I was serving as American ambassador to Belgium. On every May 30, Memorial Day, I spoke at the three American cemeteries located in that country. It was a solemn duty, and the ceremonies always touched me. One aspect, however, gave me pause. I was comfortable while speaking at Henri-Chapelle and Nouvelle-en-Condroz, in Eastern Belgium, because those gigantic establishments held the dead from the Second World War, with which I was quite familiar. By contrast, I was less assured when speaking at the six-acre cemetery of Waregem, near Ypres, where lay the American dead from the First World War. I felt my lack of background when giving honor to the dead of the First World War.

In retrospect, I regret that I did not look further into the circumstances under which those young Americans made their last sacrifice. I also regret to say that my ignorance was far from unique. It was shared by too many Americans, even those of us who have written about other aspects of the First World War. Mitch Yockelson, in this volume, is doing his part to rectify that deficiency in our knowledge. In so doing he has produced a book full of facts that anyone with an interest in things military will find of tremendous significance. Its thorough research requires the talents and training that Mr. Yockelson possesses. We are all the beneficiaries of his efforts.

The soldiers who rest in the Waregem Cemetery came mostly from two divisions, Maj. Gen. John F. O'Ryan's 27th Division and Maj. Gen. Edward M. Lewis's 30th. Together they comprised the American II Corps, the only major American formation attached to Field Marshal Sir Douglas Haig's British Expeditionary Force. Its assignment had come about as the result of a compromise between the American commander, Gen. John J. Pershing, and Haig. Pershing was exerting every effort to keep all American divisions in France concentrated under his personal command in the American First Army at St. Mihiel and in the valley of the Meuse-Argonne. The assignment of II Corps to the British, therefore, represented at least a partial defeat for American policies.

The men of II Corps underwent a unique experience. Both the 27th and the 30th Divisions came into the war relatively late, in August of 1918. After some action at the Lys Salient in the Ypres region, where they learned the basic techniques of modern war, they were assigned as the main effort of the British General Sir Henry Rawlinson's Fourth Army, whose job it was, in the Allies' last great offensive, to pierce the western end of the vaunted Hindenburg Line. The reason for the use of the corps in that role is readily understandable. Even though below strength by table of organization, each American division was twice the strength of its British counterpart and four times the strength of its German counterpart. More important, perhaps, is the fact that the American troops were relatively fresh, as had been the first British, French, and German troops in 1914. They had not yet been ground down. Their élan would make a great deal of difference.

Borrowed Soldiers contains much material in addition to the account of II Corps' actions in Flanders and the Somme. One of the areas of interest involves little-known material on the National Guard. In some ways, the National Guard underwent a more difficult ordeal than either the Regulars or, later, the National Army. In the early stages of American involvement in the war, the Regulars unabashedly favored their own component over the Guardsmen, a situation that has prevailed throughout American history. When some National Guard units, such as the 27th, were called into active service on the Mexican border back in 1916, many of the troops were forced to sweat under heavy wool uniforms in heat over 110 degrees. In the United States, the Guardsmen were housed in tent cities, whereas the Regulars (and later the National Army) lived in barracks. There were practical reasons why this happened, but it is a fact worth noting.

This early description of the National Guard, however interesting, does not constitute the main thrust of *Borrowed Soldiers*. Its principal interest lies in its comparison of the lot of the II Corps, serving with the British, as contrasted with those American troops of the First Army, who fought at St. Mihiel and in the Meuse-Argonne. That comparison leads to a broader question: Was Pershing correct in doing everything possible to keep the Americans together rather than "amalgamate" more of his divisions with British and French formations?

It is here that *Borrowed Soldiers* provides food for thought. I, for one, have never questioned the wisdom of President Wilson, with the enthusiastic support of Pershing, of keeping an American Army as such on the western front. The organization of a strictly American army, comparable to those of Britain and France, was necessary for American morale at home and as a card for President Wilson to play in the peace negotiations that followed the war. Yet it seems that once such a formation was established and recognized, additional arriving American divisions might well have been advantageously assigned to the French and British.

For the fact is that in some ways the 27th and 30th Divisions of II Corps enjoyed advantages over their counterparts in the First Army. They were, surprisingly, better fed by the British than were their American counterparts at St. Mihiel and in the Meuse-Argonne. Though the disagreeable fact has not been publicized, the men of the First Army were often poorly fed. Almost all the American supply lines relied on railways from the Bordeaux area on France's southwest coast to Verdun. They were long, and their carrying capacity was limited. These facts forced Pershing to make a choice between delivering food or delivering ammunition during periods of heavy fighting. Ammunition, of course, had to take priority; the men sometimes had to go on iron rations. In contrast, the British supply lines running between the English Channel and Ypres were short and organized; the British were never in short supply of food.

More important than supply, however, was the matter of learning the life-saving techniques of modern war, of which the British were masters and the Americans tyros. After their initial indoctrination around Ypres, the men of the II Corps, as noted above, became the main effort of the British Fourth Army striving to penetrate the Hindenburg Line. Contrary to strict orders from Pershing, Maj. Gen. George W. Read, commanding the corps, relied so heavily on Gen. Sir John Monash, in command of the Australian Corps, that he practically turned over command of his divisions to Monash, his subordinate commanders, and his staff officers. Read's courage in swallowing his pride saved the lives of many of his men. In his reports he cloaked his actions in ambiguous terms, thus avoiding censure from Pershing for doing so. Other American divisions could have attained similar benefits.

It is noteworthy, as an aside, that the unit that Read treated with such deference was Australian rather than British. It is questionable whether he would have done the same with a British division, because antagonism between the Americans, who still tended to view the British as "redcoats," and the British, who viewed the Americans as "colonists," was often strong. No such animosity existed between two nations that had both been colonized by Britain but had each become separate nations in their own right.

The author has very wisely chosen not to take sides in the question of whether more amalgamation of American formations into larger British units would have been desirable. He does, however, provide us with many quotes from British and Americans about the qualities of their counterparts, their brothers in arms. Without making arbitrary judgments, Yockelson has brought to light material too long neglected by most students of the First World War. His painstaking research makes fascinating reading for anyone who wants to know the real facts about America's first modern foreign war.

PREFACE

When darkness fell in New York City on the evening of 24 March 1919, eager crowds massed on both sides of the famed Fifth Avenue, anxious to witness the largest parade in the city's history: the welcoming home of the 27th Division. The spectators began arriving fifteen hours before the procession was to commence, and they kept coming into the night, even though there was little room on the packed sidewalks. It was later estimated that a million people witnessed the parade, but no one knows for sure. Viewing stands had been reserved well in advance, so the majority had to stand shoulder to shoulder on the hard concrete sidewalks. Many in the crowd clutched small Stars and Stripes, while larger flags waved from shop windows that also displayed red, white, and blue bunting. During the preceding days, banquets had been held with famous actors and actresses. The mayor and city council spared no expense.

From Washington Square, the starting point of the parade, Maj. Gen. John F. O'Ryan and his battle-hardened New Yorkers marched together for the last time on a route more than five miles long. His unit had just spent 363 days overseas, mostly in the shell-pocked trenches of Belgium and France. In May 1918, the division, at slightly less than 28,000 strong, had paraded up the same avenue before departing overseas. Now, almost a year later, the division had a third fewer officers and men. Disease, such as a deadly influenza epidemic, had certainly taken a toll, but modern technology's latest weaponry had claimed many of the 1,800 New Yorkers who did not return home in the spring of 1919. German artillery shells and machine-gun fire had made sure of that.

Hundreds of miles to the south in North Carolina, South Carolina, and Tennessee, from which the nucleus of the 30th Division had come, celebrations on a smaller scale took place. During the latter part of March and the first week of April, banquets, barbecues, baseball games, dances, parades, and parties were organized in Chattanooga, Columbia, Raleigh, Nashville, and Knoxville—southern hospitality in appreciation of the heroes who had served in the Great War. These celebrations were somber. Too many young officers and men were not there to take part in the festivities. The 30th had also lost heavily overseas—about 1,700. They were National Guardsmen, who previously had gathered once a month in local armories to drill and swap stories but would now be remembered with white crosses and plaques in American cemeteries. The 27th and 30th divisions were unique in that they were as much a part of the British Army as the American. Newspapers covered the welcome-home celebrations in great detail. Some published special issues to commemorate the events and exploits of the divisions.

Despite the unique relationship between the American Expeditionary Forces (AEF)[1] divisions serving with the British Expeditionary Force (BEF) in 1918, their alliance is mostly forgotten. Although the commander-in-chief of the AEF, Gen. John J. Pershing, rejected demands for full-scale amalgamation by correctly insisting upon an independent army, two of his divisions, the 27th and 30th, spent their entire service on the Western Front with the British Army. These borrowed soldiers were among the ten AEF divisions (the others were the 4th, 28th, 33rd, 35th, 77th, 78th, 80th, and 82nd) sent by Pershing to the British sector for training.[2] He insisted upon maintaining administrative control of the units and organized them into the American II Corps. Still, the British, and Field Marshal Sir Douglas Haig, the BEF commander on the Western Front, did much to make them their own. They supervised the training of their English-speaking comrades, transported them overseas, and, more often than not, provided them with the necessary equipment, arms, and food.

In the rear areas of Belgium and France, the British Tommies[3] took the American doughboys[4] under their wing when they arrived in June 1918. They did not immediately bond. There were cultural differences to contend with and the obvious confusion over the use of the common language. The inexperienced Americans also showed little sensitivity about the hardships and sacrifices already made by the veteran British soldiers, whose exhaustion from battle contrasted with the eagerness and high spirits displayed by the fresh-faced Yanks.[5] Regardless of the differences, the Americans and the British fought together to achieve a common goal, the defeat of the German army. The British prime minister, David Lloyd George, enthusiastically proclaimed the two Allies "brothers in arms."[6] Together, the BEF and the two attached AEF divisions attacked the German Hindenburg Line on 29 September 1918 during the Hundred Days Campaign and, the following month, pursued the German forces to the Selle River. This was a defining moment for both armies, as this offensive hastened the end of the war.

From the training camps of South Carolina to the bloody battlefields of Belgium and France, the 27th and 30th Divisions are viewed through the eyes of their members and those who knew them best. Along with quotes from the letters and diaries of regular soldiers, this book also follows the trials and tribulations of the commanding officers. Among them is O'Ryan. He had the distinction of being the only National Guardsman to lead a division throughout the war and afterward authored one of the best unit histories ever written. There is Col. George S. Simonds, the chief of staff and architect of II Corps. He is the one officer who truly understood the unique Anglo-American relationship. Col. Joseph Hyde Pratt, commanded an engineer regiment in the 30th Division and compiled a diary that provides a keen perspective from the field level. From the British viewpoint, the diaries and letters of Haig and senior officers such as Gen. Sir Henry Rawlinson, Gen. Sir John Monash, and Gen. Sir Charles Bonham-Carter present another viewpoint on the relationship. Their words are used along with the rich resources held in archives throughout the United States, the United Kingdom, Australia, and France. Such documentation brings to life the experience of the borrowed soldiers. This is their story.

ACKNOWLEDGMENTS

Borrowed Soldiers originated as a Ph.D. dissertation under the direction of Richard Holmes at the Royal Military College of Science, Cranfield University, Shrivenham, United Kingdom. I am grateful for Richard's thorough supervision and encouragement, as well as the assistance of Chris Bellamy, Steph Muir, and Susan Truesdale, also at Shrivenham. Along the way, friends such as Jim Beach and Peter Simkins read my early chapters and offered much-needed advice. John Bourne, Paddy Griffith, and Gary Sheffield patiently answered my long-distance questions. My research overseas included many trips to the Imperial War Museum, where Anthony Richards provided invaluable assistance. I was also welcomed at the National Army Museum, the National Archives (Public Records Office), the National Library of Scotland, the Liddle Hart Centre for Military Archives, The Kings Consort Library, The Churchill Archives Centre, and numerous other repositories.

At Sandhurst, Chris Pugsley and Paul Harris commented on early drafts of my work, invited me to address the faculty, and escorted me to France, where we walked the battlefields of American II Corps. In Australia, historians Peter Pederson, Robin Prior, and Elizabeth Greenhalgh provided warm friendship and sound advice. The research room staff at the Australian War Memorial responded to almost three weeks of constant requests with amazing efficiency. My research in France was assisted by Craig Rahanian and Murielle Defrenne at the American Battle Monuments Commission's Somme Cemetery. Through them I met Thérèse Martin, who uncovered a treasure trove of documentation on the Americans at Bellicourt, Bony, and surrounding areas and provided copies of her research. Such information helped bring this aspect of the story to life. Chris Sims at Flanders Field Cemetery was also helpful in providing information on that site. The staff of the Historial de la Grande Guerre in Peronne generously invited me to talk at their museum on the anniversary of the Hindenburg Line attack.

In the United States, many archives, museums, and libraries aided in my research. I am especially appreciative for the assistance offered by Dick Sommers, Louise Arnold-Friend, and David Keogh at the U.S. Army Military History Institute. Si Harrington and Jackson Marshall advised me about the collections at the North Carolina State Archives and Museum. Michael Aikey at the New York State Military Museum made sure his staff accommodated me. The Library of Congress, Tennessee State Library and Archives, the East Tennessee Historical Society, and many other repositories proved to be great places to research. The U.S. Army Center of Military History made my trip to Australia possible through a generous dissertation fellowship.

At the National Archives and Records Administration (NARA), where I have had the pleasure of working for twenty years, the story that became *Borrowed Soldiers* developed. Tim Nenninger, who over the years has been a friend, boss, and mentor, first helped me to conceive the idea of writing about the 27th and 30th Divisions. For this reason I owe him much gratitude. Numerous colleagues provided unsolicited encouragement, research assistance, and other help. They include Cindi Fox, Juliet Arai, Wil Mahoney, Richard Boylan, Judy Koucky, Jodi Foor, Rick Peuser, Trevor Plante, Kate Flaherty, Susan Francis-Haughton, Holly Reed, Maria Albanese, Jeff Hartley, Michael Lingenfelter, Kate Mollan, Mark Mollan, Pat Osborne, Sam Anthony, and many, many others. More recently I entered another phase at NARA with a position at its Inspector General's Office to hunt down document thieves. Here I have been fortunate to know Paul Brachfeld, Tom Bennett, Kelly Maltagliati, Matt Elliott, Rachel Wilson, Ross Weiland, and the staff in Room 1300.

First World War historians are a relatively small group, and I am lucky to be acquainted with many of them and have the benefit of their immense knowledge of the 1914–1918 period. They include Dale Blair, Jonathan Brooke, Jennifer Keene, Carol Byerly, Roger Cirillo, Tom Bowers, Jeff Sammons, Christy Leskovar, Mac Coffman, Steve Harris, Mark Whisler, and John S. D. Eisenhower, whose own books have been a great influence on my study. Lisa M. Budreau was there to help with her expertise on the commemoration of the war in the early stages of the dissertation and then the book. Robert H. Ferrell has provided scholarly support through his knowledge of history and warm personality. Ann Ferrar introduced me to Elsie Janis, and Steve Harris shared his wisdom and his newspaper articles on the 27th Division with me.

Many other historians came forward to assist in various stages of the research and writing, especially Doug Walker, Walter Bradford, Ed Slagle, Ben Byrnes, Jeff Sammons, Matt Seelinger, Henry Mintz, Jim Hurst, Tom Fleming, and Rick Atkinson.

The University of Oklahoma Press was an early supporter of this book, and I appreciate the help of Chuck Rankin, Jay Dew, Christi Madden, and others on the staff who helped make the project come together. Greg Urwin, the editor of the Campaigns and Commanders series, was also an early advocate of this book. Beyond Oklahoma, Liz Coelho worked hard on the indexing and Chris Robinson used his cartographic skills to produce the first-rate maps. Joan Maresca took the time to read the manuscript at the last minute and caught many errors. Thank you to all.

A special debt of gratitude goes out to Stacy Moran. During the writing of the dissertation she was there to turn it around with skillful editing. She came through once again with the manuscript and did so with enthusiasm for the story and a firm grasp of the red pen. She saved me from embarrassment and made it a better book. For this I will always be grateful.

I am also lucky to have the long-term friendships of Ken Markovitz and Richard Sloop. And of course my family—my mom and dad, and brothers, Gary and Rick. They have nurtured my interest in history for over four decades. Thank you for your love and support.

Despite all of this wonderful assistance and support, any errors and faulty conclusions are my own.

Borrowed Soldiers

1

ORGANIZING AN ARMY

When the 27th and 30th Divisions entered the British line in the summer of 1918, they were a far cry from the officers and men who had marched off to training camps after the United States entered the war. Like other divisions of the American Expeditionary Forces (AEF), they had developed into the effective fighting units that helped turned the tide for the Allies. Yet when President Woodrow Wilson committed his country to the conflict overseas on 6 April 1917, it was hard to imagine just how big a role the American army would play. At the time there were no organized divisions and the Regular Army numbered a paltry 5,791 officers and 121,707 enlisted men. Wilson relied upon the National Guard to strengthen the forces. Three months after the declaration of war, he called them up, and this added 110,000 officers and men. Even with the National Guard and the tens of thousands of young men who enlisted at the outset, the army was still under strength and needed to turn to conscription.[1] Since August 1914, the Western Front in France had already consumed hundreds of thousands of young men; the armies of the Allies and Central Powers were comprised of millions from each contributing nation. After three years, the war in Europe was complex.

It was breathtaking in its detailed ways of fighting and in the equipment required to fight effectively.[2]

To do its part, the U.S. government registered all male citizens and resident aliens from ages 21 to 30 (later extended to 35) under the Selective Service Act of 3 May 1917. More than 24 million men registered; over 2 million were inducted.[3] This legislation also gave Wilson the authority to mobilize the National Guard, the second time in a year he had called it into federal service. The first was in June 1916, when he sent National Guard units to the Mexican border during the punitive expedition against Pancho Villa. The 110,000 National Guard troops sent to the southwestern United States (Texas, Arizona, and New Mexico) were by many accounts ineffective. They arrived under strength, poorly trained, and lacking equipment and arms. Some units had only wool uniforms and sweltered in the heat of the region, which sometimes reached 110 degrees Fahrenheit. One unhappy National Guardsman called the environment "the most forsaken country the Lord ever made." Furthermore, he said, "we ought to clean up Mexico, and, for punishment, make them take back this part of Texas."[4]

Expecting to participate in the chase of Villa, the National Guardsmen instead fought the brutal heat and annoying scorpions while drilling and marching on long-distance maneuvers. The War Department had no intention of sending the National Guard into Mexico to join Brig. Gen. John J. Pershing and the Regulars.[5] For five months, it served as a police force under the watchful eye of the General Staff, whose officers barely respected for the state troops and considered them more of a liability than an asset. "It is a pity the militia could not have been called out two months ago," the disgusted Pershing wrote, "so that its hopeless deficiencies might have been shown up to Congress in their true light. To attempt to put dependence upon the militia is absolutely absurd and ridiculous."[6]

Such animosity toward the militia goes back at least to the Spanish-American War, when some state units irritated the Regular Army by reporting to camps grossly unprepared. As a result, only a few went overseas. Despite its conflict with the Regulars, the militia had a long military tradition that dated to the colonial period, when they were called to put down uprisings by Native American groups. During the Civil War, militia units fought alongside regular volunteer regiments in both the Union and Confederate armies. Afterward, the militia served mainly in police duty against strikers. Governors called upon the state units 700 times to preserve order in industrial disputes during the period 1877 to 1903.[7]

But the militia saw itself as more than a law enforcement agency and sought to increase the size of units and evolve as a volunteer reserve. To do so would require money from the federal government. The War Department was willing to oblige but wanted tighter control before it would relinquish funds. State militia units wanted the federal aid, but they also wanted the authority to select their officers and set the size of regiments. It was no surprise that the War Department's General Staff refused and insisted that the states comply with Regular Army tables of organization.[8] This meant balanced divisions of infantry, cavalry, artillery, and auxiliary units.[9]

The impasse was resolved with the passage of the Dick Act in 1903. Named for Congressman Charles W. Dick of Ohio, the chief creator of the legislation, the law established the Division of Militia Affairs (Militia Bureau) as a branch of the General Staff. Among its provisions were increased funds for the militia and federal pay when the militia participated in maneuvers with the Regular Army. It also attempted to standardize requirements for state officers.[10] The most noteworthy components of this law were the designation of the organized militia as the National Guard and the requirement that its officers meet more stringent obligations. Despite the best efforts of the Militia Bureau, a tug of war existed between the National Guard and the War Department. Not until another congressional intervention, the National Defense Act of 1916, was the War Department able to force the National Guard to comply with its mandates.[11]

This act ensured that the National Guard would be the country's main reserve force. The law specified that 400,000 men would be raised over an unspecified number of years and that the U.S. government provide financial support. The law was not one-sided; National Guardsmen had to take a dual oath upon enlistment. They were in the service of the U.S. Army and the state National Guard. As one historian summarized this complicated legislation: It "settled the issue of War Department authority to organize the National Guard according to General Staff dictates, and, at the same time, the National Guardsmen lost the ability to shape their units or select officers according to their own interests, while the Secretary of War could refuse federal funds if states failed to comply with the law."[12]

All of this left bad feelings between the National Guard and the Regulars, and this was one of the reasons why the state units were excluded from the action in Mexico. One National Guard formation did catch the attention of the Regulars along the border—Maj. Gen. John F. O'Ryan's 19,000-strong 6th New York Division. Stationed in McAllen, Texas, from 6 July to 14 December 1916, it was the only National Guard division on the border. The 6th Division's thorough training and professional demeanor ranked it with the best units of the Regular Army. O'Ryan's division included members of New York City's most prominent families, who served alongside farmers and laborers from the more remote northern and central areas. Despite their contrasting economic backgrounds, the men bonded well. O'Ryan made sure that lack of discipline was rarely an issue. He busied his men with constant training and physical fitness, and they had little time to slack.

Lt. Gen. Robert Lee Bullard, later an AEF divisional and army commander, met O'Ryan on the Mexican border and was enormously impressed. A "trim, well-proportioned athletic man," remembered Bullard, "who was supple, springy, and energetic in his movement, punctiliously neat, and up to the mark in his dress and personal appearance."[13] During a second encounter in 1917, Bullard observed "from the training period at Spartanburg, South Carolina, O'Ryan's thoughts seemed turned very much upon his men . . . and this feeling of comradeship continued and grew. O'Ryan held himself approachable to his men, showed himself ever thoughtful of them, not only for their comfort, supply and training, but for their personal interests."[14]

O'Ryan proved unusual among National Guard commanders. At an early age, he had prepared himself for a career as an army officer. Allegedly, he signed some of his schoolbooks "John F. O'Ryan, Major General, U.S. Army."[15] Although he attended law school, his first love was always the military. In 1899, O'Ryan accepted a commission in the New York militia. Former Rough Riders Theodore Roosevelt and Leonard Wood were among his admirers and helped him rise through the ranks and catch the eye of the War Department in Washington.[16] Wood nominated him for the Army War College, which O'Ryan attended in 1914, and, in subsequent years, he participated in Regular Army camps and maneuvers, something unheard of for a National Guard officer. Also in 1914, he published his first book, *The Modern Army in Action*, which warned of the dangers of military unpreparedness. O'Ryan foresaw the National Guard's significance in future conflicts.

He was also sensitive to the animosity the Regulars had toward the National Guard. While in Texas, O'Ryan was shown an unflattering newspaper article that quoted three unnamed Regular officers as saying the militia was "little better than 'Kitchener's Mob.'" O'Ryan fired back with a letter berating the editor for "the hostile matter that is being circulated by the press . . . a willful attempt to discredit the service." He bolstered his letter with statistics revealing the infrequency of venereal disease among his troops and bragged that they had the lowest rate of illness of the troops on the border.[17]

Conflict between the Regulars and the state units notwithstanding, the National Guard was a necessary and vital component of the newly formed AEF. Eventually one-third of the divisions serving overseas were National Guard. Still, the War Department was ill prepared for these units. To ease the problem, the National Guard was mobilized in two increments. The first call-up, on 25 July, affected units in eleven states, and the remaining units were mobilized more than a week later. Among those called up in the first wave were regiments from New York, Tennessee, and North and South Carolina.[18]

Because of a lack of training camps, it was three months before National Guard units could begin training as part of the army. To keep state regiments busy and out of trouble until the camps were ready for occupancy, the president ordered that they safeguard vital bridges, waterways, and munitions factories susceptible to sabotage.[19] The main reason that training was delayed was that the Quartermaster Corps, the War Department agency charged with constructing and supplying the camps, was woefully unprepared. It had not learned from the Spanish-American War in 1898, when the army had too few ships to transport troops to Cuba and sent many of those that did go to the hot and humid Caribbean in wool uniforms. Nineteen years later, the agency was again under strength and lacked the funds to contend with a rapidly expanding army. The Quartermaster Corps simply did not have the resources to construct the cantonments for the National Guard units. So the agency created the Cantonment

Division, and with the assistance of an advisory organization, the Committee on Emergency Construction, its board selected 1 September 1917 as the target date to have camps ready.[20] Adding to its troubles, the Quartermaster Corps did not have enough clothing for the troops. Blame was placed on the General Staff for failing to provide troop schedules so that sufficient uniforms and supplies could be on hand. The situation was remedied when factories in the eastern United States worked around the clock to reach the quotas. Still, many troops had to wait weeks before they were issued uniforms.[21]

2

WANTED: AMERICAN TROOPS

Three thousand miles across the Atlantic Ocean, the British government observed the growing pains of the U.S. military, the same process its own army had gone through over the previous three years. In 1914, the British Army entered the war with a small standing force of 247,432 that was supplemented by 300,000 reserves and territorial units.[1] In January 1916, the British government introduced conscription with the Military Service Act. Unmarried men from 18 to 41 were required to register, and in May 1917, the act was amended to include married men. In April 1918, a second Military Service Act raised the age limit to 50. The drafted troops were necessary to supplement a successful volunteer enlistment campaign organized by Secretary of State for War Field Marshal Lord Kitchener. Over 54 million recruiting posters were distributed throughout Great Britain, and by 1916, over 2 million men had volunteered for military service in "Kitchener's Army."[2]

Once the U.S. declared war, the British War Office was eager to convince the Americans to send troops to the British Expeditionary Force (BEF). The British Army General Staff addressed this issue when they drew up plans for 1917. American troops "could best be employed with the British Armies," they determined, "and so fight with men of the same language and temperament."[3]

Maj. Gen. Tom Bridges, who traveled to Washington with Sir Arthur Balfour's British mission as its military representative, hoped to out-flank the French representatives who were pressuring the White House to amalgamate American troops into their army. Bridges told U.S. Army Chief of Staff Maj. Gen. Hugh Scott, "If you ask me how your force could most quickly make itself felt in Europe, I would say by sending 500,000 untrained men at once to our depots in England to be trained there, and drafted into our armies in France."[4]

Although Scott's response is unknown, it is likely that Bridge's suggestion was ignored. John J. Pershing, now a major general, was the newly appointed commander of the AEF and had been given orders from President Wilson and Secretary of War Newton D. Baker that his troops would fight independently.[5] "It was necessary at all times to preserve the independence and identity of the American forces," Baker said, "so that they could never be anything but an instrument of the policy of the United States."[6] Initially, the Allies sought only munitions from the United States. But as the war dragged on and casualties increased, the Allies' need for manpower grew.[7]

On the Western Front, the British and French were in the midst of a new series of offensives, and if they echoed the previous campaigns of the Somme and Verdun, both armies would suffer heavy losses. Planning for the campaign took place during meetings between Allied political and military leaders even as the costly Somme campaign was winding down. A Franco-British offensive would occur on a broad front, the Allied commanders concluded, with the French attacking between the Oise and Somme rivers. At the same time, the British would operate between Bapaume and Vimy Ridge. The plans changed a short time later when French Commander-in-Chief Gen. Robert Nivelle, who had replaced Marshal Joseph Joffre, suggested an alternative plan. Nivelle wanted the British and French to carry out preliminary attacks between Arras and the Oise River to lure the German reserves from the main French attack on the Aisne River. Field Marshal Haig, commander of the BEF, wanted a Flanders operation, but the British War Cabinet intervened and ordered him to accept Nivelle's plan. Nivelle reduced the BEF to a supporting role and appeased Haig by telling him that a Flanders attack would be next if the French plan lived up to expectations.

Haig's reluctance to serve as Nivelle's subordinate echoed the uneasy coalition between France and Britain. Politically, the two European powers were longstanding rivals, a point touched upon during a private conversation between Maj. Paul Clark, the AEF liaison to French headquarters, and Captain LeBleu, a secretary at French general headquarters. The latter revealed that France had "the least affection for the Germans, and after them, for the English." Although LeBleu appreciated the excellence and magnitude of the British effort, he reminded Clark that they had been "traditional enemies throughout the last several centuries . . . and [that] the British have always worsted the French in diplomatic negotiations."[8] Of course, LeBleu exaggerated his country's relationship with Great Britain, but the tension between Haig and Nivelle was real.

A severe winter in 1917 delayed the campaign until spring. This proved costly since the German army, ignoring the harsh conditions, started withdrawing troops to a new defensive position, the Hindenburg Line, which extended from east of Arras to east of Soissons, in mid-February and completed their retirement in early April. Haig, exhibiting keen military logic, was concerned that the Germans would take advantage of the shift of his divisions to Nivelle's offensive and use their reserves to attack Ypres and cut off the BEF's communications with the Channel coast.[9] Instead, the Germans stayed on the defensive in France but launched a major attack against Russia on the Eastern Front during most of 1917. On 9 April, the British Army commenced preliminary operations at Arras with a five-day artillery barrage that preceded an attack on a fourteen-mile front. By the close of the first day, the Canadian Corps, with four divisions, had taken Vimy Ridge.

At the end of May 1917, while the death toll mounted on the Western Front, Pershing and a small contingent of hand-picked officers departed from New York harbor for Europe. Pershing would not return to America for two years. Among the 58 officers and 131 clerks, translators, and orderlies sailing with him on the *Baltic* were future generals—Fox Connor, Hugh Drum, George Patton, and James Harbord. Two weeks later, the party and its navy escort reached Liverpool,

England. There, Pershing boarded King George V's private railway carriage and traveled to London for lunch at Buckingham Palace and to meet Prime Minister Lloyd George and Chief of the Imperial General Staff (CIGS) Gen. Sir William "Wully" Robertson. Pershing liked Robertson from the start, whom he described as a "rugged, heavy-set, blunt soldier of Scottish descent."[10]

The CIGS wasted little time in explaining Britain's proposal for amalgamating U.S. troops into its army. Pershing listened patiently as Robertson detailed how the British army could establish a training, procurement, equipment, and logistical infrastructure and have Americans ready to fight in nine weeks, as opposed to the eighteen months it would take to organize the U.S. Army into a separate force. While Robertson sipped tea, Pershing quietly responded with the American plan to establish an independent army. He compared the U.S. government's attempt to increase its small Regular Army force and National Guard with new enlistments and conscripts to Britain's expansion effort two years before. What he did not tell Robertson was that President Wilson feared that American influence at peace negotiations would be diminished unless his army provided its own expeditionary force, a motive Robertson and Allied leaders already suspected.[11]

Pershing did admit to one stumbling block to bringing troops to Europe—a lack of shipping—and suggested that the British help out. Robertson said no because his government was struggling to find vessels to suit its own purposes. He was referring to the German U-boat menace of unrestricted submarine warfare that had cost Britain 520,000 tons of shipping in March and another 860,000 tons the following month.[12]

Although he understood Robertson's dilemma, Pershing would not back down. Now both sides were in a stalemate regarding amalgamation and would remain so for months.[13] Pershing left the meeting for France, where he established headquarters in the Hotel de Crillon in Paris.[14] There he began the first step in creating the American Expeditionary Forces by appointing staff officers. Pershing was now a commander with only a token division, since the National Guard and Regular Army men were just beginning training that could take at least nine months.

Meanwhile, as Pershing settled in to his new command, the British Third Army was heavily engaged east of Arras. At first it made excellent progress, but as the attacks continued in the coming weeks, the offensive turned into "another slogging match," as one historian described it.[15] The daily losses averaged 4,070 men until the operation ceased on 17 May; total casualties numbered around 159,000 men. In the south, French attacks were disappointing. A massive artillery barrage affected only a lightly held German first line, and an attempt to penetrate the second position was met with heavy machine-gun fire. By the third week in April, French casualties numbered 96,000 and there had been no decisive breakthrough. Additional French attacks during the first week of May made modest gains, but the heavy casualties and subsequent mutinies within the French army resulted in Nivelle's removal on 15 May; he was replaced by Gen. Henri-Philippe Petain.

The next offensives were split into two phases. The first consisted of an attack on the Wytschaete-Messines Ridge. This phase commenced when Gen. Sir Herbert Plumer's Second Army ordered an artillery bombardment with 756 heavy pieces against Messines Ridge, a feature that dominated the southern flank of the Ypres salient. Then, on 7 June, nineteen mines detonated under the German positions, essentially ending the attack in one day. The fighting continued until 14 June. The British lost 25,000 men. Many casualties resulted from German shelling that pulverized the infantry crowded on the ridge.[16]

From the end of July until the middle of November, the British conducted an operation known as the Third Battle of Ypres, or Passchendaele, during which losses reached about 260,000. Pilckem Ridge was the most significant gain, where on 31 July, nine divisions of the Fifth Army advanced while five divisions of the Second Army covered their right and two French divisions covered the left.

With the British army mired in another costly operation, Haig and Pershing met for the first time on 20 July at BEF headquarters in Montreuil, a little walled town a few miles to the south of St. Omer and many miles from the front lines. Haig's personal quarters were located outside town.[17] Accompanying Pershing were three staff officers who sailed with him two months earlier: Col. Benjamin Alvord, Lt. Col. James Harbord, and Capt. George S. Patton. Haig wrote that he was "much struck with [Pershing's] quiet, gentlemanly bearing— so unusual for an American. Most anxious to learn, he fully realizes the greatness of the task before him." He was less impressed with

Alvord and Harbord, who he described as "men of less quality, and . . . quite ignorant of the problems of modern war."[18]

Pershing also took pleasure in his first visit with Haig. He devoted four pages of his wartime memoir to his discussions with the BEF commander-in-chief and General Robertson, who made a point of visiting Montreuil the day Pershing and his staff arrived. Most of the conference with Haig and Robertson focused on current operations and the high number of casualties at Arras. Haig felt comfortable with Pershing and confessed to him his lack of confidence in Nivelle and the failure of the French to cooperate with the British on various occasions. "His remarks," Pershing sensed, "entirely confirmed the belief that I had long since held that real teamwork between the two armies was almost totally absent."[19]

During the remainder of their visit, the American officers listened to BEF Assistant Chief of Staff Major General Butler explain the procedures for organizing a headquarters general staff. When Pershing left British headquarters, he fully realized that creating the AEF would be more difficult than he ever imagined.[20] His visit with Haig was one of the few times the two men had such an intimate and cordial discussion. From this point on, the issue of amalgamation caused a great deal of tension between the two commanders.

3

AMALGAMATION

At the end of 1917, only four American divisions (1st, 2nd, 26th and 42nd) plus logistical support were on French soil, a total of 175,000 men. This was nowhere near the target of 1 million men that Pershing wanted by June 1918.[1] Meanwhile, the military outlook for 1918 appeared perilous, as there were indications that the German army was planning a spring offensive. After the collapse of Russia and the defeat of the Italians at Caporetto, the Germans redeployed divisions from the Eastern Front to the west. The exact date of the expected offensive remained a mystery, but the need for Allied reinforcements was immediate.

As the year came to a close, the British and French pressed for amalgamation during meetings of the recently formed Supreme War Council.[2] After getting nowhere with Pershing and other American representatives in Europe, the Allies appealed directly to President Wilson. Throughout the war, the president left matters of military importance completely in the hands of the AEF commander. As Pershing's biographer Donald Smythe reminds us, "Perhaps no field commander in history was ever given a freer hand to conduct operations than was Pershing by Wilson."[3]

An urgent Christmas Eve cable from Secretary of War Baker arrived at Pershing's Chaumont headquarters the following day, supporting this point.[4] It informed Pershing that "both the English and French are pressing upon the President their desires to have your forces amalgamated with theirs by regiments and companies." Baker said that "we do not desire loss of identity of our forces, but regard that as secondary to the meeting of any critical situation by the most helpful use possible of the troops at your command." He added that "the President desires you to have full authority to use the forces at your command as you deem wise in consultation with French and British commanders-in-chief."[5] Pershing was in no hurry to respond and waited almost a week to do so.

He knew he had the upper hand regarding the amalgamation issue. The British needed his troops, but Pershing was in no hurry to give them up. Despite his impatience with the American general, Field Marshal Haig remained enthusiastic about the AEF officers he met. He wrote his wife in December 1917, "Our idea of what American men are like is quite wrong. Those we are working with are quiet, unassuming fellows—entirely unlike the fashionable Yankees we used to see in London following in the wake of some loud-voiced Yankee beauty! Personally, I am finding the American men connected with the U.S.A. Forces very much like our own officers. I need give them no higher recommendation."[6] As amalgamation dragged on, Haig's high regard for the Americans diminished.

"The winter of 1917-1918 was the most severe of the war," General Pershing remarked in his memoirs.[7] He was referring to the freezing temperatures and heavy snows that tormented both France and the United States. Yet he easily could have meant the frigid relations that formed between him and senior British and French commanders. They were pulling him in opposite directions, and his own government also was beginning to question his reasoning for withholding troops from the front.

On 1 January 1918, Pershing finally replied to the Christmas Day cable by writing to Maj. Gen. Tasker Bliss, the American representative on the Supreme War Council, not Secretary of War Baker. His long message assured Bliss: "I do not think an emergency now exists that would warrant our putting companies or battalions into British or French divisions."[8] Pershing reiterated his long-held convictions that if American troops were amalgamated they would lose their national identity and that the methods of instruction in the Allied armies might interfere with AEF training doctrine. "Attention should be called to prejudices existing between French and British Governments and Armies," he wrote, "and the desire of each to have American units assigned to them, and the exclusion of similar assignment to the other."[9] A cable to Bliss three days later showed he was beginning to soften his views, albeit slightly. He now entertained the idea of the British transporting and assisting in the training of American troops as long it was "strictly supplementary to our own regular program" of fielding an American army. Pershing recognized that British help was needed to transport troops to France, and he had to make a concession.[10]

Sir William Robertson met with Pershing on 9–10 January 1918. The two men had last conferred in November 1917, but that discussion had accomplished little. Now it was a new year and a fresh start for both. Robertson brought a proposal that offered to transport 150,000 troops (150 battalions) from divisions still in the United States that were not already scheduled for overseas duty. He also suggested breaking them up as the British had done with Territorial Force and New Army divisions in 1915 to supply reinforcements and lines of communication troops. The proposal, he reiterated to Pershing, related only to infantrymen and machine gunners the British needed to reinforce under-strength units. Robertson also sought to reassure Pershing by reminding him that he in no way wished to interfere with the buildup of an independent American army.

The British were willing, temporarily, to forgo the shipping used to import food and raw materials from abroad and use it to provide the immediate transport of American troops, if only Pershing would approve. Sensing that Pershing was not going to accept the proposal, Robertson played to his emotions. He told him that unless the Americans provided men to fill up the British army's decimated divisions, it could very well exhaust its manpower and the Allies would lose the war.[11]

Pershing later recalled that he was bewildered when the British suddenly offered to transport troops because previously he had been told that no shipping was available. Furthermore, it bothered him that Robertson's current proposal was not current at all; it was essentially the same as that submitted to Lloyd George by the House mission a few weeks earlier.[12] But Pershing was overreacting, because the British, particularly Robertson, were in no way trying to be deceitful. On the contrary, they were attempting to be amenable by offering to sacrifice tonnage to bring the Americans to Europe as soon as possible.

After Robertson finished outlining his proposal, Pershing responded that instead of carrying 150 battalions, the British should carry full divisions to France. If they could find shipping for battalions, he reasoned, they could certainly find space for divisions. Robertson anticipated this reaction and had a ready answer: the infantry battalions were needed badly, not the support units attached to a division. Those could come later. He left the meeting with the proposal still open. On 13 January, Pershing cabled the War Department: "This whole question seems to me to be one of necessity, and we must consider the probability of strong German attacks in early spring and summer. . . . The emergency requires this temporary supply of men for the British."[13]

The War Department agreed with Pershing and submitted a recommendation to President Wilson, who approved, but cautiously. Sounding much like Pershing, he warned: "Whatever they may promise now, the British will, when it comes to the pinch, in fact, cut us off from some part of the tonnage they will promise us for our general program in order, themselves, to make sure of these battalions, or will promise us less for the general program than they would otherwise have given, had their plan for these reinforcements for their own front not been accepted."[14] How America's role on the battlefield might affect the peace negotiations greatly concerned Wilson.[15]

A few days later, Pershing had second thoughts. He wrote to Bliss on 21 January: "We should be very guarded in making any concessions to the British."[16] He met with Robertson on the 25th, this time in Paris. Here Pershing broke the news to him that he would not approve the shipping plan, which greatly shocked Robertson, and with good reason. Robertson learned that less than a week before Pershing met privately with Haig and Petain and expressed no dissatisfaction with the proposal. Now Pershing claimed it was in the best interest of the American army that the British transport whole divisions, not individual battalions. Once the divisions arrived in

France, the British would supervise training and, should the need arise, the troops could be of limited use in combat. Pershing's change of mind also surprised Bliss, who favored the British plan and was prepared to present it to the Supreme War Council. But Pershing did not back down. When the two American generals met, the AEF commander stressed that a unified front was important to the Allies and argued that the transport of complete divisions was the only acceptable course. Bliss reluctantly agreed. Pershing then persuaded the British that this was the best plan, and they agreed a week later.[17]

Accordingly, Pershing and Bliss met with Lloyd George, Lord Milner, Robertson, and Haig on 29–30 January 1918. After two days of tense discussion, both sides reached an agreement.[18] They settled on the American plan by which the British would transport six complete divisions, less artillery, to France for a ten-week training program. The artillery units would be trained in American camps located in the French sector, and the British took responsibility for feeding and supplying the Americans. Pershing emphasized that the American divisions were on loan to the British army and could be recalled at his discretion.[19]

Pershing made sure that the agreement clearly outlined how training would proceed. Perhaps the most important proviso of the agreement stated that once platoons, companies, battalions, and regiments of each division completed training, they would be designated ready "to take the field . . . and would then be handed over to the American commander-in-chief, under arrangements to be made between the various commanders-in-chief."[20] This gave Pershing the assurance he insisted on that American divisions were only temporarily assigned to the British. The British also enhanced the agreement by proposing that American commanders and staff officers be attached to corresponding British headquarters for additional instruction. This clause benefited Pershing since it gave his inexperienced officers training they never would have received in the United States.

On 4 February 1918, the American and British representatives met again to finalize the training agreement, but it was not a straightforward process. Pershing insisted upon a few changes. One stated that the six divisions would form an American corps, another that the training program was to be designed by the Americans after consulting the British. To the British, these revisions were of little concern, and on 12 February 1918, the arrangement became official. In a memorandum to Haig the same day, Pershing promised "my full and earnest cooperation in ensuring successful execution."[21] Although the training agreement would undergo many minor changes in coming months, it began a relationship between two armies that had a profound effect on how they fought the war.

Mostly forgotten during the negotiations were the French, and their reaction to the British proposal was one of disappointment. Since December 1917, Petain requested that AEF divisions be transferred to France to his army for amalgamation. He was anxious to strengthen his divisions before the impending German attack. Although Pershing rejected this request, he had great fondness for Petain and wanted to ensure that good American-French relations continued.

As a matter of courtesy, Pershing met with Petain on 21 January to inform him of the British proposal. He refused to say why his troops were headed to the British, but he did indicate that he hoped this decision did not hurt their friendship or show any lack of respect toward the French army. It was necessary to accept the British offer to transport troops since the Americans lacked shipping, he explained. Pershing promised that his troops would then go to the French for advanced training, but did offer them four black infantry regiments that were formed into the 93rd Division.[22]

4

THE SUNNY SOUTH
Training in the United States

Back in the United States, mobilization and training were in full swing as the General Staff put its war plan into action. The AEF would consist of the National Guard, the Regular Army, and the National Army. The Regulars were professional soldiers, and the men of the National Army had been selected in the draft. National Guard divisions were assigned numbers 26–75, although 50 divisions would never be formed. Divisions below 26 were Regular Army; those above 75 were assigned to the National Army. Because of this numbering system, O'Ryan's 6th Division was federalized as the 27th Division, and the southern National Guard units in North and South Carolina and Tennessee became the 30th Division.[1]

True to its word, the Quartermaster Corps completed the cantonments by the end of summer 1917. The General Staff sent the National Guard regiments to camps constructed in the warm climate of the southern, southwestern, and western states. There, canvas tents sheltered the troops and semi-permanent structures housed utilities. Each tent was large enough to hold a squad (10 or 11 men) and was set over a wooden floor with wooden sidewalls. A wood-burning cone-shaped Sibley stove (a Civil War invention by Confederate Gen. Henry Sibley) stood in the middle, its chimney protruding through the top.[2] Some unlucky soldiers were assigned tents without floors, so when it rained, as it often does in the South during the warmer months, they were surrounded by mud. The army did provide the men with canvas cots.[3] Regular and National Army regiments were housed in more permanent barracks that were lavish compared to the National Guard tents.[4]

In early August, O'Ryan's division began arriving at Camp Wadsworth in Spartanburg, South Carolina. His men were happy to be in the sunny South. Although it was hot and humid there in the summer, they looked forward to a winter away from the bitter cold in the Northeast. Close to Asheville, North Carolina, and within sight of the scenic Blue Ridge Mountains, the camp was named in honor of Gen. James S. Wadsworth, a former U.S. senator and Union Army officer who was killed at the Battle of the Wilderness in 1864. In 1917, Spartanburg had 27,000 residents, many of whom were employed in the cotton industry. Families in Spartanburg were generous to the homesick doughboys. Merchants welcomed the soldiers and assured them that they would receive courteous and fair treatment. Notices were posted in town announcing that "no overcharges to men in the uniform of the United States would be tolerated."[5]

The naive doughboys learned quickly that few shop owners abided by this credo. It was even worse for the black 369th Infantry (formerly the 15th New York Infantry), which shared Wadsworth as a training ground. Although not attached to the 27th Division because of the army's strict segregation policy, the 369th was commanded by white officers. In Spartanburg, which the regimental commander referred to as "a region hostile to colored people," the citizens treated the black doughboys poorly. The 369th was subjected to racial insults and fights until the War Department removed the unit from the unfriendly environment and sent it to France. There, it was eventually placed in the incomplete 93rd Division and distinguished itself in several battles.[6]

Camp Sevier in Greenville, South Carolina, was designated as the training cantonment for the 30th Division. Located at the foot of Paris Mountain, part of the Blue Ridge Mountains, Greenville had 16,000 inhabitants in 1917. The camp was named in honor of John Sevier, a hero of the 1780 Battle of Kings Mountain and the first governor of Tennessee.

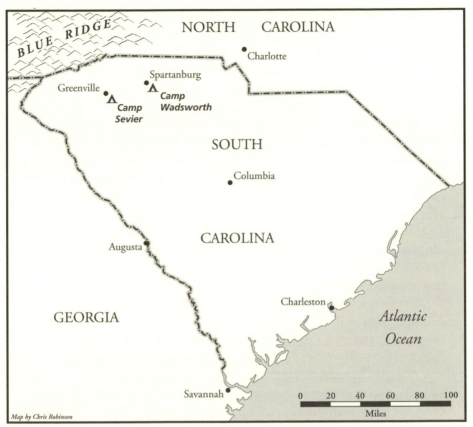

Camps Sevier and Wadsworth, South Carolina, 1917–1918

Company K of the 3rd Tennessee Regiment, the first to reach Sevier on 15 August 1917, found that before the men could pitch tents, they had to uproot a cotton field. Then they had to build a company street and clear a road for supplies.[7] Another unit spent so much time clearing trees for drill grounds that it referred to itself as "The South Carolina Land and Development Company."[8]

Unlike the 27th Division, which had one commander throughout the war, in the 30th Division, nine different general officers commanded from 1917 to 1919. In 1917, it was mostly under Maj. Gen. John F. Morrison or Maj. Gen. Clarence P. Townsley. Morrison had been a respected tactics instructor at Fort Leavenworth before taking command of the division. Like most general officers, he had graduated from the military academy and served in the Philippines. Townsley was a former superintendent of West Point.

Men in units of the 30th Division came from all over the three states of North Carolina, South Carolina, and Tennessee. For instance, those in the North Carolina National Guard lived in the central and piedmont sections of South Carolina and mobilized on the U.S.–Mexican border near El Paso. At Camp Sevier, the 1st and 2nd North Carolina units were redesignated as the 119th and 120th Infantry Regiments and formed into the 60th (Tar Heel) Brigade under Brig. Gen. Sampson L. Faison, a Regular from North Carolina. His men came from communities such as Lenoir, Gastonia, Orangeburg, Crossville, and Etowah and cities such as Raleigh, Asheville, Knoxville, Nashville, Charleston, and Columbia. According to the 30th Division's official historian, its regiments "were organizations whose history reached far back into the early period of our nation's life." Many in the division could trace their lineage to the War of 1812. For that reason the 30th was nicknamed Old Hickory, after the hero of the war and future president, Andrew Jackson.[9] In honor of the division nickname, the men adopted an insignia with a blue, elliptically shaped letter "O" on its side. It surrounded a blue letter "H" with blue Roman numerals XXX inside the crossbar of the "H," which was superimposed on a maroon field.[10]

The division's members were generally Scots-Irish whose ancestors had emigrated to America for economic reasons in the early to mid-1700s and inhabited the southern United States. Added to the mix were English, German, Huguenots, and Welsh immigrants who settled there around the same time to escape religious persecution.[11] The historian of the 120th Infantry described his unit as "a thoroughly American organization" that had inherited the "best tradition of a fighting stock, which had proven its worth in the War of the Revolution and the War Between the States." Veterans of the regiments referred to their recently graduated reserve officers as "Sears and Roebuck Lieutenants"[12] because they reminded them of new clothes purchased from one of America's best-known mail-order companies.[13]

To prepare for war, the War College Division overhauled the army's structure.[14] Large divisions (approximately 28,000 men), twice the size of those of the Allies, were created after consultation with the British and French General Staffs.[15] A division was now square since it had two infantry brigades with two regiments in each brigade. The realignment worked well for the Regulars but created havoc among the National Guard divisions, which were now forced to meet the new tables of organization. State units, for example, had an excess of infantry and a shortage of artillery. As an expedient, the War Department switched units between arms of the service. Infantry regiments became artillery regiments or machine-gun battalions, and in some cases two regiments became one.

Cavalry units were also abolished. After more than three years of fighting, both the Allies and Central Powers recognized that barbed wire and machine guns made cavalry impractical. In 1918, horses were still used for transport to the front, but as tactical tools they had been replaced mostly by tanks.[16] When Secretary of War Baker encouraged the chairman of the Committee on Military Affairs to empower the president to deploy cavalry units as foot regiments, Congress passed legislation federalizing National Guard cavalry regiments as artillery and machine-gun units.[17] Both the 27th and 30th Divisions converted cavalry regiments to machine-gun battalions and trench-mortar batteries with mixed results. As one historian points out, "Many field-grade infantry officers lost their commands, while others were placed in charge of units for which they had no training."[18] The realignment threatened the heritage of some National Guard units, resulting in further resentment toward the War Department. State military and political leaders protested to Secretary Baker, who could do little but urge the commanders of National Guard divisions to try to preserve the identity of the oldest regiments.

To their dismay, units of the National Guard received drafted men from all over the United States. This caused the state units to lose their local flavor. To some in the National Guard system, this was a deliberate attempt by the War Department to weaken the states' authority in wartime.[19] The 30th Division received recruits representing practically all of the United States. One soldier from Indiana wrote to his mother how the "southern boys are very nice" and said that "it sounds kind of funny to hear them talk . . . just like a colored fellow talking."[20] Local men enlisted for a variety of reasons. Cpl. Joe Thompson from Goldsboro, North Carolina, joined the 119th because his "home was broken up through the death of his parents, and he had nowhere else to go." Thompson fit in quite well among the National Guardsmen because they were like him: farmers who "accepted discipline easily."[21]

O'Ryan and other National Guard officers recognized that the War Department depleted local pride by sending replacements.[22] During the Civil War, the army had learned that units formed from the same home towns fought better for the simple reason that men feared that word of misbehavior would trickle back to their families and friends. After the war, O'Ryan testified that what Congress referred to as an unfortunate replacement system was flawed because it allowed new troops to destroy the unity local units produced. The Allied armies, he suggested, were more sensitive. "Certainly the Scotchmen would not be willing to serve in any other commands than Scotch divisions, and I believe the Australians would refuse to serve in any part of the British Army, and would serve only with Australian units."[23] The committee carefully noted O'Ryan's comments, but he was incorrect. In late 1915 and during the first half of 1916, the British army began to transfer men from New Army and Territorial Force units to ostensibly Regular battalions. This was in response to the perceived poor performance of two New Army divisions at Loos.[24] The British had proved that strong local identity of units was not the secret of success; better tactical methods and weapons systems were the key.[25] O'Ryan's testimony did little to affect how the National Guard would be used in future wars, as the same problem occurred in World War II.

It also appeared that the War Department had little regard for members of the same family who served together. Such was the case of the nine Warlick brothers from Shelby, North Carolina, five of whom served in the 115th Machine Gun Battalion of the 30th Division. All of them survived the war, although William Warlick was wounded twice—once near Ypres and the second time during the Hindenburg Line attack.[26]

Soldiers entertained themselves by attending stage shows at the camp theater, making visits into town, reading and writing letters (at a YMCA-maintained building), or enjoying a home-cooked meal at a hostess house.[27] They looked forward most to the coveted weekend leave or furlough, which was issued in rotation so that every man was granted a Saturday and Sunday holiday at least once every six weeks.[28]

During the first month at camp, divisions concentrated on the schooling of the soldiers—disciplinary drills and physical exercise.[29] In late October 1917, the French and British armies began to send instructors to America. Eventually, 286 French officers, predominately artillery specialists, and 261 British officers, primarily for training in gas warfare, physical fitness, and bayonet drill, spent several months in the United States. Through a special congressional appropriation, the War Department set aside funds to pay the foreign officers $10 a day plus train or bus fare when they traveled and had to find accommodation in a city or town. When British and French officers stayed on an army post, this extra pay was reduced to $6 per day.[30]

British instructors spent more time than their French counterparts at Sevier and Wadsworth and greatly influenced the way the 27th and 30th Divisions trained. Physical training, the British army had shown, was essential to both the minds and muscles of soldiers. Maj. J. B. Sharp was ordered to Wadsworth to serve the 27th Division as an advisor in physical and bayonet training. A member of the Buffs (the East Kent Regiment), he impressed the Americans with his "high standard of disciplined efficiency" and devised games that tested a soldier's physical ability. When lecturing American officers, Sharp claimed that experience had proved that groups of fighting men were most effective when training to respond as a team. This was particularly true during the height of noise and confusion in combat.[31]

Physical fitness, it was reasoned, would "tighten the relation between the mind and muscle, so that the latter would become automatically and instantaneously responsive to the former, and the former instantaneously resourceful in applying methods to aid the latter when hard pressed."[32] British officers encouraged squads from each regiment to specialize in a branch of warfare. Hence, one squad might be proficient in grenade throwing and another might have special skills with machine-gunning. This was enshrined in the British doctrine in early 1917. Manuals such as the *Instructions for the Training of Platoons for Offensive Action* (*SS 143*) provided four areas of concentration: Lewis guns, hand grenades, rifle grenades, and rifles. Fresh from the printing press, *SS 143* incorporated all that the British had learned from the costly Somme operation, where nearly 60,000 had been killed or wounded on 1 July 1916. Its doctrine prescribed small-unit tactics. No longer would the Tommies fight in massed ranks as they had since 1902, when the object was to repel cavalry.[33]

The physical training schedule devised by British officers consisted of three hours of drill in the morning and three in the afternoon. Lectures for noncommissioned officers were held each evening. Sgt. Maj. William Tector of the British Army Gymnastic Corps was also sent to Wadsworth. His tremendous skill as a physical and bayonet instructor appealed to the Americans.

As training progressed, other components of soldering were emphasized, such as the use of the bayonet and the Chauchat machine gun and instruction in adjusting and using the gas mask. Gas drills were held until every man could don and adjust his mask in less than six seconds. At the end of gas training, all infantry regiments were put through a gas chamber in the camp with actual (nonlethal) gas filling the room. This was supposed to simulate the kind of gas attack soldiers would encounter on the front line.[34]

Maj. H. D. Matson, a British specialist in machine-gun training, was sent to Camp Sevier to instruct the 30th Division.[35] Along with other British instructors in the United States, Matson helped establish schools to provide instruction in handling bayonets, bombs, and Stokes mortars, as well as in sniping and scouting. Classes formed for special courses in tactics. During later weeks of training, almost every man was a student at one of these special schools.

Officers serving with the British training mission in the United States refused to openly criticize their American pupils, but their superiors in England learned their true feelings. Lieutenant Colonel Murray wrote to his commanding officer in England that the training was difficult. Each American division was more than 20,000 men, and the five officers assigned to each of the camps were overwhelmed. Murray spoke of the weak discipline between American commissioned and noncommissioned officers and hoped that the British instructors "affected a great deal in the required direction, and that the necessity for strict discipline is now understood."[36]

Not surprisingly, the American officers found reason to fault their well-intentioned British instructors. "Intolerable and overbearing," commented Lt. Kenneth Gow, a machine-gun company commander in the 27th Division. "There is only one way which is right—their way." He much preferred French instructors because they were "considerate, polite, and will always take suggestions."[37]

Training was hindered by the fact that not all the men had received a full complement of equipment yet. The commanding general of the 30th Division complained to the War Department that it was two months before all units had rifles, which prevented them from instruction in the army's most relied-upon weapon.[38] The standard-issue service rifle in the army was the U.S. 30-caliber magazine rifle model 1903, known as the "Springfield 03," the "03," or the "Springfield." The 43.5-inch weapon, which weighed 8.69 pounds and had a 24-inch barrel, has been called "the finest bolt-action military rifle of all time."[39]

The infantry rifle was at the heart of Pershing's open-warfare doctrine. He criticized both the British and French armies because they had "become mired in trench warfare" and as a result, their offensive capabilities were diminished to a defensive posture on the Western Front.[40] Pershing was fearful that if his own army adopted trench warfare, it would also lose the offensive spirit. He envisioned aggressive movement and pursuit to force the enemy into the open. His thinking drew from experiences of the old frontier army during the Indian wars, when part of the infantry consisted of expert marksmen and scouts.

He seemed to long for the days on the Plains and in the Southwest, where there were no trenches in which to take cover. Developing an aggressive, self-reliant infantry was his training goal.[41] Pershing did not create this doctrine. It was based on the tactics prescribed in the army's Infantry Drill Regulations (IDR), particularly the 1914 edition. The IDR was first published in 1907 and remained the army's doctrinal bible well after this world war. One of Pershing's biographers describes open warfare as "fluid, open-ended, and flexible. . . . Oriented to the earth's surface, rather than its bowels, it is inclined to go around strong points rather than into them."[42] Much to his dismay, Pershing heard that training in the United States at camps such as Sevier and Wadsworth focused on trench warfare with little emphasis on open-warfare tactics. He repeatedly cabled the War Department to complain that training with the rifle was not being sufficiently stressed at home and stated that when the divisions arrived in France, they would be retrained to his liking. One historian referred to the lack of coordination in the training of U.S. soldiers in 1918 as "tactical dysfunction."[43]

At Camp Wadsworth, for example, an elaborate, eight-mile specially constructed trench system covered a front of 700 yards. The system included shelters and bomb-proof dugouts. "It afforded opportunity for every unit to engage in practical instruction in the use of pick and shovel, trench sanitation, the construction of listening posts, barbed-wire entanglements, saps, mines, machine-gun emplacements, and lines of communications," O'Ryan later wrote.[44]

On 22 September 1917, O'Ryan received orders to proceed from Camp Wadsworth with two 27th Division officers to France to observe the British and French fronts. Although the War Department was months away from sending divisions to the British for training, the trip would prove to be a valuable training lesson.

O'Ryan's observations provide insight into the Allied armies and influenced his own theories on command. His party spent most of its time with Gen. Sir Hubert Gough at British Fifth Army headquarters and with the 29th and 31st Divisions on the front lines. While in the trenches with the 29th Division, O'Ryan learned the importance of duckboards, which were essential for moving to forward lines over the terrain of slippery mud that was so prevalent in France and Belgium. At the front, O'Ryan saw a number of German prisoners and was surprised at their poor stature and physical condition.

Discipline within the British army greatly impressed O'Ryan. "The main manifestation was quietness," he wrote. "Neither in the front trenches nor in the back areas did I ever hear, among the thousands of soldiers I saw, any soldiers shouting or cursing at their horses or mules, or, in fact, shouting or calling in a loud voice to other men."[45] O'Ryan made a favorable impression upon the British as well. The British evaluated every American officer who spent time with them and forwarded the comments to Pershing. Major General O'Gowan of the British 31st Division considered O'Ryan "a keen and capable officer, with considerable knowledge of his profession, and a facility for mastering the detail of trench warfare and the administration of a division."[46] O'Ryan spent his last week with the French 38th Division, a quiet sector headquartered in Soissons. His final day in the French sector was at an army school where "training seemed to be thorough. There was continued evidence of snap and ginger in everything that was done."[47]

When he returned to South Carolina, O'Ryan observed there were 35,000 men at Camp Wadsworth, 7,000 over the authorized strength of 28,000. At Sevier, the strength of the 30th was only 17,557 officers and men in mid-October, and not until 10,000 more were posted in was it was at full strength. Yet both divisions had problems keeping its best officers and men. If a soldier was skilled in pneumatic riveting or fluent in French, he was considered a valuable commodity and was likely to be transferred by the War Department. This occurred in all of the army training camps and remained an issue overseas when the most qualified men were taken out of line for special training on the eve of combat.

Through the last part of the summer, the health of both divisions remained reasonably good. This was largely due to the warm weather. In the case of the 30th Division, less than 1 percent had to be hospitalized. However, the temperature turned cold at the end of October and remained so for the next four months. When winter arrived in December, ice, sleet, and snow were more prevalent than clear skies and balmy conditions. "It was the coldest god dam winter they had in the history of South Carolina," insisted one soldier.[48] Fuel was scarce and was doled out for cooking purposes only. Some of the more desperate soldiers took matters into their own hands and stole wood and other burnable materials from the quartermaster depots. "Nights were bitterly cold," recalled Pvt. William F. Clarke of the 104th Machine-Gun Battalion, "but the sun would be scorching hot during the day." He vividly remembered coming back from either "a day on the drill field or from a 10-mile hike, perspiring profusely, and then almost freezing to death at night."[49]

In the winter of 1917, a measles epidemic broke out. Men were forbidden to leave camp for fear of spreading the disease, and anyone caught violating the order was punished. At Wadsworth, the Spartanburg newspaper reported, "a guy went to town from the quarantine a few nights ago and got for his troubles six months in the guard house."[50]

Weather was certainly a factor but not the only reason for this outbreak. The failure of the Quartermaster Corps to provide warm uniforms (the men were still wearing the light khaki variety) and the fact that men were sleeping in crowded tents were partially to blame. Yet the quartermaster had a legitimate excuse for the problem. After the debacle in 1898, the Quartermaster General had repeatedly requested appropriations from Congress to purchase large reserves of clothing but was refused each time. When the National Guard was mobilized in 1916, the meager stocks on hand were depleted. A final attempt to secure appropriations also failed when Congress adjourned on 4 March 1917 before it could vote on the legislation.[51] Concerns over the clothing shortage prompted the head of the Chattanooga branch of the National League for Women's Service to press the governor of Tennessee to buy warm underwear for the cold soldiers at Camp Sevier. The lack of a war contingency fund prevented the state from helping out, although Governor Thomas Rye promised to write to the 30th Division commander on behalf of the league.[52]

Keeping the men out of trouble when they were on leave was a constant concern of the division commanders. Despite their rural locations, both Sevier and Wadsworth were affected with high rates of venereal disease when the camps were first populated. But the U.S. Army surgeon general, who compiled weekly statistics on such matters, surmised that most cases were preexisting. He suggested that men from large cities, such as New York, Charlotte, and Memphis, had contracted the disease before enlistment. His theory provided correct when cases leveled off, then increased only when recruits and drafted men arrived at both camps in the autumn of 1917.[53] To prevent an increase in syphilis and gonorrhea, prophylactic stations, where soldiers were checked and treated for venereal diseases, were maintained in the camps and in nearby towns like Greenville and Spartanburg. Medical officers and social workers were dispatched to the camps by the Committee on Training Camp Activities to lecture the naive troops about vice and show them upbeat films such as *Fit to Fight*.[54]

Drinking also concerned the straitlaced O'Ryan. He got an early jump on the potential problem of alcohol abuse. Before departing for South Carolina, he issued a plea for sobriety to his division: "You will notice in reading this letter that no reference is made to the effect upon your morals of the use of liquor or uncommendable associations," he wrote. "You are largely the custodian of your own morals."[55] His preemptive attempt to induce soldiers to control their own drinking was likely prompted by a report from the construction crew at Wadsworth that they had found a liquor still only a few feet from where O'Ryan's headquarters was to be located.[56] After the New Yorkers arrived in Spartanburg, he assigned fifty men from his military police company to stand continuous post in the city's streets as a deterrent to would-be drunks.[57] Ironically, the soldiers who later developed a taste for alcohol in France were forced to give up drinking when they returned to the United States after Prohibition was introduced in 1920 with the Volstead Act.[58]

5

ORGANIZING II CORPS

With the amalgamation issue behind him, at least for a while, Pershing could put his energy into organizing his much-sought-after army. The creation of the corps was an important move in this direction. He formed American II Army Corps on 20 February 1918 to establish administrative control and supervise the training of the six American divisions scheduled to arrive in the British sector over the next two months.[1] Pershing chose Lt. Col. (later Brig. Gen.) George S. Simonds as its chief of staff. It was a wise selection because Simonds already knew many BEF staff officers from his work with the Baker mission the previous year.[2] Also, he was a good officer, as his already-impressive career had shown.

After graduating from West Point in 1899, Simonds was commissioned in the 22nd Infantry and took part in eleven engagements and expeditions during the Philippine Insurrection before helping to suppress the Boxer Rebellion. His superiors thought highly of him, one rating Simonds "an excellent, conscientious and painstaking officer, capable and fitted for any duty."[3] During the years before the United States entered World War I, he served mostly as a training officer. After returning from France with the Baker mission, Simonds was appointed the 26th Division chief of staff, remaining with the "Yankee

Division" only a short time before being transferred to AEF G-3 staff (Operations). His fluency in French probably had some bearing on his return to France.[4]

As a corps chief of staff, Simonds "faced with aplomb the tremendous task of formulating training programs," as one historian points out, "solving logistical problems, and adapting American principles of organization and administration to those of the British."[5] Since Pershing did not immediately select his corps commanders, for a period, Simonds was the highest-ranking American officer in the British sector. He reported to Brig. Gen. James G. Harbord, who by that time was the AEF chief of staff.

Only days after Simonds's appointment took effect, Harbord presented him with a two-and-a-half-page directive outlining his duties. It gave him the background on arrangements for bringing divisions to France—when they would arrive and how long they were to train with the British. More important, it made clear that Pershing had the authority to determine the disposition of each division after training was completed.[6]

Such tight control over administrative matters was typical of Pershing. As AEF commander, he continually managed the minutest details and was not averse to relieving staff officers who failed to follow his orders. It is understandable why Pershing was not willing to relinquish control after his experience of the difficult negotiations with the British. Simply put, Simonds was to carry out Pershing's proposals and ensure that the British did not exceed their authority. This was unfortunate for Simonds because the limited power often hindered his performance as a corps chief of staff.

Recognizing the difficulties Simonds was about to confront, Harbord offered some much-needed advice. He urged him not to rush into the job but to take his time organizing a staff at the AEF headquarters in Chaumont. After all, the first of the six divisions was not scheduled to arrive until early April, so there was plenty of time to sort out the administrative details with the British. Harbord's suggestion notwithstanding, Simonds was anxious to start working. It would be more prudent, he thought, to schedule a visit to British general headquarters and discuss the training program with Haig's staff before selecting corps staff.

So Simonds left Chaumont on 20 February 1918 with two aides and arrived at the rail station near Montreuil the following morning.

Several British officers and the chief of the American mission at British general headquarters, Col. Robert Bacon, enthusiastically greeted him at the train. Bacon, a lawyer, banker, diplomat, and now a soldier, would work well with Simonds. He and Pershing were also longtime acquaintances, and, for that reason, as well as his "intimate knowledge of the French people, and his tact and discretion," Bacon was a natural for the job.[7]

Simonds and his party moved on to Montreuil, where he "found great excitement and enthusiasm about the American troops coming to the British front."[8] After the usual formalities, they went to work in a conference attended by the British deputy chief of staff, the director of training, the quartermaster, and the heads of the various supply branches. Shortly afterward, it became obvious that two problem areas existed in making the preliminary arrangements for American divisions: logistics and training. Complicating the second and more important of the two was the apparent misunderstanding by British staff officers regarding their role in supervising training.[9]

Practically ignoring Simonds, the British officers openly discussed plans to train the Americans at the battalion level, then place squads, platoons, and companies in line. Simonds did not expect such frank discussion, and he was unprepared to talk about these matters so soon. For the moment, he kept quiet. Yet he knew from his briefing with Harbord that only American officers were to supervise training and that it was his responsibility to ensure that arrangement.

As the meeting ended, Simonds addressed some of the issues brought to the table. Regarding supplies and equipment, he spoke candidly. The supply officers in attendance told Simonds that the British were quite willing to provide the Americans with whatever they needed as long as resources were available. In turn, Simonds promised to make their task less complicated by creating supply and equipment tables and adapting the British items and system of issue to the American organizations.

Simonds avoided the sticky question of who would instruct the Americans. He requested that the British provide one training area for each American division and warned that at a later time he might require an increase and modification of the areas to suit the needs of the American training system. Overwhelmed and exhausted from traveling and the complexities of his job, Simonds asked that they meet again the following day, when he promised to be more prepared. He retired to his temporary corps headquarters in Colonel Bacon's office, "a dingy little building" at Montreuil. There, he and his aides were supplied with transportation, clerks, typewriters, and batmen (servants to British officers).[10]

The next day's conference was more productive. Simonds came organized and started off the agenda with a plan for the British to supply II Corps with all items except the distinctive articles of uniform: overseas caps, overcoats, blouses, and breeches. He learned that accommodating an additional 150,000 troops was going to be a burden on the already-stretched British supply system. To complicate matters, the British army had no organizations that corresponded to an American regiment and therefore needed to adjust accordingly to the AEF system. A British infantry brigade equated to an American regiment, and the various components of a regimental headquarters "seemed to them like excess baggage."[11]

To comply with the American regimental tables of organization, the British supply system had to provide for such units as the headquarters company, machine-gun company, and supply company. Another issue was horse transportation for combat units. Here Simonds was willing to compromise. British tables of organization also gave a greater proportion of personnel to animals than the American tables, and he agreed that his units would conform to the British practice of handling and care for animal transportation.

Simonds saw the need to adjust and compromise over certain issues. As the meeting continued, much progress was made regarding supplies and equipment, but Simonds had yet to broach the sensitive issue of training. When this subject was finally raised, the meeting intensified. British staff officers repeatedly questioned Simonds's authority, and he had to remind them that direction, supervision, and control of training were done at II Corps headquarters. These were the instructions given to him by AEF general headquarters. All arrangements for training were to be handled by him until he appointed an operations officer.

Although the British seemed willing to accommodate Simonds regarding general training and provide an area for short-range rifle training, they refused to make provisions for open warfare and long-range rifle practice. Both were integral components of American training doctrine and there could be no compromise about the issue. "After a somewhat lengthy and spirited discussion," he was promised that American specifications would be met "in so far as time and conditions would permit."[12]

Now that the foundation for training was set, Simonds could breathe a bit easier and start to build his staff with officers from Chaumont. The British provided him Château Bryas at St. Pol-Sur-Ternoise (commonly known as St. Pol) for his headquarters. It was centrally located near the divisional training areas, about 70 kilometers from the front in the direction of Arras. He spent most days attending conferences and inspecting training areas and the ports of Calais and Le Havre, where newly arriving troops would disembark. One of the British officers who conferred frequently with Simonds was Lt. Gen. Sir Charles Bonham-Carter, the BEF director of training.[13]

Bonham-Carter was 42 years old and had a background typical of most World War I general officers of the British army. Educated at Sandhurst and the Staff College at Camberley, he had served in the South African War in 1900. Prior to his appointment as training director, he was a staff officer of the 50th Division in 1915. A year later he was promoted brevet lieutenant-colonel and appointed General Staff Officer Grade 1 to the 7th Division. Afterward, he went to general headquarters as a training officer, and from there, he served on the staff of III Corps for seven months before Haig chose him to set up a new training section in early 1917, where he was to produce manuals and develop tactical doctrine.[14] Previously, training was not standardized but conducted as seen fit by the various army, corps, division, and brigade commanders.[15] Bonham-Carter would prove a great asset to II Corps, especially as a liaison between Simonds and the British staff officers charged with supervision of the American training.

As the weeks passed, American officers were seen frequently in the British sector. Most were students of the General Staff College established by Pershing in September 1917 at Langres. Its mission was "to train selected officers for staffs of divisions, corps, armies, and lines of communications."[16] Many of its instructors were British and French, who lectured on subjects such as military map reading, staff organization, and intelligence. After graduating, the American officers were ordered to observe British and French divisions at the front, and some officers were also attached to New Zealand battalions for up to six days. Confidential reports on the Americans were then compiled by the hosting officers and submitted to Pershing's staff. One AEF officer was deemed "very keen and energetic during his attachment," and another "showed intelligent and critical interest in what he saw."[17]

While most of the Americans were out of harm's way, the Western Front erupted on 21 March, a foggy Thursday morning, when the Germans launched an attack that has been called commander of the German forces Erich von Ludendorff's last hope of victory.[18] Code-named "Michael," it started at 4:40 A.M. with a five-hour artillery barrage—the greatest of the war so far—against the British defenses near St. Quentin. Reportedly, the guns could be heard as far away as London. The Germans fired 3.2 million shells on the first day, one-third of which contained gas. "It seemed as though the bowels of the earth had erupted," recalled a private in the British 24th Machine-Gun Battalion.[19]

Although poor visibility affected the accuracy of the barrage, the Germans were proficient. The creeping barrage was designed to move forward on a fixed schedule, but because of poor communications, it was difficult to modify or stop once it started. The St. Quentin attack depended on the infantry advance complying with the rate of the creeping barrage that supported the infantry assault. Because there was little flexibility in adjusting the firing schedule, some infantry units had to run to keep up with the pace of the barrage.[20] The Germans were initially successful because they used the newly developed storm trooper tactics that the German high command (the Oberste Heeresleitung, or OHL) had published in January 1918. *The Attack in Position Warfare* called for destroying the enemy position rather than "nibbling away at the enemy front lines."[21]

Five hours after it started, the creeping barrage began moving forward under cover of fog with the infantry following closely behind. The Germans pushed forward enormously fast, as sixty-two divisions left the defenses of the Hindenburg Line and attacked the British Third and Fifth Armies on a 50-mile front between Cambrai and La Fere. The Third Army, under Gen. Sir Julian Byng, held its front after being slightly pushed back, but Gen. Sir Hubert Gough's Fifth Army retired ten miles back toward the Somme. Among the ranks, reaction to the German attack was one of disbelief. An Australian soldier, H. G. Taylor, overheard some the troops in his battalion bemoan that the "territory that has taken months of hard fighting to acquire has now been recaptured by the Germans in a matter of a few days."[22]

The OHL had begun to seriously consider an offensive in October 1917. Ludendorff was optimistic that if the general situation of the war stabilized and enough troops could transfer from other theaters, an assault, or *Kaiserschlact* (imperial battle), was possible against weak British positions. His object was to separate the British and French armies and capture the Channel ports. He considered three possible locations for attack: Flanders, where the ports were vulnerable; the Somme, where British and French lines met; and the south, against the French positions. After Russia and Romania suspended hostilities in December 1917, the Germans had been able to transfer thirty-three divisions to France and Belgium by the end of the year.[23]

Along with strength came surprise. The Germans caught the British unaware with the main thrust of their attack. With light machine guns, satchel charges, flamethrowers, and stick bombs, sixty-two German divisions attacked twenty-six British divisions in the Fifth Army zone. The offensive eventually penetrated forty miles after confusing the Allies about the location of the main thrust. Using elaborate deception measures, the Germans made it seem that the main attack would be in the French sector, near Rheims. Haig also expected an assault farther north and concentrated on strengthening the Flanders front to protect the Channel ports, the lifeline of the BEF, counting on the French to cover the south.[24] Instead, the Germans directed a major thrust against the British positions east of Amiens. The British Fifth Army bore the brunt of the attack and took terrific losses before falling back. It also seemed that the French capital was in peril. In Paris, more than half of the population left the city after tiring of the frequent German air raids. An estimated 20,000 tickets were issued at the main rail station, more than double the usual number of departures.[25]

Because American II Corps headquarters was situated in the British sector, Simonds became an eyewitness to the German offensive. On 23 March, Harbord ordered him to serve as a special observer of the battles and send a weekly bulletin to Chaumont. For two weeks, Simonds visited a portion of the front to the east of Amiens and was able to get as far as brigade headquarters, frequently even to battalion headquarters. In one bulletin, he wrote about the Germans' impressive use of machine guns, which were moved forward in large numbers with their infantry units. An American doctor assigned to a British hospital informed Simonds that most of the wounds he was treating were the result of machine-gun fire, the highest number he had encountered since coming to France.

Simonds also reported on how the British used automatic weapons to great effect, and that one or two Lewis guns supported small units of infantry, which "time and again held up German infantry until the guns could be pulled out and gotten away."[26] His later bulletins were less optimistic about Allied progress. One reported that men at the front told stories of "determined rear guard actions where men and guns simply stayed until they were engulfed by the oncoming masses of Germans." Simonds saw firsthand the withdrawal of tired divisions that showed the effects of what they had been through. "The companies are small, and the survivors look worn out," he reported.[27]

Each day when Simonds returned from the front, he read the numerous intelligence communiqués sent by the British. They were summaries of information that provided the economic, military, and political conditions of each of the Allied and Central powers. He found the ones written by the Italians particularly amusing because they frequently contained such phrases as "retreating for strategical purposes" or "being covered with glory." To break the monotony of his everyday routine and relieve the tension of the military situation, he wrote his own bulletin that parodied the Italian style of reporting. There was much to report, since the German drive into British territory caused some of the training areas allocated for the American divisions to be moved farther west to the vicinity of Calais south of the Somme.[28]

Simonds was also forced to relocate his headquarters from Château Bryas to Furges, closer to the coast. He wrote an embellished account of the movement of headquarters by informing Chaumont that "II Corps has this day retired 75 kilometers. The move was a great success. Our brave clerks, stenographers, batmen, and other camp followers would have defeated the enemy with great loss had he dared attack. The move was ably supported by our noble allies."[29] Simonds's bulletin circulated throughout general headquarters, and the amused staff responded by sending him congratulatory notes on the success of the move.[30]

On 9 April, the Germans commenced another offensive, this time to the south of Ypres in the area of the Lys River. In Operation Georgette, the German Sixth Army struck the British First Army in an advance to take the rail junction of Hazebrouck. Like Operation Michael, the attack started with great intensity. The next day, the German Fourth Army enjoyed an advantage over the under-strength British Second Army and seized Armentières. Further gains forced General Plumer to abandon Messines and Wytschaete, which his men had fought so hard to occupy a year earlier. The desperate situation prompted Haig again to request assistance from the French. General Foch, now generalissimo of the Allied Armies,[31] had introduced a system of rotation that allowed British divisions to move to quiet French sectors and be replaced by French reserves. But he was unable to coerce Petain to release his reserves. On 10 April, Haig told Foch that the German offensive now extended from La Bassée Canal to Messines and that the British Army needed the French to take immediate steps to relieve some part of the British front and actively participate in the battle.[32] Foch relented, and although he refused to relieve British forces in Flanders, he ordered the French V and X Armies to the north of the Somme to relieve British positions in this section of the front. Also, he promised to send troops to Arras, but they did not reach that zone until three days later.[33]

When news of the latest attack reached Chaumont, Simonds again was ordered to observe the fighting. On his way to the front, he and his driver got caught in part of the action. The Portuguese Corps (1st and 2nd Divisions) was holding a large portion of the line between Armentières and the La Bassée Canal when nine divisions of the German Sixth Army attacked. The Portuguese Corps received the brunt of the assault, and during its hasty withdrawal, the automobile in which Simonds was a passenger became mired in the confusion. Fearful of capture by the onrushing Germans, his "chauffeur had to make some time and do some skilful driving to keep up" with the fleeing Portuguese troops in order to reach the safety of the rear.

By 11 April, the Germans were within five miles of Hazebrouck, and Haig issued a special order telling his men they had their "backs to the wall. Every position must be held to the last man: there must be no retirement."[34] His troops heeded the warning, and two days later, the tide turned slightly in favor of the Allies when the Germans suffered heavy losses after being battered by the British artillery. On the Lys, stiff resistance from the British 5th and 33rd Divisions, supported by the 1st Australian Division, stopped the German drive and even recaptured some of the lost ground. The Germans were now the desperate army and they launched another attack on 24 April toward Amiens at Villers-Bretonneux, but this attack too ran out of momentum and was halted by Australian and British troops. Five days later, Ludendorff called off Operation Georgette.[35]

6

GOODBYE, SOUTH CAROLINA
The Final Weeks of Training

Across the Atlantic, springtime in South Carolina brought a welcome relief to the troops training at Camps Wadsworth and Sevier. With the difficult winter behind them, the men were no longer cooped up indoors. They had tired of watching such films as *The Training of a Soldier* and craved outside activities. The warmer climate helped reduce the sick rolls, and morale noticeably improved.[1] Free time was now spent playing baseball and other sports that had been neglected during the past few months. The men were in high spirits for another reason—rumors had spread throughout the camps that they would soon be heading overseas. In the case of the 30th Division, it was more than a rumor. Its commanding general learned from the War Department on 14 March 1918 "that your division will be prepared to embark for overseas service late in May and will undergo a 10-week course of training with the British Army in France."[2] It was one of the six divisions, along with the 77th, 82nd, 35th, 28th, and 4th, chosen for transport on British vessels as part of the training agreement with Pershing. Similar news was not received at Camp Wadsworth, and O'Ryan had no idea when his division was slated to embark.

Before departing Camp Sevier, the 30th Division needed to be brought up to strength. This was accomplished with new recruits from Camp Dodge, Iowa, and Camp Jackson, South Carolina. They were formally assigned to depot brigades, units organized to train soldiers who needed special help and were thought unready for service overseas. These organizations supplied manpower to under-strength combat divisions throughout 1918. The men who arrived at Sevier were immediately placed at the mercy of noncommissioned officers and taught the rudiments of soldiering and other skills.[3]

With overseas service on the horizon, both divisions received intense training for the remainder of March and the entire month of April. Officers who had been away at schools such as the one for brigade commanders and field officers at Fort Sam Houston, Texas, were brought back to the camps, newly proficient in map reading, training methods, guard duty, and military law.[4]

Despite Pershing's call for training in open warfare, men were spending up to three days at a time in the trenches at Sevier and Wadsworth. Infantry units also focused on training with the artillery. In the mountains, an enlisted man in the 107th Infantry marveled at the fact that after reaching the artillery range, "you could see all over the country for miles." Even more fascinating to Private Pierce were the stereotypical local mountaineers, who he guessed "shave only once a year." Furthermore, "they think it is a wonderful sight to see a company of soldiers," he observed. "They all flock to the front door as if the world had come to an end."[5]

Typically, the divisions concentrated on the fundamentals of machine-gun instruction and gas training. In the latter, infantry battalions were taken company by company and instructed in the use of respirators as gas clouds passed by.[6] A private in the 30th Division described the ordeal of gas training. The troops were taken into the woods where shots were fired. Officers told the men it was gas and instructed them to put on their gas masks. "You clamped your nose, so you had to breathe through your mouth, through chemicals in your mask," Private Clodfelter recalled. "It kept the gas from getting in your lungs."[7]

At Wadsworth, gas training was more sophisticated. The men marched to the trenches, where an elaborate alarm system of bells and iron bars was used. As soon as the smell of gas was detected, a sentinel at the head of the stairs leading down into the trenches would kick a pail. The noise was intended to be the first warning to the men to put on their masks. Another soldier would then ring the bell or beat on the bars to alert the others of an attack. If a more general attack was suspected, warning was sent from the headquarters by telephone.[8]

To help with the training, more Allied instructors were brought in. This included fifteen Canadians, some of whom were veterans of Vimy Ridge, to teach the raw Americans the correct way to operate a machine gun. All of this training, according to a major in the 27th Division, was "to make the American soldier the best-trained, most self-reliant and thorough soldier the world ever knew." After becoming skilled with the bayonet and rifle, he would become a "dangerous foe to combat."[9]

Inspections of the 27th Division exposed a number of problems. Foremost was discipline within regiments. During an inspection of the 106th Machine-Gun Battalion, O'Ryan was appalled to see men in one company wearing "nondescript clothing," such as sweaters and overalls. He observed half the company drilling while the other half slept in cots or played games in the street. Supervision appeared to be insufficient; the captain of the company was in his quarters, leaving two lieutenants in charge. "There was an entire absence of steam, snap and punch," O'Ryan complained. He also inspected Company H of the 106th Infantry and found their dugout "in disorderly and unsatisfactory condition. Mess kits, books, papers and equipment were scattered about."[10]

As punishment, O'Ryan ordered the delinquent captain to report before an efficiency board, where he was reprimanded but allowed to stay with his unit. To the division commander, the 27th may have appeared more like a collection of amateur soldiers and less like the professional outfit that had impressed the Regulars on the Mexican border the previous year. But there was little that could be done at this point in the training. In reality, discipline within the 27th Division was quite good. Divisional court-martial orders show that few cases went to trial. Drunkenness and unauthorized absences were the main infractions, and they were dealt with by regimental commanders. The same was true in the 30th Division; there were no general court-martial hearings reported that winter or spring.

O'Ryan's strict command style was reflected in an incident that occurred in early January. The two main British trainers, Sergeant Major Tector and Major Sharp, held a séance at Wadsworth. Although they clearly enjoyed a humorous moment with a group of naive New Yorkers, O'Ryan found the incident less than amusing. He responded with a general order stating there would be "no more indiscriminate hypnotism in this camp."[11]

During a routine inspection in February, the 27th Division almost lost its commanding officer. O'Ryan rode to the artillery range at Glassy Rock Mountain, twenty-five miles outside camp, accompanied by the 52nd Artillery Brigade commanding officer, Brig. Gen. Charles Phillips. When the two were seven miles from the range, one of the guns fired. The tremendous noise scared the general's horse as he led it up a mountain pass, and the startled animal kicked O'Ryan so hard in the stomach that he was unconscious for fifteen minutes. The party was far from the first aid station at the range, and it was feared the 27th Division commander might die before receiving medical attention. However, O'Ryan surprised everyone, and after several days of rest and nursing, he was back at work.[12]

One can only speculate on the effect O'Ryan's death would have had on the division. He had done much to shape the division up to this point, and the affection of the men of the 27th for him can hardly be overstated. This became evident when he solicited ideas for the division insignia. The men unanimously voted in favor of an elaborate design that consisted of the letters NYD (New York Division) monogrammed within a red-bordered black circle, along with the stars of the constellation Orion, a tribute to their commanding general.[13]

For the New Yorkers at Camp Wadsworth, the training was tiresome and they grew impatient. Soldiers wrote home to complain that the division was being ignored; they worried that maybe it was destined to sit out the conflict. This prompted Senator J. W. Wadsworth of New York, a descendent of the family after which the training camp was named, to write the War Department that the "delay in sending the 27th Division abroad has received considerable notice, especially when the quality of it is compared with the other divisions already gone over." Assistant Secretary Benedict Crowell replied: "We fully appreciate the excellence of the 27th Division, and it is far from forgotten. The officers and men, and their friends at home, can rest assured that the War Department intends to use the division to full advantage."[14]

Finally, on 15 April, O'Ryan received orders for overseas deployment. His instructions were extremely vague; they made no mention of when the New Yorkers were to leave Wadsworth or what would happen once they arrived in France. One part told O'Ryan to "prepare various parts of your division for shipment overseas by 1 June and the remainder a month later, since there was not enough shipping available to take the entire division over at one time." O'Ryan was also told to "be prepared for movement to concentration camp at any time for possible earlier shipment." Four days later, another telegram ordered O'Ryan to "send advance detachment of 314 officers and men, designated therein for your division, reported ready and equipped for overseas duty."[15] All of this meant that he had about two weeks to prepare his men.

Deployment of the divisions was based largely on the reports filed from the first round of inspections in late 1917. They were reviewed at the War Department, and a ranking system rated the divisions from the most to least deployable based on the inspectors' remarks. Although a second round of inspections was scheduled for the spring, these would have little bearing on when the divisions were to be sent overseas. The General Staff assumed that any deficiencies could be corrected in the training areas in France. Still, the Inspector General's Office took the next inspections seriously, as evidenced by the reports filed on both the 27th and 30th Divisions.

Brig. Gen. Eli Helmick, who had conducted the first round of National Guard inspections at the end of 1917, again was charged with visiting the training camps. He made no effort to hide his disdain for the state units and wrote detailed reports on their alleged problems. He arrived at Camp Wadsworth on 2 May and found most of the camp nearly deserted. One unit that had not yet headed north for embarkation, the 106th Infantry, received a thorough review. Helmick's report was particularly hard on the regiment's officers. He wrote that the camp was "lacking definite control on the part of the officers, which is an index to good discipline." Helmick noted that the 106th's problems ran deep, and his only suggestion to alleviate its troubles was for the regiment to get extensive training before being allowed to enter the front lines. His analysis was correct. Four months later, the 106th engaged the enemy during its first major offensive and suffered significant casualties, largely the result of poor leadership on the battlefield.[16]

Helmick inspected the 30th Division on 10 May, but by then Maj. Gen. George W. Read, who had taken command of the division from Faison, had left for the port of embarkation. Thus, Helmick's inspection was largely based on interviews with the few officers remaining in camp and internal reports that had been left behind. He and two assistants spent five days at Camp Sevier but found that a full inspection was impossible. As a result, he was unable to "arrive at any definite, just conclusions as to the training."

Yet, in an angry tone, Helmick wrote that he was "satisfied training was defective, and discipline was far from satisfactory. It would not be possible for me to attempt to fix the responsibility for this condition." He concluded that "numerous changes of division commander made it practically impossible to hold any one officer responsible for the training and discipline." Furthermore, it was his opinion that it "will take from 30 to 60 days intensive training for the infantry regiments, after they get abroad, to become ready for active service in the field."[17]

The thrill of finally going overseas was evident throughout Sevier and Wadsworth. At the former, Sgt. Judson W. Dennis, of the 119th Infantry, noted the excitement in his letters home. He wrote from South Carolina for the last time on 28 April. Dennis and the rest of his company were placed in quarantine, a standard procedure for troops preparing for overseas duty, he told his mother Minnie, who lived in Tip Top, Tennessee. However, they were allowed to celebrate the night before leaving South Carolina. "The girls of Greenville gave the soldier boys a farewell reception at all the dance halls in Greenville last night," Dennis proudly told her, and "they sure did treat us so nice." He then turned serious and reassured his mother:

> Don't be uneasy or worry about me, for we are going to make it alright. We are willing and ready to sail, for we feel it is our duty and a debt we owe to our country to be loyal sons. We feel that we are going to be cared for and someday return to our own native land of the free.[18]

Dennis also wrote to his brother, Tom, on the same day, to say that his company was "longing for the time to come for us to see sunny France. We want to see the front and go over the top."[19]

An advance party of the 30th Division left Camp Sevier on 30 April 1918 and moved north for embarkation overseas. It was customary for an officer and small detachment to sail ahead to make arrangements in France to receive the division. Other elements of the 30th departed shortly thereafter, and by the end of May, the entire division had left South Carolina. Typically, it took two days by train to reach the embarkation ports of the Northeast. Cheering crowds greeted the troops when they passed through the towns of North Carolina and Virginia. During stops in Washington, D.C., and Philadelphia, Red Cross workers served apples, cigarettes, coffee, and sandwiches.[20]

For the men of the 30th Division, many of whom had spent their lives in the rural south, the departure elicited fear and excitement. Sergeant Dennis noted that when the train approached New York City, the sight of the Statue of Liberty in the distance "did much to ease his nerves."[21] He then wrote his brother: "Don't spend another year in the South. Come to the northern states. They are the garden spot of the world." Dennis was impressed by a "big reception" given by the New York City YWCA where the girls "sport diamonds as common as an old shoe" and "are the friendliest people I ever met."[22] Dennis would have the chance to write his mother and brother only a few more times throughout the next six months. He was killed near the Selle River in mid-October.[23]

Troop movement was conducted with detailed efficiency. Because so many men were heading to terminals in New York and New Jersey at the same time, trains going north moved at a slow pace so they would not all arrive together. This gave soldiers ample opportunity to write letters or sleep. Some men rested in passenger or overnight sleeping cars, while company cooks took up residence in baggage cars that had been converted to kitchens.

Upon entering the New York City area, men were assigned to an embarkation camp—either Camp Mills on Long Island or Camp Merritt in New Jersey (seventeen miles north of Hoboken). Merritt was the larger and busier of the two camps, and by the time the war ended, more than 578,000 men had passed through there.[24] Facilities included a base hospital, thirty-nine warehouses, and a bakery that produced 22,000 loaves a day. Troops were expected to stay in the camps a few days before moving to the port at Hoboken.[25]

Days were marked by inspection, instruction in behavior aboard ship, and indoctrination. For officers, it was a busy time, as they had to ensure that service records were in order and that men were issued clothing and equipment. Canvas leggings and campaign hats were exchanged for woolen puttees and caps. As a grim reminder of war's potential consequence, each soldier was issued two aluminum identification discs that contained his name, rank, unit designation, and serial number. In the event of death, one disc remained around the neck of the deceased man when buried while the other was sent to the Graves Registration Service headquarters for inclusion in the casualty file.[26]

Soldiers also received their final pay before leaving the United States. The War Department recognized that converting foreign currency might be a problem, so to eliminate unnecessary money-changing, soldiers were paid in French francs or British pounds. The army encouraged families to visit loved ones, and through efforts of the YWCA, hostess houses provided relatives with meals and lodging. Commanding officers were discouraged from issuing leave passes in an effort to keep men from the vices of New York City.[27]

Before a soldier was allowed to board the transport, there was a final physical examination, and anyone diagnosed with a contagious disease was not allowed to sail. To prepare for what lay ahead, there were motion pictures about lifeboat drills and lectures about the threat of German U-boat attacks. Soldiers were required to sign and address cards to next of kin indicating that "the vessel on which they sailed had arrived safely." The cards were kept at the port of embarkation and mailed when a ship was reported arrived.[28]

By the time the entire 30th Division reached France on 2 July 1918, it had used twenty-five transports to take it across the ocean. Most transports were British, although the 105th Engineers was "carried over" on the *Talthybius*, a "leaking and dirty" Canadian transport that was once used as a cattle boat.[29] Before any of the ships left the docks, precautions were taken to prevent sabotage. Portholes were closed, and all men, with the exception of guards, were sent below deck. Once the transports entered open water, the troops were assigned submarine observation duty. Each ship had a specific place for observation, with posts connected to a central station by telephone.[30] Ships were equipped with 6-inch guns and traveled in a convoy, normally with ten others and a group of navy destroyers. A zigzag course was developed in an effort to confuse and dodge the prowling enemy submarines.[31]

Although none of the transports carrying the 27th or 30th Division troops encountered danger, U-boat attacks were a serious threat, as shown by the sinking of the *Tuscania* on 12 February 1918. On its way to Le Havre with 2,013 men aboard, the transport was struck by two torpedoes fired by a U-boat and sank seven miles north of Rathlilin Island. The attack cost 230 lives. Despite stringent efforts to protect the ships, several more transports were attacked in 1918.[32]

A typical voyage was that taken by the 119th Infantry. It sailed on the *Haverford* alongside a school of porpoises that joined the convoy and unknowingly provided entertainment during the slow trip across the Atlantic.[33] It took twelve days to reach England; this was the average time for a transport. Ships to France took two days more. Seasickness was prevalent, and when a man was well enough to eat, he was fed British fare. Instead of fried chicken, pork chops, hot biscuits, and other American delicacies, a meal might consist of mutton and orange marmalade. "Six meals a day—three up, three down" is how one soldier described the difficulty of eating.[34]

The journey of the 27th Division was similar, except that a few of its regiments sailed from Newport News, Virginia. It was a minor port compared to Hoboken, and prior to sailing, the men were housed at Camp Stuart—smaller than Camps Merritt and Mills. The 107th Infantry spent a week here, where men slept in "warm, comfortable barracks, furnished with spring beds instead of canvas cots."[35] They traveled aboard the USS *Susquehanna*, a captured German vessel previously named the *Rhein*. The *Susquehanna* was slightly larger than other troop transports, and men called their quarters "the black hole of Calcutta" because they were located so far below deck. Officers and men in the 107th had shown stamina during its months of training at Wadsworth, but General O'Ryan was concerned they would go soft during the voyage.[36] He therefore issued orders for the regiment to continue physical exercise aboard the ships. It was to be done as long as it did not interfere with the policing of quarters, guard duty, administration, and kitchen policing.[37]

To help pass the time on board, newspapers printed wireless news and ship gossip. The *Calamares*, which transported the 53rd Brigade and the 104th and 105th Machine-Gun Battalions, produced *The Sea Serpent*. It attempted to bring humor into the boring passage. The paper announced the weather forecast as "dry—until we reach France" and indicated the regulation uniform would be "life belts—day and night." Another transport called its paper the *Mid Ocean Comin' Thru*; still another named its publication the *Rail Splitter*, in honor of the ship's name, the *President Lincoln*.[38] Crews were made up of sailors from the Naval Reserve Force, and an entrepreneurial camaraderie existed between them and the doughboys. Aboard the *Antignone*, the 107th Infantry could have their uniforms cleaned by the sailors, who used the revenue for a day's outing in the ports of France. The crew also peddled candy and pickles, and soldiers with a supply of money were happy to indulge.[39]

7

ARRIVAL

Units of the 30th Division, such as the 117th Infantry, docked in Liverpool, England, and remained there for a day before being transported by train to Dover for the passage to Calais, France. As the train passed through London, people waved flags and handkerchiefs to welcome the Americans. In Dover, the effects of the war on the home front were evident. At restaurants, soldiers signed food cards before being served anything to eat, and throughout the city signs pointed to places where people could go if they were caught on the street during an air raid. Some of the shelters were built in cellars and some in cliffs.[1]

After a two-hour trip aboard a channel steamer from Dover, the regiment reached Calais. Instead of cheering crowds, the doughboys heard distant artillery fire, their introduction to the war zone. The nights brought further reminders of what war was about in the form of German air raids.[2]

At Calais, the men had their first look at the devastation of four years of war. When a soldier from the 105th Engineers wandered through the city, he was shocked by the sight of "hundreds of little children on the streets all day begging" and roads that were "narrow and dirty, with a few street cars in operation, manned by women conductors and motor women."[3] Calais was supposed to be a rest area for the 30th Division troops, but as Col. Joseph Hyde Pratt, in command of the 105th Engineers, recalled, the "rest is questionable. This is the dirtiest camp we have been in yet. Officers are in large tents, about twenty-four to a tent. The men are twelve to sixteen in small tents, no beds or mattresses, just their own blankets." During a sightseeing excursion, Pratt observed that "all around the center of town are dugouts for the civilian population. Many of the houses are banked up with sand bags for protection. Absence of young men is noticeable, and a great many women and girls are in black."[4]

Over many years, Calais had seen its share of destruction. Located twenty-two miles from the English coast, it was once the eighth largest port in France, known for factories that processed silk and cotton tulle. In 1347, the city put up a heroic stand before capitulating to the English, and it was more than two centuries before the French could recapture it. By 1918, the French maintained control of the city, but numerous German air raids had laid much of it in ruins.[5]

O'Ryan's division sailed directly to France and disembarked at Brest to await training orders. The port city, which dated back to Roman times, had a population of 90,000 just before World War I. In 1918, the U.S. Army and Navy took over Brest, including its famous château.[6] Sergeant Jacobson, along with two other men from the 107th Infantry, played tourists one day during their brief stay in the city. After "turning the corner of a particularly beautiful avenue," Jacobson recorded, "we forgot the warbling birds and the idyllic quiet of the sleeping city. We saw our first Germans! We beheld perhaps 50 prisoners marching between blue-clad poilus. Never could one imagine a motlier crew. They were unkempt of hair and person, shockingly in need of razoring, and their uniforms were of every cut and color ever issued in Germany."[7]

A more frequent sight in Brest and other French ports was troops on leave. For the right price, a meal, a hot bath, or female companionship could be found. The brothels in France were in great demand, as witnessed by British Capt. Robert Graves. On one occasion in Calais, he passed by a brothel and saw a "queue of 150 men waiting outside the door, each to have his short turn with one of the three women in the house."[8] They were probably visiting one of the houses licensed by the French. Even though legal prostitutes were supposedly inspected on a weekly basis, British and French authorities recorded high numbers of venereal cases. This was no surprise to Col. Hugh H. Young. The Johns Hopkins urologist witnessed some of the so-called medical examinations of prostitutes. He was appalled by the unsanitary methods employed and advised General Pershing to keep Americans away from the houses.[9]

Pershing's previous experience with organized brothels was during the punitive expedition in Mexico. In 1916, he had established a fenced-in compound where prostitutes were kept and routinely examined. Upon entering the area, soldiers were examined, and when they left, they were given a tube of prophylactic ointment. There were no documented cases of disease during the expedition. Despite the success in Mexico, Pershing never seriously considered a similar operation in France, for the simple reason that he did not want families back in America to think he condoned immorality in the AEF. Whereas the punitive expedition was conducted with Regulars, the army was now comprised overwhelmingly of citizen soldiers.[10] Pershing issued three general orders in 1917 to warn the troops already in France and as a preventative measure for those soon to arrive.

First, he urged officers to lecture men on the virtues of staying clean and instructed medics to conduct examinations every two weeks. Pershing established prophylactic stations in every command, and any soldier who failed to get treatment within three hours after an infection became visible was subject to court-martial. Another order set up regimental infirmaries so soldiers could be at the front for treatment with their units and not crowd hospitals in the rear. The third was more severe; it demanded that officers "give personal attention to matters pertaining to the prevention of venereal disease. No laxity or half-hearted efforts in this regard will be tolerated." At Brest and Calais, Pershing declared houses of prostitution and saloons off limits. Soldiers' passes were limited, and commanding officers were required to report infection rates.[11]

While some commanders turned a blind eye while their men consorted with prostitutes, O'Ryan paid close attention to the commander-in-chief's third general order. Wherever the 27th billeted in France and Belgium, he ordered military police to stand picket in front of houses of ill repute to discourage his men from visiting.[12] This measure apparently worked, since only five men from the 27th were reported to be infected at the end of June. The 30th Division was even healthier that month; only three cases were reported among its men.[13]

After a short stay in Calais, the 30th Division left the city during the final week of May and moved south to the Eperlecques training area. Before departing for the training area, the division commander, Major General Read, issued a general order to help protect the men of the 30th against the dangers they might encounter. "Where troops are in tents, it is not necessary to pitch tents in regular order," he warned. "They should be pitched under trees and alongside hedges, where as much concealment can be secured as possible. Furthermore, embankments, 3 feet high and 2 feet wide at the top, will be thrown up around each tent, in order to give protection from bursting bombs. This work will be done at once."

Inglinghem was the site of the first overseas training camp for the 30th Division in Belgium. There, the 30th was affiliated with the British 39th Division, originally composed of locally raised battalions mainly from the south of England. Like many British divisions on the Western Front, it had suffered enormous casualties during the Somme offensive and at Third Ypres. The 39th had been reduced to a cadre in May 1918 and was never reconstituted.

During the first week of June, the 27th Division left Brest, and any concern O'Ryan had about the physical condition of the men was put to rest. Regiments hiked through one village after another, carrying packs, ammunition, and rifles, a load weighing about eighty pounds, without a soldier lagging behind.[14] At this time, the division received word that it was going to be trained by the British in the Rue-Buigny area. O'Ryan regarded this decision with pride and told his men: "Without a doubt, our division was selected for cooperation with the British not only because of its military excellence, but also the well-known intelligence of its personnel and their ability as New Yorkers to get along with strangers under any circumstances."[15]

O'Ryan's division commenced training on 10 June 1918, attached to the cadre of the British 66th Division, which was formed from second-line troops of the Territorial Force units in the 42nd Division. It had supplied drafted soldiers to overseas units before heading to France in March 1917, where it fought with distinction. The 27th Division commander knew from the inspections at Wadsworth that his division had some minor disciplinary problems and that these

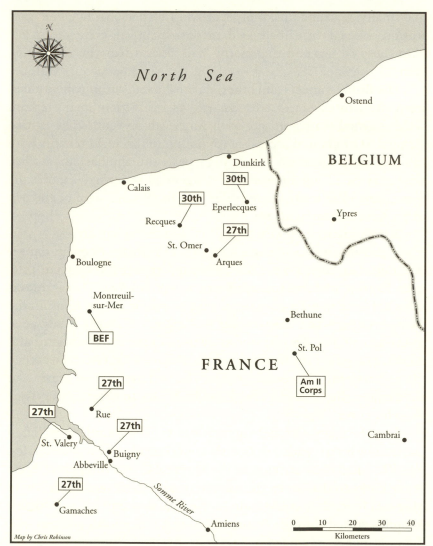

British training areas used by the American divisions, June–July 1918

would have to be addressed immediately, before training with the British got underway. On 9 June 1918, he issued Bulletin #39 "to each squad in the division armed with the rifle . . . to be frequently read and discussed by the men of the squad." Among the points covered in almost three pages, he stressed: "Be disciplined; shoot to hit; preserve your morale; never be surprised; know your gas defense;

and finally, read and follow orders governing personal hygiene, sanitation, rules of the road, and march discipline." He promised: "Do these things and the enemy will always fear the 27th Division."[16]

The British officers and other ranks who had accompanied them from the United States after serving as instructors in the camps were assigned temporarily to both American divisions. The British General Staff granted special permission "for them to remain with the American divisions during their period in the back area since they may be of use to assist in the general training."[17] Once the Americans were ready to enter the line, the British were to go back to England for reassignment.

British instructors were eager to teach the newly arrived Americans, and the first lesson was how to deal with the frequent danger of air attacks. Lights were not permitted at night, they were told; even lighting matches outside tents was prohibited. These precautions did little to deter persistent German pilots. Bombs fell "almost every evening when the weather was clear," a doughboy recorded in his diary.[18] The British, who were used to the constant bombardments, headed for the dugouts, while the green Americans watched the air raids and "appeared to enjoy the performance as much as a child enjoys the circus."[19] They would not have to be reminded twice to go for cover.

Since February, Colonel Simonds had worked countless and often frustrating hours with his British counterparts to prepare for the 280,000 doughboys arriving in the spring. He had ironed out most of the kinks so that when the ten divisions set foot on French soil in May and June, they could train in the British sector without delay. Simonds sorted through British training publications, such as *The Training and Employment of Divisions*, *Bayonet Training*, and *Scouting and Patrolling*, that Pershing had ordered Colonel Bacon to send to II Corps for its officers.[20] Simonds also dealt with more complicated matters, such as soldiers' mail and the issue of rations. The censorship of mail had concerned the British army since the Boer War, and in 1914 all mail sent from France was passed through a censor, who blacked out any mention of location or numbers of troops. On the outside of the envelope only the soldier's name and unit could appear. Any words the censor thought potentially helpful to the enemy were deleted. Simonds and British intelligence agreed before the first Americans arrived that they would follow the British procedure and use the green envelopes and Field Service cards the British soldiers had been using since the war began.

Because sending and receiving mail was complex, lectures were arranged to explain the regulations and encourage doughboys to use the Field Postcard, which had fixed phrases, such as "I am quite well," "I am wounded," "I have received your letter," and "I have received no letter from you." The soldier would cross out the inapplicable phrases and send the card home. Most preferred to write letters, which kept censors busy as they crossed out certain phrases or, in some instances, confiscated the correspondence altogether.[21]

Despite the great effort Simonds and the British devoted to the mail issue to ensure a smooth operation, the Americans still managed to complicate matters. First, the AEF Postal Service at Chaumont failed to establish an Army Post Office (APO) in the British area. As a result, mail sent to officers and men in American II Corps either went astray or was routed to a BEF post office at Hesdin. From there, it was sent by motorcycle sidecar to the II Corps statistical office for distribution. The long process caused much delay. Not until early September 1918 did the Americans in the British sector have their own post office, APO 790.[22]

There was also the problem of men blatantly violating the censorship regulations. Each month, the British issued a report on censorship of mail sent by American troops, since outgoing mail passed through the BEF. One serious case involved Pvt. Curtis Conion of the 412th Telegraph Battalion. In a letter to his mother in Texas, in which he inquired about her health, he inserted a small map that showed the location of his unit between the envelope and the folded pages. The letter was stamped approved by his unit censor, but it was opened by the British War Office censors and confiscated. Private Conion was tried by a court-martial, found guilty, and forced to forfeit two-thirds of his pay for a month and to perform hard labor for the same period.[23]

An even more important issue to contend with was feeding the troops. To simplify matters, Simonds agreed that the British would handle rations. A British officer was detailed as a senior supply officer, and, along with two assistants and a detachment of seventy-five men, he distributed rations at a railhead. From there, the rations were delivered daily by horse or motor transport, known as pack or ration trains. They were then handed over to American division senior supply officers and distributed to the regiments.[24]

Despite the best efforts of the American regimental quartermasters, there were early difficulties in distribution, as noted sarcastically by British Lt. (later Maj. Gen.) J. M. L. Grover, who was assigned to train the American 107th Infantry. "They had little organization for meals and lined up in single file to receive their portions," Gower noticed. "The result was that as the last man got his dinner, the first man was back for the next meal. There wasn't a single night that I was with the Americans when at least one company failed to get anything, although they'd been working with us then for some weeks."[25]

Once the rations found their way to the hungry troops, the men often found the food disagreeable. The Americans never took to the British food and complained bitterly. Accustomed to large portions, the doughboys were issued a small meat ration, tea instead of coffee, and cheese. Simonds, who received the brunt of complaints, appointed a board to investigate the alleged problems.

British rations, the board concluded, were slightly less than those issued by the U.S. Army. The meat ration was deemed sufficient, and the board suggested that American soldiers would get accustomed to eating cheese. To appeal to the American palate, the board recommended more vegetables and coffee rather than tea. The latter, according to O'Ryan, was peculiar to the British soldiers. Every afternoon at 5:00, he claimed, "they had a tea break, no matter what the battlefield situation or where they were located."[26]

8

TRAINING OVERSEAS COMMENCES

Simonds prepared for instruction in the British sector with help from an AEF-produced guide, *Program of Training for American Divisions with the British*. Copies were ready for distribution when the divisions arrived. It outlined each training period and the hours needed to train each unit. Its calculations were based on a minimum six-hour day, excluding Sundays and holidays.[1]

The ten weeks allotted to train infantry and machine-gun troops were divided into three periods. Period A, a minimum of four weeks, included drill, musketry, and physical exercise. This involved tutoring in infantry weapons, such as Lewis guns, light trench mortars, bombs, and grenades. Signalers, engineers, and medical personnel also received their specialized training at this time. During Period B, the Americans were attached to British troops in the line for three weeks. Officers and noncommissioned officers entered for a 48-hour period; men combined with British companies and platoons for shorter periods. For Period C, each regiment trained in a rear area for three to four weeks for advanced instruction in procedures, such as the maneuvering of battalions and companies.[2]

An advantage of training with the British was the extensive experience their officers and noncommissioned officers provided. But there were problems with this relationship. One was that the Americans refused to allow training to be dominated by British doctrine. Simonds sensed that "the tendency of the British was to actually take over the training of the platoons and regiments" from the inexperienced American officers, who "wanted to be friendly and cordial" with their allies. He sent a tersely worded memorandum to division commanders: "A clear understanding has been reached with the British Training Section that American authorities retain absolute control of, and responsibility for, the training. British instructors will lend assistance to American officers, mainly by going through the work beforehand with them and during the actual instruction of the troops. In no case during this training will British officers take command of American troops."[3] Such feelings were known to Haig, who told Bonham-Carter: "Our officers are not to command and order the Americans about, but must only help American officers by their advice and experience to become both leaders in the field, as well as instructors."[4]

Bonham-Carter took a strong interest in the Americans. His diary and correspondence show that he met with Simonds or visited training areas on a daily basis. He wrote: "Spent all day visiting Americans; officers good—NCOs bad; men first rate; and the men in the ranks did not appear to render their officers the respect given by ours to officers on account of holding a commission, nor the trustful obedience and devotion our men give to any officer who proves his worth. They always seemed to be keeping their end up."[5]

The British soldiers Bonham-Carter assigned to instruct the Americans were fresh from combat in some cases. Three years before, they had been recruits heeding the call of Field Marshal Lord Kitchener. Now they were survivors of the Somme and Passchendaele. The weight of their experience was quite apparent to a private in the American 105th Machine-Gun Battalion, who viewed his British instructors as "a tired, inarticulate crowd."[6] But such experience would be an advantage when the two allies went into battle together. Lt. Col. Sir Phillip A. Christison, a former battalion commander in the 15th (Scottish) Division, was ordered to help train the Americans. He commanded the 7th Cameron Highlanders (Training Battalion), one of the many skeleton units formed for the purpose of assisting the doughboys. After his month-long assignment with the American 119th Infantry, he bemoaned: "I never saw my old and loved battalion again."[7]

Christison's first meeting with the Americans was frustrating for the veteran British officer. He was asked to address them with a few personal experiences and lessons he had learned during the war. "When I had ended," he wrote home, "an old colonel, dressed more like a sheriff, said Gentleman I would like you all to give the Scottish major a healthy round of thanks for his very interesting lecture. Then he shook his finger and went, but I'll have you know that the British have been trying these tactics for nearly four years and they ain't done much damn good."[8]

Remarkably, spirits remained high within the British ranks despite heavy losses during the 1916 and 1917 campaigns and the more recent German offensives in the spring of 1918. At this stage in the war, the British were ideal tutors. As historian Paddy Griffith wrote: "By 1917, BEF infantry units had come of age . . . as some of the battalions had maintained a reputation for good discipline, cohesion, and an aggressive desire to dominate no man's land at every opportunity."[9] Although perhaps they did not appreciate it at the time, the Americans would receive the benefit of the British experiences of hard fighting at the Somme, Passchendaele, and, later, St. Quentin. While French units also trained AEF divisions in their sector and had much to contribute, the British offered them even more. At French headquarters, Maj. Paul Clark observed that for "their first period of instruction, the Americans are just as well off, if not much better off, with the British as with the French. There is a community of language, and there is no doubt that the discipline of the British is superior to the discipline of the French."[10]

In 1918, the composition of the American army in many ways resembled that of the British army when it had first entered the war. Four years later, the British army consisted of small cadre of prewar Regulars supplemented by a larger Territorial Force that nearly doubled the original BEF. The latter was organized much like the American National Guard regiments. By January 1918, the British army was filled largely with conscripts.[11]

It is true that losses in their battles over four years had changed British units. But such changes in British army divisions from 1914 to 1918 had little effect on their ability to keep fighting. "In 1918, as in earlier years," according to a study of morale in the BEF, "some units were more effective than others, and a host of reasons determined military effectiveness. Leadership, morale, training, and tactical ability were among the most important." Recently drafted men survived by blending with veterans, and "the survival of distinctive traditions and ethos in some units supports this contention. Conscription did not, in itself, affect combat performance to any great degree."[12]

One issue that neither Simonds nor the British could prepare for was how the American and British officers and men would actually get along as allies. Such a relationship was tainted because resentment toward the Americans ran deep, and some in the British officer corps were still annoyed by Pershing's rejection of amalgamation. One fervent critic was Maj. Walter Guinness (later the first Lord Moyne). As a staff officer of the British 66th Division, Guinness became well acquainted with the 27th Division and its commanding officer, who he described as "a typical Irish soldier of fortune." Guinness's diary is replete with negative comments about the American officers and their ability to command: "The senior American officers were very poor indeed. Many of them had been Regular Army officers, physically and mentally unfit for responsible commands under the strenuous conditions of modern war."[13]

Guinness mocked the training program Pershing's staff organized for the doughboys and considered him "to be the stupidest man in France, showing quite remarkable narrow-mindedness and obstinacy. He [Pershing] worked out a so-called 'schedule' of training, which itemized, almost hour by hour, what the American troops were to do. In many respects, the schedule was perfectly absurd. For instance, it made no provision whatsoever for route marching, and although in our weekly confidential reports on the American troops, which we had to furnish our G.H.Q., we continually emphasized this omission, there was nothing we could do to get it remedied."[14]

Furthermore, Guinness found it ludicrous that "all troops, wherever they were billeted, had to do exactly the same program for each week of their course. We were obliged to organize the area to afford special facilities near the coast for long-range musketry and in the southern part for maneuvers of, say, a whole brigade at a time. The third area was only suited for elementary training, owing to the difficulty of getting large tracts of land for maneuvers and the impossibility of

making safe rifle ranges. Nothing, however, would induce American
general headquarters to remodel its 'schedule' so as to conform to
the necessities of the training ground."[15]

While there is much truth in Guinness's comments, he was
probably incorrect in one area. "Many of the American divisions no
doubt would have liked to take advantage of our organization and
advice, but they were often too afraid to do so," he claimed, "because
they had a vicious system under which the inspector's staff used to
arrive unexpectedly, look at troops at work, and send in a report to
American G.H.Q."[16] Guinness exaggerated the system of inspection
in the AEF. Inspectors made every attempt "not to interfere with the
program of instruction," according to one historian.[17]

Less cynical than Guinness was Lt. L. G. Pinnell of the British
57th Machine-Gun Battalion. He took it upon himself to assist Americans in adopting "British principles of tactics and organization. With
all due respect to our French allies," Pinnell thought, "we are admit-
tedly more advanced than they." He surmised that "the system of
organization adopted by the Americans is halfway between ours and
the French." His commanding officer responded firmly but sympa-
thetically: "It is out of the question to attempt to influence the
course of training or system that they will adopt. I am afraid things
must take their course."[18]

How well the American and British troops interacted with each
other varied. One advantage was that both spoke the same language.
It was exciting for the majority of soldiers from both armies to hear
their native language spoken for the first time with a far different
accent. To the British soldier, the popular stereotype of an American was that of the cowboy. No doubt this image was perpetuated
by popular works of western fiction published since the 1870s that
circulated around the world and was enhanced by the success of
Buffalo Bill Cody's Wild West Show, which had toured Britain three
times. Cody's last tour was in 1916, and "by then, the show had
become the best-known representation of America," according to
one chronicler of this period.[19]

One only needs to look at the letters, diaries, and published histories from both the doughboys in the 27th and 30th Divisions and
the British Tommies to know how they interacted. The relationship
between the southern soldiers in the 30th Division and their British

instructors is a good example. Lt. Col. Graham Seton Hutchison of the British 33rd Division was typical of those troops who believed the cowboy stereotype. He couldn't understand why none of the doughboys in the American 30th Division resembled "a gentleman in a wide-brimmed hat, aiming sly shots at peaceful drinkers, rifling his pockets, and disappearing into the vastness of the mountains of Arizona," as portrayed in the movies. On the contrary, the "North Carolinians from the hills of southern America" struck him as more like his own division's Highlanders.[20]

Still another surprised British soldier wrote that the men in his battalion "had decided that these quiet, thinking men of North Carolina were not at all like the popular type of 'Yankees.' Some of them were proud to claim English descent! We wanted to justify our conception of the slack-jawed, keen-eyed man of quaint jargons and turns of speech that Mark Twain and others had introduced to us."[21] British troops repeatedly reflected on the impressive stature of their American allies. The 33rd Battalion Machine-Gun Corps historian commented that they "struck one at first glance as a concourse of very grave men with extremely tight uniforms."[22] A philosophical Tommy opined that "it is impossible to lay down any characteristics of the American soldier, owing to the large and varied area from which he may be drawn, and the mixture of races to be found in the large cities. . . . At the same time, the general impression gained is that the American is quicker witted than the average British soldier, and men from the country districts are undoubtedly of very fine physique."[23]

A member of the 26th Royal Fusiliers observed Americans camped next to his unit as "men with cowboy hats, who wore their packs the way Indian women carried babies."[24] Major General Grover echoed the conclusion of Haig that the rawness of the American National Guard troops was much like that of the British Territorial units in 1914. "They came from all walks of society," he commented, "and did stupid things, like shooting their ammunition when there was nothing to shoot at, and throwing grenades when there was nothing to throw them at."[25]

The Americans were often just as bewildered by their British allies and, at first, had no particular affection for them. The 27th Division had a large population of Irish Americans from New York, and it was no surprise to hear some of the men openly express their dislike for the British and make it known they would much rather train in the French sector. There were also a fair number of German Americans in the division, and like their families and friends at home, they may have secretly wished for a German victory.[26] But O'Ryan, whose bloodline was also Irish American, kept his opinions to himself and as a good officer insisted that his soldiers cooperate with their British hosts. The 30th Division's ranks were heavy with men of Scots-Irish descent, and it is likely that anti-British sentiment existed there as well. Recognizing the potential for dissension, the British officers and men were cordial to the American troops, and over time the two groups warmed to each other.[27]

Lieutenant Gow of the 107th Infantry perhaps best summed up the American attitude in a letter home in early June. Only a few months before, he had complained about the British officers who had helped train him at Wadsworth, but Gow now had a complete change of opinion after entering the line with the Tommies. "I like the Britishers," he wrote to his family. "The Englishman has a reserve that's very hard to break through, but when it is down, he is very much a human being."[28] Gow understood that because most officers were likely to be of a very different social class than other ranks, they exhibited different social behavior.[29]

Gow's division commander thought highly of the early days of the Anglo-American relationship. "We trained about one month with the British," O'Ryan wrote, "and having British officers assigned to each regiment helped us learn all the little things that we wanted to pick up on. We were given problems in field exercises and trained on a larger scale in war than we had ever been trained before, as the British had large training grounds about 20 miles south of Calais, and every sort and kind of school."[30]

While the training of the Americans was under way, the British brought up the amalgamation issue again. Although Pershing had already made his position very clear, he was put back on the defensive. This time the pressure came from Lt. Gen. J. C. Smuts, South Africa's representative in the War Cabinet. He insisted to Prime Minister Lloyd George that Pershing should be replaced since he was "without real war experience, and is already overwhelmed by the initial difficulties of a job too big for him." As a compromise, he suggested that "Pershing remain in charge of all organizations in the rear, but let the fighting command over the American Army be entrusted to another commander."[31] Smuts, who sought a field command, was probably referring to himself.

For some reason, Lloyd George took such talk seriously and called a meeting with Pershing on 2 June. He read a proposal requesting that Pershing "agree to leave entirely in the hands of the BEF the decision as to the schedules of training of American divisions assigned to the British, and also the power to put these divisions into action."[32] Pershing held his temper but very firmly objected to this proposition and stated that he "could not, should not, and would not surrender my prerogatives in this manner."[33] Lloyd George backed off. He then tried to make amends by stressing the importance of establishing good relations between the two English-speaking allies. A short time later, he met privately with Secretary of War Newton Baker during one of his trips to France and communicated a "desire for opportunity of American and British soldiers to fraternize." Lloyd George became oratorical: "The future peace of the world depends upon the American and British peoples understanding one another, and the best hope of such an understanding grows out of the intermingling of the soldiers of the two armies."[34]

Perhaps at the urging of Lloyd George, Sir Douglas Haig did his part to make the Americans feel welcome when he inspected a brigade of the 30th Division. During a private conversation with Col. Robert Bacon, he remarked that "they were some of the most splendid men I have ever seen . . . and very well drilled." Because they were National Guard troops, which "corresponded to our old militia," Haig said, "they pick up the work very quickly and, I think, should be able to go into the line much sooner than was anticipated, which is a good thing."[35]

9

Division Training

Despite Haig's enthusiasm for the fresh Americans, they needed more training. The overwhelmed doughboys were struggling to learn the system of areas and subareas the BEF used in the zone of the advance, which were complicated and nothing like what they had learned at Camps Sevier and Wadsworth. According to Sergeant Jacobson of the 107th Infantry, "each British unit was assigned to a certain longitudinal sector running westward from the battle front, and these sectors were divided laterally into three areas—the battle area, the forward area, and the training area." Billeting was very rudimentary, especially for enlisted men. While the officers had the luxury of sleeping in comfortable rooms at private homes, accommodations such as the barn one New Yorker slept in "next door to cows, pigs and horses" were not unusual for the enlisted men.[1] The men rarely, if ever, knew the names of the villages where their billets were situated, while many officers, just as ignorant, were forced to brush up on the geography of the area.[2]

Gradually, the Americans became accustomed to serving with the British. As the days passed, the regiments began to receive all sorts of British equipment—limbers, water carts, officer's mess carts, rolling kitchens, harnesses, animals, ordnance, and the important

British gas masks and steel helmets.[3] Cartridge belts and bayonets were collected and replaced with British Lee Enfields, British belts, and British bayonets. Reluctantly, the doughboys turned in their reliable "03" rifles in exchange for the unfamiliar British short magazine Lee Enfield (SMLE) rifle. Ordnance experts have called it one of the finest military bolt-action rifles ever produced. The SMLE weighed slightly less than the U.S. Model 1903 and was chambered for the standard British .303 cartridge. This meant that the smaller American ammunition was not compatible.[4] British noncommissioned officers instructed the Americans in loading and firing their new rifles with imitation bullets and "scores of other things a fellow should know about it."[5]

Training was basically the same each day, and it started early. The early hour made little difference to the doughboys, since nearby artillery firing commenced around 4 A.M. and made sleep impossible. After breakfast, a detachment of British noncommissioned officers arrived in the American areas to instruct U.S. noncommissioned officers in the use of gas masks, rifles, and bayonets. The officers, in turn, taught this to their men. Sergeant Jacobson described this instruction by the British as "up-to-the-minute, vigorous, and very interesting."[6] More advanced training was given in trench warfare, bayonet-running, and marksmanship at a short-range rifle pit. The doughboys drilled in grenade-throwing and trench movement under a gas cloud. In all this, according to a soldier from Tennessee, British instruction "was valuable beyond estimation."[7] One of the British lecturers boasted he had been "over the top 19 times without the loss of a single one of his men."[8] Yet all of this should have been familiar to the Americans, since they had already learned it at the camps in South Carolina.

Leisure time, as one New Yorker recounted, consisted of cooling off once or twice a week in a nearby lake or visiting a nearby town, such as St. Omer. The town was a short hike from camp and gave the doughboys an opportunity to see the wartime damage to some of the village's dwellings and pavement.[9] At night, the British entertained American officers with horse shows and dinner parties.[10]

Later that summer, Elsie Janis visited the 27th and 30th Divisions. The vaudeville star had thrilled audiences from the stages of New York and London with "her lilting voice and acrobatic dance routines," as one writer described her act.[11] Arguably, she was the Bob Hope of her day. For six months she traveled throughout the Western Front with her mother, performing shows for the American and British troops. Janis almost missed the troops training with Haig's army when the British at first refused to grant her access to their sector. It was a policy of the BEF to "never permit women to visit any of the front line areas under any conditions, at any time." Janis took her request to Pershing, who ordered his chief of staff, Maj. Gen. James W. McAndrew, to intervene. Pressure from the AEF commander forced the British to relent, and "after having stated their objects, they did not desire to refuse further."[12]

Janis entertained each division separately, and according to the 27th's commander, "her visit was greatly appreciated. She was the first American woman we had seen in several months."[13] Janis was also enthralled by the New Yorkers and described O'Ryan as "a blue-eyed, spick-and-span fighting Irishman with more 'it' than most." She got a good sense of the wartime conditions the troops were living with during one performance for the thousand or so doughboys of the 30th Division. She later recalled that "guns that had been murmuring started to roar, artillery clanked by, and just as I was yelling the point of a story, the men who were lying in the ground around my platform began to steal glances at something overhead."[14]

Along with the 27th and 30th, eight other American divisions were training in the British sector. But this was short lived. On 3 June 1918, Foch informed Haig he planed to remove five of them from the British sector. Foch was concerned that the German offensive at the Chemin des Dames on the Aisne had battered the French Sixth Army along the ridge, and there were few French divisions to hold off the enemy, which had about 4,000 guns. Haig, as expected, adamantly opposed this move. He considered it "a waste of valuable troops to send half-trained men to relieve French divisions. In three weeks time, these Americans will be fit for battle," he said, and he doubted "whether the French divisions they relieve will ever really fight in this war."[15]

Lloyd George sided with Haig, fearing that German reserves were still a threat to the British in Flanders and that the shift of divisions would be harmful. But it was Foch's call since he was general-in-chief of the Allied armies in France. Pershing made no effort to intervene, since the proposed move meant that the divisions would be closer to the main body of the AEF and he could use them once the crisis subsided. So on 15 June, five divisions (35th, 77th, 82nd, 4th, and 28th) in the British area were transferred to quiet sectors on the French front.[16]

As a gesture of goodwill between the British and French, Haig sent Bonham-Carter and a quartermaster to help coordinate the transfer. It was a long trip by Rolls Royce for the British officers and their drivers that was made longer because of "two or three tire punctures and no spare wheels." After arriving in the French sector, Bonham-Carter "had little to do except deal with administrative matters and answer questions about training."[17]

More important news occurred around that time; Pershing finally selected a commander for II Corps. Although he created a corps headquarters staff, he waited to appoint a corps commander until he evaluated the performance of his general officers at the division level.[18] His choice for II Corps was Major General Read, "a handsome, tall cavalryman, who looked to one acquaintance as if he might have been a model for one of Frederick Remington's drawings of a frontier cavalry officer," as a historian described the former recruiting officer and 30th Division commander.[19]

Impressed with Read for some time, Pershing recommended him for promotion to brigadier general in 1917.[20] Read's appointment was well received by the divisions attached to II Corps. The officers of the 30th Division, in particular, were elated to see one of their own selected, and O'Ryan was pleased since he and Read were classmates at the Army War College. The British too, especially Haig, were comfortable with Read. "He seemed to me too old for the duties of a G.O.C. Division," the BEF commander thought, "but he knows the fundamentals of war, and should do well as a corps commander." Haig was being generous. Read may have known the fundamentals of war but he had no battlefield experience to put his knowledge into practice. After graduating from West Point in 1883, he had taught military science in Iowa, then commanded a troop of the 5th Cavalry Regiment at a remote western post. He served in Cuba during the Spanish-American War as Fifth Army Corps staff officer, never facing the enemy.[21]

Haig's approval of Read was probably self-serving. He must have felt a sense of security when Pershing selected a corps commander, since he could then assume that there was no immediate plan to remove the other divisions from the British. When Haig and Pershing met on 30 June, they discussed the appointment of Read and agreed that "four divisions are too large a force for an inexperienced corps commander. Two divisions are ample."[22] This is peculiar, since the other AEF corps had at least four divisions under command of officers who had about the same level of experience as Read.

Little is known about Read's work as corps commander. He left minimal trace of his experience in the war. Read is rarely mentioned in the correspondence of others, either American or British, and did not leave behind a body of papers. Those who do mention Read describe him as amiable. The British Fourth Army commander, Gen. Sir Henry Rawlinson, considered him a "nice calm gentlemanly man who does not get rattled."[23] After the war, Read wrote a brief unpublished narrative of his experiences in France. The manuscript is superficial and shies away from intimate or controversial moments during the war, although there is one instance that offers some hint into Read's personality. He humorously tells of breaking up a gambling party during his first week at II Corps headquarters. Read warned the culprits that any future behavior would not be tolerated unless he was invited to join.[24]

It also is difficult to gauge the command style of Read as a general officer. An examination of the orders issued from II Corps headquarters reveals that most were written by Simonds, and it appears that Read allowed division commanders wide latitude in day-to-day functions. He can be judged as a commanding officer who wanted to be liked by everyone and tried to avoid controversy.

Once Read was promoted to corps commander, a vacancy existed in the 30th Division. Brig. Gen. Lawrence D. Tyson, 59th Brigade commander, expected to fill the post. He certainly had leadership qualities. A future U.S. senator, Tyson graduated from West Point and attended law school after his obligatory service in the army. He was an attorney in the private sector until he was commissioned as a colonel during the Spanish-American War. Afterward, he affiliated himself with the Tennessee National Guard and served with the 30th Division since its formation. An even more logical replacement for Read would have been Brigadier General Faison, another West Point graduate, who was also with the division since the beginning. For a short period he commanded the 30th Division and by virtue of his experience was qualified for the permanent post. But Pershing had other ideas. He brought in Maj. Gen. Edward M. Lewis from the 2nd Division as the 30th's seventh, and final, commanding officer. He had led the 3rd Brigade, 3rd Division, at Belleau Wood, earning glowing admiration from Pershing's close friend, Maj. Gen. Harbord.[25] Lewis perfectly fitted the description of a Pershing commander. Not only was he a West Point classmate of the commander-in-chief, but he was also a graduate of the Army War College. Praised as "a model commander," Lewis remained with the 30th Division until it returned home in 1919.[26]

Tyson's reaction to Lewis's appointment was predictable. "Faison and I have borne the brunt of the day," he moaned to a friend in Tennessee. "We trained the division and brought it over here, and made it all ready for somebody else's benefit."[27] But neither he nor Faison had a chance at being named division commander. Tyson's officer rating, which was compiled after the armistice, illustrates how lucky he was to have been a brigade commander. He was a good disciplinarian but was "not deemed aggressive enough." Another officer judged Tyson's ability more harshly: "I do not recommend him for promotion. If active operations were to continue, I would be disposed to recommend him for duty at a depot, rather then for the command of a fighting brigade."[28]

Faison's rating, on the other hand, showed him to possess "the essential qualifications of leadership and an excellent, well-trained mind." Yet Pershing did not have a high opinion of Faison. During a visit to the 30th Division training area on 1 July, Pershing was angered that Faison "had not arranged any program for visiting his troops; consequently, we did some aimless wandering through his sector." Furthermore, he noted, Faison "seemed to have no energy or grasp of the situation."[29] Nevertheless, Faison and Pershing remained cordial until Faison died in 1938.[30]

There was also a change of officers on the British side that impacted the Americans. On 23 June 1918, Lt. Gen. Sir Ivor Maxse was appointed inspector general of training of the BEF. By virtue of this new position, Maxse directly oversaw the training of the American divisions in the British sector. At 56, he was a career officer who had trained and commanded the 18th Division until January

1917 and had shaped it into one of the BEF's best units. Maxse had then been promoted to command XVIII Corps. Haig had long considered creating a BEF inspector general of training, and in a letter to Secretary of the War Cabinet Sir Maurice Hankey, he wrote: "I consider it a matter of the highest urgency to take steps to improve the efficiency of training throughout the armies in France."[31]

Maxse's new position of inspector of training eclipsed that of Bonham-Carter. Although disappointed that he was no longer a field commander, Maxse worked hard in his new assignment and made inroads in coordinating a unified training doctrine, which had been lacking within the British army in France. But this took time, and there is no evidence that his work had any direct influence on the training of American soldiers. Bonham-Carter, on the other hand, did have some effect on the doughboys. In reflecting upon his experience with II Corps, he wrote to his sister: "My work with the Americans is now practically finished, and the most backward of the divisions now with us is very nearly fit to stand on its own feet and walk with help. Their freshness is very invigorating; one only realizes after being with them how tired we all are."[32] He had done his bit.

During training, the doughboys also became acquainted with Canadian troops, their North American neighbors, and, as was true of the British, they learned from the Canadian divisions. It was not hard to run into them. By the time of the armistice, more than 458,000 Canadians were overseas in France as part of the Canadian Expeditionary Force. Initially, one-third of staff officers in the Canadian force were British. Eventually, the Canadians formed into their own corps of four divisions under Lt. Gen. Sir Arthur Currie. Although they never trained or served together with the doughboys, the two forces had many similarities. As it had for the American II Corps, the British army provided supplies and artillery to the Canadian Corps. The Canadians were not responsible to the British government but to the government of the Dominion of Canada. Political pressure from the Canadian government ensured that its divisions were not split up but served together as a Canadian corps.[33]

On 22 June, Maj. Lloyd C. Griscom, the American representative at the British Embassy in London, made an official proposal to have the Canadians play a more active role in training the Americans. He met with the premier of Canada, Sir Robert Borden, about this matter.

Griscom wrote to Pershing in Chaumont that Borden "considered the rapid training of our troops the most important single factor of the war today, and he believed that Canadian officers could train our troops as fast, and possibly faster, than anybody else." Borden also believed that the "Canadians had developed some things in the art of war that were peculiar, and which would be of value to the American Army."[34] As recent historiography suggests, Borden's biased assessment of his army is correct. One historian called it the "shock army," and its attack across the Canal du Nord in late September 1918 substantiates this opinion.[35] But Borden's proposal was for naught. Sir Henry Wilson thought that the offer had come too late and would disturb the training schedules already in place for the American divisions.[36]

Also charged with helping instruct the Americans were the Australians, who ultimately influenced them greatly. By most accounts, the Americans and Australians had a natural affinity with each other. Upon seeing the Americans, an Australian officer remembered that "we amused ourselves watching a lot of very brand-new-looking Yanks arriving with their extraordinary-looking equipment. Some of the officers carried leather suitcases and umbrellas and looked more like commercial travellers than soldiers."[37] Another was entertained when he saw some Americans "coming up the road with bayonets fixed and rifles ready kilometers away from the front line. They wore their gas masks when there was not a whiff of gas about."[38] The Americans were also fascinated by the "diggers," as the Australians were known. A 27th Division staff officer recalled that the Australian soldiers he encountered were "dressed in olive-drab uniforms, wrapped puttees and broad-brimmed hats fastened up the side," and they reminded him of "Roosevelt's Rough Riders at San Juan Hill."[39] Another remembered how he was "greeted by and impressed with the Australians at Haute-Allaines. A battalion marched by, preceded by a band playing Mademoisselle [sic] from Armentières, and there was a general interchange of greetings between our men and the Aussies."[40]

In many ways, the diggers served as mentors to the doughboys. They frequently reminded them to avoid capture by the Germans at all costs, since escaped Australian soldiers claimed to have been tortured by the enemy.[41] Australian troops were legendary as tough

undisciplined soldiers.[42] This myth was largely perpetrated by newspaper correspondent C. E. W. Bean, who was later the official historian
of the Australian Imperial Force (AIF). To Bean, the Australian soldier
was a "bushman in disguise." After observing them in Gallipoli, he
noted that the "wild pastoral life of Australia, even if it makes
rather wild men, makes superb soldiers."[43] There was some truth to
Bean's rhetoric, according to the American troops who fought side
by side with the Australians in the summer and autumn offensives.
"As individual fighters, they were superb," a couple of American II
Corps officers wrote about the Australians after the war. "Their initiative, vigor, and bodily strength enabled them to surprise, wear
out, or overpower the foe in almost every encounter."[44] Lt. Gen. Sir
John Monash commanded the five divisions of the Australian Army
Corps, part of the British Fourth Army. Not a typical officer, he was
an engineer in civil life. Historian John Terraine credits Monash with
studying "the military profession in peacetime with a thorough-
ness that few Regulars could match."[45] The Americans would be
given ample opportunity to form their own opinions about him in
the coming weeks.

10

WE HAVE FOUND
EACH OTHER AT LAST

Although the Americans were still in the early stages of training, the British were anxious to bring them into the line sooner rather than later. Pershing and Haig agreed from the beginning that the AEF divisions could serve as reserves only if an emergency necessitated such action. But Haig's army commanders, Second Army's Gen. Sir Herbert Plumer in particular, wanted to accelerate Period A of training and made a formal request to Colonel Simonds. He thought it imperative that the Americans should be "brought in closer contact with frontline conditions at an earlier stage of their training" and wanted them in the sector near Ypres that was in danger of being overrun by the Germans.[1]

Simonds said no. The forward areas did not have adequate training facilities for bayonet practice, target practice, and other exercises that were essential to the completion of Period A. It made more sense, Simonds argued, to continue the current instruction in the rear until Period B commenced and then consider allowing the divisions to enter the line. However, he would consider the idea if the British "furnished this office with such information as you may deem necessary as regards your plans and lines of defense" so that "proper steps could be taken to utilize these divisions by preparing tentative plans, making reconnaissance, and in other ways preparing to assist in the defense of this sector."[2]

Haig stepped in and appealed directly to Pershing. Although he recognized that facilities would not be "quite so good as those in the areas [the troops] now occupy, and the training might be, to some extent, though not seriously, delayed, . . . it was a necessary action to support the under-strength British units."[3] Probably tired of Haig's badgering, Pershing relented with the understanding "that the training of these divisions will be continued insofar as conditions permit and necessities require."[4]

Therefore, on 9 July, the 27th and 30th Divisions were assigned to the British Second Army and moved to its sector southwest of Ypres, Belgium, and ordered to organize and defend a portion of the East Poperinghe line. The position took its name from the town of Poperinghe (situated several kilometers north) and consisted of an irregular system of unconnected trenches, strongholds, and pillboxes. A great many concrete machine-gun pillboxes with steel turrets had been put into position along the line. Pillboxes were constructed in parts that consisted of curved cement blocks and adjustable steel turrets. First, a foundation was laid in concrete, then the blocks were fitted to each other on the foundation, and finally the steel covering was put in place. This was shaped at the angle calculated to best withstand the shock of hits by high explosives.[5]

The 30th Division moved near Poperinghe and Watou, where it came under the tactical control of the British II Corps, while the 27th Division assumed the second, or reserve, position in the British defenses near Mt. Kemmel, under the command of British XIX Corps. This included Dickebusch Lake and the Scherpenberg area.[6]

Two days later, the 30th moved to the same reserve sector as the 27th, and the divisions were practically next to each other. Both were on the north face of the Lys salient, a front that covered 4,000 yards. The salient was formed in the Allied line south of Ypres that spring, when the Germans had attacked along the Lys River during Operation Georgette and took Mt. Kemmel from the French. A British officer wrote that the "loss of Kemmel by the French is good; we held it anyhow; it should make them [French civilians] less uncivil."[7]

British soldiers referred to the Ypres sector as simply "The Salient" and to Ypres as "Wipers," "Eepriss," or "Ee-pray." Ypres was the medieval center of the Flanders wool trade and had played an important role in the war since 1914, when the Germans first entered the town on 13 October and the next day met with opposition from the BEF. This was the beginning of the first battle of Ypres, and for the remainder of the war, the salient continued to be one of the most active parts of the Western Front. The Menin Gate memorial near the town's center is a grim reminder of the terrible losses the British suffered in their four years there. It commemorates the almost 55,000 British and Dominion anonymous officers and men who died in the Ypres salient area up to 15 August 1917; these men have no known grave. Another 35,000 names are recorded, including the names of the missing from August 1917 to the end of the war, at Tyne Cot cemetery near Passchendaele.[8]

The salient extended from Zillebeke Lake, at one time the chief water supply for Ypres, to southeast of Voormezeele. It was shaped by the fighting of the first battle of Ypres, and subsequent battles created deep craters. The ground was very low, and shell holes became little pools when it rained. Surrounding the salient was the high ground of Observatory Ridge, Passchendaele Ridge, Wytschaete-Messines Ridge, and Mt. Kemmel, all of which were in German possession. It allowed the enemy a clear field of fire in all directions. An American observed that often the "men in the forward systems believed they were being shelled by their own artillery, when, as a matter of fact, the shells were from the enemy guns on the right and in the rear."[9]

On 16 July, the battalions of the 119th and 120th infantries began occupying portions of the front in the canal sector ten miles southwest of Ypres. One regiment had its camp at "Dirty Bucket," about four miles from Ypres. Men were housed in huts built by the British in a grove of oak trees big enough to house an entire company (256 officers and men). Quarters were far from luxurious; the lack of cots or bunks meant sleeping on the floor.[10] For the commanding officers of the 27th and 30th, it was much different. The 27th maintained headquarters at Oudezeele, while the 30th Division set up its command in Watou, where O'Ryan and Lewis slept in relative comfort.[11] A regimental commander also described his billet as "very comfortable." He called them "Armstrong huts." They were collapsible and could readily be moved. The sides of the sleeping part of the hut were banked with sandbags to protect the sleeper from shrapnel and pieces of shell. The banks were three feet high, "just enough to cover you when lying on the cot."[12]

Both divisions were now only four miles from the front and well within range of enemy fire, as Pvt. Robert P. Friedman learned. A member of the 105th Engineers, he died as a result of wounds from shellfire on 13 July, the first combat casualty suffered by the 27th Division.[13] Friedman was one of many Jewish soldiers, several high-ranking officers among them, in the 27th; his loss was mourned by all in the division.[14] The 30th Division experienced its first combat-related death a month earlier when 1st Lt. Wily O. Bissett of the 119th Infantry was killed on 17 June 1918.

In Belgium, the Americans witnessed the hardships of the civilian population. Shelling had destroyed villages around Ypres but failed to break the spirit of the Flemish people. They continued to cultivate their fields, and the engineers from the American divisions on the East Poperinghe defense line were specifically instructed not to damage the crops. This was a difficult order to follow since laying wire entanglements near the front meant clearing some of the crops despite the protests of the farmers.[15] Colonel Pratt of the 105th Engineers was amazed at the skill of the Flemish farmers. "We came back through the wood and through several farms, all these latter being intensely cultivated," he wrote. "The grain is rapidly ripening, and it makes the field look luxurious. All of the reaping in this section is done by hand. I have not seen a single mowing machine, reaper, or planter here."[16]

Continuous fighting in this region caused untold casualties among the civilians, and one unit, the Headquarters Company of the 106th Infantry, "adopted" a 13-year-old orphan and fed him for the entire time it was overseas. In early 1919, as the regiment prepared to return to the United States, the men brought him to Brest as a passenger, but the military police wouldn't allow the young boy to travel on the troop transports.[17]

One of the objectives during this phase of training was to teach American officers how to command in the line, so each company commander rotated to the front for a few days. An early student in the lines was Capt. Henry Maslin, a company commander in the 105th Infantry. For four days, he was assigned to A Company, 7th

Battalion, London Regiment, British 58th Division and entered a portion of the line opposite Albert. "At all times, day and night," Maslin accompanied the commander when he inspected and visited his company and went with him out of the trenches and "over the top" at night. He observed how the British had a "battle surplus" of two officers who did not enter the trenches during a tour of duty. That way, if there was a heavy loss of officers, "there will be some officer who can assume command with knowledge of the company's administration." Maslin was also impressed that "hot tea was served to men for breakfast, as well as one-half dry tea ration for the remainder of the day." Water was scarce, and "men had to either go unwashed or go without tea."[18] He reported afterward that "all officers with whom I came in contact were very willing to give me all information."[19]

Another company commander, Capt. George P. Nichols, 107th Infantry, reported to the British 41st Division a month after Maslin. Assigned to the 124th Battalion in a sector opposite Mt. Kemmel, he spent three days in the line and afterward reported observations on three specific topics: the intelligence service and the "keenness of the men in each platoon assigned to the work"; the highly trained platoon and company runners; and the "high morale attained by the continued efforts of platoon commanders to instill 'platoon spirit.'"[20]

At the 30th Division, battalion officers went into the line with the British 49th Division, which had been in the Ypres sector since 1915. It was still a dangerous section of the front three years later. German shells killed four officers and twenty-two men during the month of July.[21] The Americans were tutored in reading maps and occupying and defending the line. Terrain exercises were also scheduled, but the British cancelled them because of the frequent shelling.[22] Despite the danger, the experience was a positive one for the Americans. "The relations that prevailed between the units of the American 59th Brigade and the units of the British 49th Division," Major General Tyson later remarked, "were always of the most cordial nature. The men of my brigade cooperated in every way possible and were on the best terms with the British, and they cooperated in every way with us, and there was never anything, so far as I am informed, but the best of feelings, in every respect."[23]

The British officers did find weakness in the American troops after conducting "state of training" inspections to ascertain progress by the Americans. A report drawn from the inspections showed that although training was progressing satisfactorily, it was hampered by significant delays in issuing British rifles and Lewis guns. One division (the 27th) had little training beyond drills and physical exercises.[24] Pershing's training section responded by extending Period A by two weeks.

As Haig had noted, the 27th Division would lose almost a week of training by moving closer to the front, and this had to be made up before the division passed to Period B. Additionally, the division suffered a slight setback when Col. Willard C. Fisk, in command of the 107th Infantry, became seriously ill with stomach trouble. Now 60 years old, he had been with the 7th New York for forty years and was considered one of the National Guard's most competent and experienced officers. Under his leadership, the 107th was the pride of the division, achieving high marks in efficiency ratings. O'Ryan ordered Fisk home and another National Guardsman, Col. Charles I. DeBevoise, replaced him. Formerly in command of the 1st New York Cavalry, he was fresh from the Army School of the Line at Langres, where he graduated first in his class and remained as an instructor until O'Ryan brought him back to the division. He proved capable in combat and kept up the morale of his regiment during its darkest hours in the attack on the Hindenburg Line. After the armistice, DeBevoise was promoted to command the 53rd Brigade.[25]

Within the 30th Division, the southern soldiers were having their own setbacks. A frustrated Brigadier General Faison, the acting division commander, observed that his infantry brigades were "badly handicapped by the lack of suitable and well-trained officers." He alerted Read to the problem and offered a solution; any officer not doing his job should be relieved. Faison blamed the War Department regulations that allowed incompetent officers to remain in command and feared that "under present conditions, this division is not capable of maneuvers, and the prospects are not bright for this state of affairs to come about." Read ignored Faison, and the 30th continued training with its regimental commanders in place.[26] When Lewis took over as division commander and Faison stepped aside, the problem persisted. Lewis used the excuse that he was new and wanted to give his officers a chance to improve.[27]

11

VISITORS AND INSPECTORS

During the second week of July, Pershing visited the Ypres sector and stopped in to see the 27th Division. On his way to the training area, he spotted one of the New York regiments on a road west of O'Ryan's headquarters and stopped for an impromptu inspection of the startled soldiers. He later remarked to their division commander that the "men look fit, but carry too much equipment. Get rid of some of it."[1] It is not clear what he meant by too much equipment. Men of the 27th and 30th had the same amount of equipment as any other soldier in the AEF. The only difference was their outer clothing, as well as their shoes, breeches, and tunics, which the British had mostly provided. This was done out of necessity since the American supply depots were slow to refill, and Read had given the authority to fit the men from British stores.[2]

Before leaving the 27th Division area, Pershing complimented O'Ryan on the "splendid spirit" of his men but also pointed out a number of deficiencies. In particular, he noted that "one major saluted him with a riding whip, and another was seen going through the streets not wearing a belt." Pershing also observed that when reviewing the men in one battalion, their packs "had too much in them and were carelessly made."[3] Such sloppiness within the division had been previously noted at Camp Wadsworth, and now it appeared that the National Guardsmen had brought their bad habits overseas, despite O'Ryan's best efforts to correct their deficiencies.

Colonel Bacon also came to the 27th Division training area when Pershing was there, but he stayed much longer. He accepted an invitation to have lunch with some of O'Ryan's staff and spent much of the occasion filling in the news-starved officers of events in the other AEF sectors, such as the French front, where some of them longed to be. Bacon told them of the recent operation of the American 1st Division when it relieved the French at Montdidier and captured Cantigny on 28 May, despite heavy losses from German counterattacks. It was the first offensive operation by an American division since the Americans had come to France. From there, Bacon's enthralled audience learned of the accomplishments of the American 2nd Division at Belleau Wood a week later. There, two regiments of marines had encountered some of the German army's best storm troops and suffered great losses. But after three days, the Americans drove the Germans from the wood and captured the village of Bouresches. As Col. Franklin W. Ward, commander of the 106th Infantry, recounted, Colonel Bacon's stories were the "first graphic news that has been received by the 'lost' division from their comrades on the American front." Ward's reference to his division as "lost" revealed just how isolated he and the other officers and men training with the British felt from the main body of the AEF.

On 25 July, the divisions began Period B training. One battalion of each infantry regiment was sent to the front lines for a period of eight days. Up to this point, only American officers had seen combat with the war-weary British, but now the men would experience it for themselves. "Battle, whatever its frequency—or lack of it—is the end towards which most military training is directed," one historian noted, "and is an event which comes to loom large in the soldier's mind."[4] The first time in the line was confusing for the Americans, and they relied heavily upon the British for guidance. In one instance, an officer from the 105th Infantry questioned why a party from the 1st Battalion had not completed its work on the Dickebush reserve line. He was told that the British guide had failed to show up to direct the lost Americans to the area to which they were assigned.[5]

A regimental historian recalled a few years later that "the first trip to the front line trenches will ever remain graven upon the memories of the men of the 107th Infantry." The unit made the journey under cover of darkness "along shell-torn roads that were fringed in many places by hidden batteries of British guns."[6] Once at the front, the British soldiers teased the green American troops and offered lots of "practical" advice. One frequent suggestion was: "Don't stir up Jerry, Yank; you shoot at im, he'll shoot back twice."[7]

Because of their inexperience, the Americans were impatient to learn from the veteran British. In one instance, four officers from the 120th Infantry, who were detached for instruction with the 9th (Glasgow Highlanders) Battalion, demonstrated such eagerness. One evening, the Scottish officers from the Highlanders were sent on a raiding party, and one of the American officers insisted upon accompanying them. He was advised to stay behind for lack of experience. Yet despite the best efforts of the Scots to keep him away, 2nd Lieutenant Bellamy somehow coaxed a uniform from one of his instructors and tagged along with the raiding party dressed as a Highlander. When they entered the enemy trenches, the party lost one man to capture and five others were wounded. Perhaps to the disappointment of the Scottish officers, Bellamy was neither captured nor wounded.[8]

After leading another AEF regiment to the front lines for the first time, a bitter British corporal was still angry more than a month later. He was tired of "the big talk of what they were going to do, but had not done yet. . . . All I hope is that when they do start, Jerry will smash them to atoms, for they are nothing more than human garbage, and this is the best I can say about them."[9] But most British officers had positive experiences with the Americans. A sniper with the Worcestershire 2nd Regiment recalled that when he and other officers visited with some excited Americans recently brought into the line, "they took us along to one of the huts, and talked away about being shelled by them goddamned Bosches." The British officers reciprocated with words of encouragement while they "drank their excellent coffee." The Americans then treated them to an evening meal of chicken, potatoes, and peas, "the likes of which we had not tasted for many a long day."[10]

That summer, Pershing returned to the British sector for another inspection, this time to see the 119th Infantry before it moved to the front. In typical fashion, he arrived six hours late and "made no apology," a British officer observed. He "walked along the front ranks with a forbidding scowl on his face and did not talk to a single man. All the officers seemed dead scared of him."[11] Pershing's comments on the regiment are not recorded, so it can be assumed that he was mostly pleased with its appearance.

During the second week of August, Read conducted his first inspection of the two divisions to determine their "state of training, general preparedness for active service, and general efficiency." Along with various General Staff officers, Read spent two days with each division, and he came away disappointed. For the 27th Division, Read reported that it was "deficient in map reading, sketching, scouting and patrolling, and rifle and hand grenade practice." He also concluded that the division's officers were not sufficiently zealous in their care of men. On a positive note, Read thought the noncommissioned officers were exceptionally good. Comments on the 30th Division were also mostly unfavorable. Unlike the 27th, its officers were zealous. But "sketchy methods have been used in the 119th and 120th Infantries. Both regiments exhibited inadequate instruction in map reading, sketching, and scouting and patrolling."[12] Faison tried to tell Read this the previous month, but Read paid little attention.

The British XIX Corps also inspected American units, and its findings contradicted those in Read's report, as least as far as the 27th Division was concerned. Brigadier General MacMillan determined that "the keenness, intelligence, and spirit of all ranks have left nothing to be desired" among the New Yorkers. Although the inspector reported some minor deficiencies, such as the improper wearing of caps, insufficient knowledge of trench cooking, and a general lack of sanitary education, he thought all of this was attributed to "inexperience and faulty administrative arrangements."[13]

One area in which the British could not criticize was discipline. Despite some sloppiness, it had remained good since the start of the first phase of training, with some exceptions. While on leave in Calais, the occasional officer or enlisted man failed to produce the proper passes, and this meant the military police had to return the guilty parties back to their units. When the II Corps inspector general visited the regimental billets, he also noted irregularities. He observed that saluting was "not yet uniform in all units of the same division" and that "soldierly bearing" was "generally good, even though many recruits in all divisions bring down the average." But none of these infractions was excessive, and his report for July was positive.[14]

To boost morale, it was announced that King George V would visit the soldiers at the front. One hundred men from each American division and the same number from the British divisions were instructed to assemble before the king on 6 August. The troops were formed without arms, wrote the historian of the 120th Infantry, because "the British were afraid some of them would take a 'pot shot' at their ruler."[15] On the day of arrival, a British chaplain delivered a sermon, then a band in a field across the road played while the divisions marched by. The king sat on a raised platform to greet the troops, and after the parade, he visited the 30th Division headquarters with the king and queen of Belgium. According to an eyewitness, the queen pulled the lanyard of a gun in the back area, thus "hurtling potential death among the Germans, her own kin."[16]

Read was also concerned about the fact that neither division had its own artillery. It was never intended for the II Corps divisions to have their own artillery, and from the moment artillery units arrived in France, they were assigned to the French army for instruction. There was never any indication that these divisions would be reunited with their artillery while training with the British. Still, Read wrote to the AEF operations branch: "With regard to divisional troops, the division, at present, has with it the British artillery, and it is presumed that these arrangements can be continued as long as the divisions remain on this front. Our experience here has shown that the combination of British methods with our own, which is necessary to a certain degree where British equipment is used in our organization, and where the smaller units serve together in a mixed larger unit, leads to unavoidable complications and results in a hampering of the proper development of our units along our lines."[17]

His concern was justified, since the artillery regiments that trained for nine months with the 27th and 30th at Camps Wadsworth and Sevier would never enter the British sector. Instead, the infantry and machine-gun units were forced to operate with the British artillery, whom they had not trained with. The two divisions never entirely adjusted, and this became a real problem during the Hindenburg Line operation.

Another anxiety for the Americans (and all the soldiers who fought during World War I) was the terror of gas warfare while at the front. In one horrific experience, twenty-two men of the 30th Division died as a result of a friendly gas attack that backfired. A similar mishap occurred three years before at Loos, when the gas companies of the British 2nd Division released chlorine during an unfavorable wind, resulting in numerous casualties within this division and other units nearby.[18] This time, 400 men and officers of the 105th Engineer Regiment, under supervision of the British, transported 2,520 cylinders of gas, phosgene, and chlorine in nine trains of seven 3-ton trucks each. The trains were pulled by a light railway to the Trois Rois Spur on a tramway system organized by the commander of the Royal Engineers Special (gas) Brigade, Maj. Gen. C. H. Foulkes.[19] The cars were pushed by hand to positions just below the outpost line. When all troops were withdrawn from the outpost line, the gas was released simultaneously from all cylinders as the wind blew about four miles an hour directly toward the enemy lines.

Shortly after the cylinders were released, a steady wind changed direction and blew the gas clouds back over the Allied lines toward the trains. Recognizing the confusion, the Germans fired machine guns that caught soldiers from the 119th and 120th Infantries, who were on patrol at the front, by surprise. Casualties mounted when one of the gas cylinders containing phosgene fell nearby and poisoned the men before they could adjust their respirators. When inhaled, phosgene was so lethal that only one or two breaths could result in mortal respiratory wounds.[20] Other soldiers walked unknowingly into the gas cloud and were also immediately affected.

According to prisoner interrogations a week later, the Germans lost a few animals but no men from the botched attack.[21] There were two investigations of this incident. The 30th Division gas officer conducted the first, and he concluded that officers should "pay closer attention" and that "no one be permitted to remove his respirator before receiving an 'all is clear' command." The chemical advisor to the British Second Army carried out the other investigation, and his suggestions were more practical. He surmised that the "leak-age of gas around the edges of the mask is important and greatly emphasizes the need of the nose-clip and mouthpiece with the present type of mask."[22] One bright spot was the conduct of Sgt. Guy R. Hinson, who led the men of his platoon away from the gas cloud to safety, then returned to the cloud on four other occasions to rescue men overcome by the gas. His excellent leadership was rewarded with the Distinguished Service Cross.[23]

Little could have been done to prevent this incident, since both the officers and men who were involved had received extensive training in gas warfare. A report written more than a month before by the AEF chief of the Chemical Warfare Service informed Read that in addition to the regular training of the corps gas personnel, many of its officers and noncommissioned officers had taken a special four-day course taught by the British. Also, two hours each week was devoted to gas lectures.[24]

Minor problems aside, the Americans were learning quickly, thanks in part to the British and Dominion troops and their patience with the inexperienced doughboys. Yet there was still much to be taught, and this would become evident as the two divisions were given more difficult tasks. The experience of being at the front had already hardened the doughboys. An even greater opportunity to test their ability was coming up as the second phase of training came to an end.

12

ALONE WITH THE BRITISH

In mid-August, Pershing surprised Haig by telling him that the American divisions would be withdrawing from the British. Pershing's diary describes the uncomfortable moment for both himself and Haig and how the conversation was "not pleasant for a while, though we both kept quite within the bounds of politeness." Pershing presented his usual argument that he was forming an independent American army and that it was never meant for his divisions to remain permanently with the British. Haig disagreed, saying that it was his understanding that the ten divisions were sent to him to fight, but now they were all being withdrawn without having participated in any battle.[1] This was not true. Companies from the American 33rd Division took part in the Hamel operation on 4 July and most recently in a small engagement at the Chipilly Spur.

By claiming that the American divisions should be allowed to fight under his command, Haig grossly exaggerated. Pershing made it known at the outset that the divisions were to train only temporarily with the British and would be allowed to fight only in emergencies. Pershing reminded Haig that "we are all fighting the Germans, and the best way, at present, for my troops to fight the Germans is in my army." In the end, Pershing compromised and allotted the

British two divisions, the 27th and 30th. The reason why these two divisions were chosen and whether Haig had much influence over the decision is not known. O'Ryan claimed that the 27th was selected because Haig had been impressed when he reviewed a detachment during the first week in June.[2] Whatever the reason, the 27th and 30th were now with the British permanently. But Pershing made sure that Haig understood they would continue to function under their own commanders.[3]

Their meeting ended, Pershing claimed, with Haig confessing "to seeing my point of view and agreeing to the withdrawal of the divisions."[4] However, Haig's diary reveals a different conclusion. "A VERY HOT DAY" is how he began his diary entry for 12 August. Although Haig was obviously referring to that day's dreadful summer heat, he was perhaps making a reference to his most recent discussion with Pershing. "I have done everything to equip and help these units of the American Army," he wrote out of frustration. "So far, I have had no help from these troops. If he now withdraws the five American divisions, he must expect some criticism on his action, not only from the British troops in the field, but also from the British government."[5] Haig then wrote: "All I wanted to know was *definitely* whether I could prepare to use the American troops for an attack. . . . Now I know I cannot do so." Furthermore, he called Pershing "very obstinate, and stupid" because "he did not seem to realize the urgency of the situation" and "hanker[ed] after a great, self-contained American Army."[6]

This reaction was far too dramatic. Pershing was within his right to remove the divisions, but he should have expected a negative response from Haig. The previous month Pershing was awarded the Grand Cross of the Order of the Bath by the king of England. Afterward, he received a congratulatory letter from Sir William Robertson. The two were at loggerheads during discussions over amalgamation earlier in the year and had not corresponded since Robertson was fired as chief of the Imperial General Staff in March. He was now assigned to the General Headquarters at Horse Guards in London, and the tone of his letter suggested a lingering bitterness toward Lloyd George. Robertson warned Pershing to be "careful in looking after the best interests of the American Army." Pershing responded: "You may be sure I understand what you mean."[7]

Yet even Pershing was unsure about this recent decision and doubted his actions. On previous occasions, he turned to the French for advice, and this time was no exception. In January, he sought guidance from Petain regarding amalgamation, and now he went to French Premier Georges Clemenceau for counsel. Pershing told him about his recent exchange with Haig and the constant pressure from him and Lloyd George to keep his divisions with the British. Clemenceau revealed how he had originally agreed with the British that the idea of forming an independent American army was a mistake. But after giving this subject more consideration, he was now less inclined to side with the British. He was of the opinion that "everyone who was against the Americans on this proposition was wrong." The AEF "should operate separately as an American Army, and you [Pershing] should not give it another thought."[8] The conversation with Clemenceau had a positive effect, and the change was noticeable in Pershing's next letter to Haig:

> My dear Sir Douglas: I have already directed the commanding general, II Corps to place, at your request, the 27th and 30th Divisions in the line. I have, however, informed General Read that these divisions must remain under their own division commanders. We have so often discussed the question of bringing American forces together in large units that I am sure it is unnecessary for me to insist upon the reasons why my division commanders should exercise tactical as well as administrative control over their own troops. As I wrote you some time ago, I would be very glad if you could find it practicable to utilize the II Corps staff in an actual tactical command at an early date. I may add that I think the realization of this would be desirable from every point of view.[9]

Pershing closed by thanking Haig for approving the removal of the divisions but hinted that the decision resulted from pressure by Foch:

> The task that Marshal Foch has confided to me makes it essential that the 33rd, 78th and 80th Divisions join my forces in this region at the earliest possible moment. I spoke to you of this when we last met, and I am now writing Marshal

Foch and pointing out that the assistance of these divisions is essential to the success of the forthcoming operations. I wish also to thank you for your cordial cooperation and the prompt manner in which you have met our desires in the matter of transferring divisions, especially as at this time, I realize how much this may have disarranged plans that you had already made.[10]

Haig's response was more to the point. "I always know when I am dealing with *you* what your opinion is on the question at issue!" he wrote Pershing. "This is not always the case with the French. I am very glad to assist you with the entry into the line of the 27th and 30th Divisions, and I feel certain that the withdrawal of the remaining divisions will appeal to you as being in the general interest." Furthermore, he told Pershing, "I trust that events might justify your decision to withdraw the American troops from the British battlefront at the present moment. But, I have no doubt that the arrival in this battle of a few strong, vigorous American divisions, when the enemy's units are thoroughly worn out, would lead to the most decisive news."[11]

Fifty thousand American soldiers were now attached to Haig's forces for the foreseeable future. He wrote Foch on 27 August: "In order to exploit the present favorable situation, I am strongly of the opinion that it is desirable that American divisions should take an active share in the battle without delay." Foch responded favorably. "It was not only permissible," he wrote Haig, "but desirable that we should use both American divisions at present with us in the battle after 31 August."[12]

Pershing's close friend and advisor, James G. Harbord,[13] who had been promoted to major general, was a keen observer in the game of politics the Americans and British were playing. His postwar narrative covers, in detail, the often-stressful relationship between Pershing and Haig.[14] Harbord visited Pershing at Chaumont on 23 August and "found the general full of his plans and problems." Pershing hoped that "Marshal Foch would direct that certain of our divisions serving with the British would be returned to their own First Army," Harbord observed, since "Marshal Haig had always played the game with General Pershing in an understanding way. Foch, as Allied commander-in-chief, could easily have ordered them back and saved General Pershing a rather uncomfortable visit to British Headquarters. But he left the child on Pershing's lap." Harbord correctly surmised that the "two men [Pershing and Haig] understood each other, and their friendship had never faltered from the day they met."[15]

As the five American divisions from II Corps left his sector on 25 August, Haig was still seething. His diary records: "What will history say regarding this action of the Americans leaving the British zone of operations when *the decisive battle* of the war is at its height, and the decision is still in doubt?" Would events "justify his [Pershing's] decision to withdraw such a large force of American divisions (over 150,000 men) from me at the height of battle?" Haig asked rhetorically. "For the present, I am convinced that if they had taken part in this battle, they would, owing to the present tired and demoralized state of the Germans on this front, have enabled the Allies to obtain immediate and decisive results."[16] Haig was exaggerating again. The American divisions attached to the BEF would prove to be more than enough strength for the coming offensive.

After Haig had time to let the recent news sink in, he wrote to Pershing about various matters and ended the otherwise businesslike letter with a warm sentiment: "I take this opportunity of expressing my deep appreciation of the cordial way in which all ranks of the American Forces have worked in conjunction with the British Army since their arrival in the British zone, and I trust that the friendly relations already established may continue for all time."[17]

When word reached II Corps headquarters about the reduction of its size, the chief of staff took the news poorly. Simonds wrote a confidential letter to Brig. Gen. Fox Connor, now the operations officer under General Pershing, with a few carefully considered suggestions that indicated his preference that the entire II Corps be moved to the main body of the AEF. "I believe that if you had hit them for the five [divisions] instead of the three, they would have turned them loose," Simonds advised. "I think the sooner we can get these divisions with our own army, the better it will be, and I suggest that since both divisions will finish their tour on the front lines about the same time, the termination of that tour will be the psychological time to get them away."[18] This was a strange comment for Simonds to make since there was no prior indication of his displeasure with the II Corps arrangements. Connor did not respond, and Simonds apparently let the matter drop.

Despite their troubles, Haig and Pershing had survived their latest struggle, and both had come out on top. Pershing gained Allied backing for his own army, while Haig had use of American II Corps for the foreseeable future. Composed of only the 27th and 30th Divisions, it was the smallest corps in the AEF. After 12 August, Pershing stopped visiting corps headquarters for inspections because he was too busy organizing the American First Army and making preparations for its first independent operation. Read would have to step up and make decisions as a commander without Pershing looking over his shoulder. Although he still had to keep Chaumont informed of how the two divisions were being utilized, he had much more latitude to act on his own.

13

YPRES

After the 27th and 30th Divisions had completed the second period of training, Read placed them under tactical control of the British Second Army, and they were ordered into battle for the first time. Some officers and men of the two American divisions had already seen action in the form of raids and patrols during rotation to the front with British units. In mid-August, sizeable infantry units and their accompanying troops, such as machine-gun battalions and engineer regiments, went forward to occupy their own sectors with no supervision except the local British corps commander.

From August 16 to 24, the 27th and 30th Divisions prepared for combat at night. The 30th Division ordered its 60th Brigade to take over the Ypres-Comines Canal sector from the British 33rd Division, which was located on the north face of the Lys salient, southwest of Ypres. The 119th Infantry was on the right side of the line, the 120th Infantry on its left. In reserve was the 59th Brigade (117th and 118th Infantries). A week later, the 53rd Brigade (105th and 106th Infantries) of the 27th Division relieved the British 6th Division in the Dickebusch sector. It took over the front and support positions with regiments side by side, with the 54th Brigade (107th and 108th

Infantries) in reserve. The British divisions left their artillery units to support the Americans.[1]

Troop movements as well as the transport of supplies were accomplished by light railway and were conducted during the night because daytime movements toward the front attracted the fire of German artillery on top of Mt. Kemmel. The 102nd (27th Division) and 105th (30th Division) Engineers arrived in advance of infantry and machine-gun units. They had the difficult and dangerous task of repairing pockmarked roads that were nearly impassable after three years of shellfire. When the troops reached the front, they were quartered in wooden huts built by British engineers that one occupant described as spacious.[2] Two squads of eight men plus a corporal in charge slept in each hut. To coordinate liaison between the infantry and the artillery, work details had to lay cable. This meant digging a six-foot trench through the hard Flanders clay that was not unlike the soil of South Carolina.[3]

Each day involved surveillance from observation posts and aeroplanes. The first few days were reported as calm. "Quiet, inoffensive" is how the 30th Division operation report summarized this period.[4] But the quiet did not last. Suddenly, as the division's historians noted, "the scene . . . shifted to the battleground of the World War—a stern and terrible reality to the men of all ranks."[5] They were referring to night patrols sent out as far as 1,000 yards to probe enemy defenses. Troops patrolling too close to the German outpost lines were greeted with blasts of machine-gun fire.

At first, the Germans were unaware that Americans had entered the sector opposite them, but according to a POW interrogated at 27th Division headquarters, this changed when the rifle fire became "more brisk and haphazard." When asked to elaborate, the soldier from the German 93rd Infantry Regiment explained that soldiers "who have been in the war for some time only fire individually when they are sure they have a target, whereas new troops are apt to fire more or less constantly at night, whether or not they have a target." He said the considerable shooting during the previous few nights and the flashes from the guns allowed the Germans to better pinpoint the American line of advance. Once they recognized that untested American troops were opposing them, it became a daily ritual to

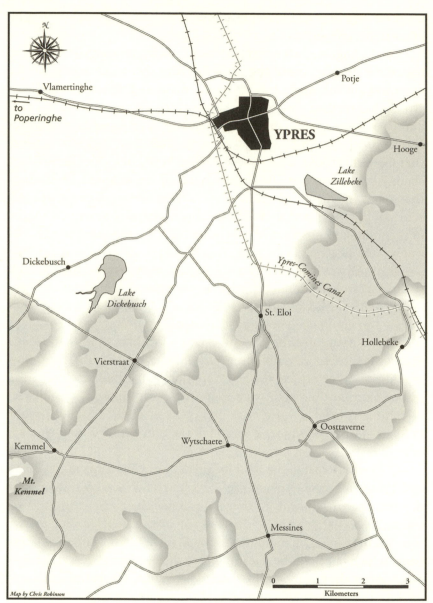

Ypres and vicinity

try their mettle with harassing artillery fire, lobbing shells into back areas to hit crossroads and villages.⁶

On 30 August, the enemy conducted a surprise move that further tested the doughboys. In the early morning, heavy clouds of smoke crept toward the American lines. An initial report said it was a gas attack, but further observation revealed the Germans were burning dumps of some kind to mask a withdrawal. A prisoner captured near Mt. Kemmel confirmed the updated report when he told interrogators that German troops were retiring to the Wytschete-Messines Ridge about 7 kilometers east and slightly south of Mt. Kemmel. He claimed that a new line had been established in front of Armentières, directly south of the ridge, and that eight men per company remained behind in machine-gun posts on Mt. Kemmel. They were there to give the impression of strength.⁷

That night British XIX Corps headquarters sent O'Ryan a telegram to order patrols from his brigades to reconnoiter the left of the line, opposite the 30th Division. But the request to engage the New York division in combat was actually more informal than that. Earlier in the day O'Ryan and the Second Army's General Plumer met and Plumer remarked casually after tea: "Oh, by the way, O'Ryan, how would you like to have a go at our friends on the ridge?" O'Ryan responded that "his men were there for that purpose," and Plumer told him to have a word with his chief of staff. That was when O'Ryan discovered that the details of the plan and a tentative corps order were already in place.⁸

O'Ryan instructed the 53rd Brigade to send elements of the 105th and 106th Infantries toward the German trenches to determine the depth of the withdrawal. As they approached the German lines, there was minor resistance from scattered machine-gun posts. The patrols were accompanied by members of the British 184th Tunneling Company, which checked the vacant enemy dugouts for mines and booby traps. After they reached the enemy positions, the patrols reported back to brigade headquarters that the prisoner's statement was correct; the Germans had given up Mt. Kemmel, although not completely.⁹ Additional American patrols were organized and told to be ready to advance in support of those sent out.¹⁰ The Americans were gearing up for their first battle as entire regiments.

On 31 August, British II Corps ordered up the 30th Division to send out patrols in its sector to determine enemy strength and location. Major General Lewis chose the 60th Brigade and made it clear that if strong resistance was met, they were to return to their entrenchments. Lewis was not ready to commit to a battle. Small parties from the 119th and 120th Infantries were sent out, and like those of the 53rd Brigade, they found the German defenses at Mt. Kemmel mostly abandoned. Additional parties from the 30th Division held nearby positions at the Voormezeele Switch (the former German trenches) and Lock 8 of the Ypres-Comines Canal. The Germans were still nearby in strength, and Lewis ordered his troops to hold tight and await further orders. Relaying the messages was difficult because the Germans kept a close eye on the runners and frequently fired on them, so the Americans mostly communicated by wire. To ensure that there was little delay in this method, the 105th Signal Battalion laid 15,000 feet of cable along the Voormezeele Switch to establish a forward communications post.[11]

At 7:30 A.M. the next day, Lewis gave the order to advance; he was now ready for a battle. After a short barrage, a platoon of forty men from Company I of the 120th Infantry moved forward toward Lankhof Farm. There, the Germans had constructed a cluster of pillboxes in the ruins of an old farm building and positioned machine-gunners and snipers. As the Americans advanced, the Germans withdrew to the canal and abandoned their defenses at the farm, suffering only two casualties. The platoon then pushed beyond the farm and established contact with the 119th Infantry, which was advancing on the right of Lock 8. Artillery from the British 33rd Division fired in support, but some shells fell short and Americans were wounded.[12]

Friendly fire incidents were an unfortunate consequence of war. The 30th Division had recently lost two men this way. In the initial instance, 1st Lt. Robert H. Turner of the 115th Machine-Gun Battalion was struck on 24 July by a shell from the 186 Battery of the Royal Field Artillery while he and another officer were on patrol near Belgian Chateau. In the second incident, an officer in Company M of the 120th Infantry, 2nd Lt. Lowell T. Wasson, was shot by a private from his unit on 7 August. Wasson apparently became confused after returning from a patrol near Swan Chateau and entered a listening

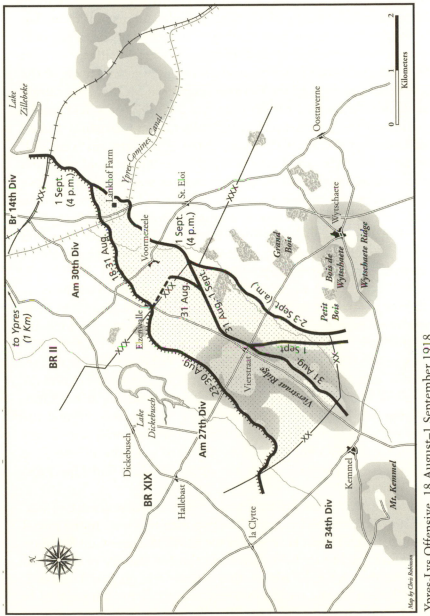

Lake Zillebeke

Br 14th Div

Ypres-Comines Canal

Lankhof Farm

1 Sept. (4 p.m.)

St. Eloi

Am 30th Div

18–31 Aug.

Voormezeele

1 Sept. (4 p.m.)

to Ypres (1 Km)

BR II

31 Aug.

Elzenwalle

31 Aug–1 Sept.

2–3 Sept (a.m.)

Grand Bois

Bois de Wytschaete

Wytschaete

Petit Bois

Wytschaete Ridge

Oosttaverne

Viertraat

1 Sept

31 Aug

Viersraat Ridge

2–30 Aug.

Am 27th Div

Lake Dickebusch

Dickebusch

BR XIX

Hallebast

la Clytte

Kemmel

Mt. Kemmel

Br 34th Div

Kilometers

0 1 2

Map by Chris Robinson

Ypres-Lys Offensive, 18 August–1 September 1918

post unannounced. The private guarding the post was ordered to fire on Wasson by his superiors, who thought the intruder was a German conducting a trench raid.[13] Both friendly fire cases were investigated, and while Turner's death appeared to be an accident and "entirely unavoidable," Brigadier General Tyson concluded that in Wasson's case, the shooting could have been avoided. "Orders will be issued to prevent a recurrence of such deplorable results," Tyson wrote in his report.[14]

With the 119th taking fire from both its own artillery support and the Germans, two more platoons from the 120th Infantry were sent forward to help relieve the chaotic situation. After advancing 1,000 yards, they retired, having lost touch with both flanks. The Germans complicated matters with fire from trench mortars and machine guns hidden in Ravine Wood, about 6,000 yards to the southeast of the location of the 119th. At 10 A.M., the second battalion of the 119th Infantry advanced and held on against heavy resistance.[15] During this action, a patrol that included Cpl. Burt T. Forbes of the 30th Division's Company I, was acting as a flank guard when a squad of eight Germans approached. As the enemy started setting up their machine guns, Forbes crawled by himself and charged the Germans. He single-handedly killed three and drove the other five away. For this act of bravery, he was awarded the Distinguished Service Cross and the French Croix de Guerre.[16] Word of the action was sent to the rear by pigeon. It was the first time the 30th used this means of communication, and it was successful. Remarkably, only one hour and five minutes elapsed between the time the message was sent and the time it was received and transmitted by the division staff.[17]

After intense fighting, the 30th Division's contribution to the operation was over, and the results were impressive. It had gained one square mile of ground, inflicted 100 German casualties, and captured sixteen prisoners, two machine guns, one grenade launcher, and a small amount of ammunition and stores. Mount Kemmel was now in Allied possession and, as one doughboy remarked, "it sure is a blessed relief to move around without feeling the German eyes watching you."[18] In the process of taking this coveted piece of land, the 30th lost two officers and thirty-five men.[19]

In the 27th Division sector, British XIX Corps ordered O'Ryan's men to advance at 10 A.M. on 31 August and occupy a line along the Vierstraat Switch, 1,000 yards from their starting location. Patrols from the 106th Infantry advanced along the line until they were held up for three hours by machine guns concealed in numerous nests near Siege Farm, west of Vierstraat Switch.[20] The Americans retaliated with their own machine guns, and units of the British 66th Division fired artillery. By 5:30 P.M., the enemy was driven back, the objective gained.[21]

August ended as another bloody month on the Western Front, and September started off the same way. On the morning of 1 September, the 27th Division's 105th Infantry went forward on its right to pivot on the 30th Division at Vierstraat Village. As it attempted to advance to the east crest of Vierstraat Ridge, the Germans resisted and drove the Americans back to the village. Again, the Americans used creative methods of communication to send messages to the rear. In this case, the 102nd Signal Battalion sent messages with pigeons and dogs; amazingly, the latter were able to maneuver through the lines and across ground while subject to heavy fire.[22]

Despite such valiant efforts, communication was difficult. The 1st Battalion of the 105th Infantry sent an urgent field message to communicate its situation: "Our new position very heavily shelled, making communications almost impossible. . . . Request that artillery open fire on hill opposite our new position."[23] Yet the battalion continued to wait for the assistance it had requested. Information on why the regiment was stalled did not reach brigade headquarters until late in the day on 1 September: messages were delayed because shellfire had cut the forward line. To help remedy the troubling situation, Cpl. Kenneth M. McCann of the 102nd Field Signal Battalion worked for seventy-two hours, while being subjected to repeated gas bombardments and machine-gun fire, to replace the forward line near Mt. Kemmel. For his extraordinary efforts, he was awarded the Distinguished Service Cross.[24]

More discouraging news reached the rear from an officer who observed at the front that on the left of the 106th Infantry, two battalions had become badly mixed up and crowded into the line.[25] When word reached Brig. Gen. Albert H. Blanding, the 53rd Infantry Brigade commander, he ordered the commander of the 106th, Col. William A. Taylor, to the front to investigate. Taylor reported two hours later that the officer in command at the front, Maj. Harry S. Hildreth, had

"apparently entirely lost control and seemed at a loss as to what to do."
Blanding ordered Taylor to immediately relieve Hildreth from command and take charge. Not until daylight the following morning was
the situation under control.[26] Hildreth was only temporarily reprimanded.
He was lucky this was his only punishment, since it was common
in the AEF, as well as the BEF, to permanently relieve commanders
from their units for poor performance. Hildreth was allowed to regain
his post as a battalion commander in the 106th a few days later.[27]

On 1 September, Blanding ordered his brigade not to make a general attack but to advance the front line as far as possible. With the
help of artillery harassment, the two regiments moved forward and
by the afternoon of the next day had captured the southern slope of
Wytschaete Ridge. At noon on 2 September, Taylor phoned Blanding
and requested permission to dig in on the line of the first objective
and wait for relief. His request was denied. Instead, he was ordered
to advance farther, and after another day of hard fighting, the 106th
permanently occupied the Chinese Trench, which ran for 1,000 yards
to the east of Vierstraat Village between the Berghe and Byron Farms.
The Germans by now had retired in some strength to Wytschaete
Ridge.[28] The two-day operation ended with the 53rd Brigade losing
two officers and seventy-seven men, mostly from artillery fire.[29]

14

AFTERMATH OF BATTLE

Two days before the Battle of Vierstraat Ridge (as the 27th Division's portion of the Ypres-Lys Offensive was called), O'Ryan received a visit from the portrait painter John Singer Sargent. The British War Memorials Committee of the Ministry of Information had commissioned him to paint a large-scale war scene for exhibition in a Hall of Remembrance.[1] The subject was to be a picture of the British and American troops cooperating. Sargent arrived in France on 2 July 1918 and was attached to the XIX Corps. During his visit with the 27th Division, he became part of A Mess in his quest to learn about the American troops.

Sargent found little inspiration to paint New Yorkers in Oudzeele and persuaded an American staff officer to take him to Ypres. Roads packed with troops and trucks slowed the journey. Instead of despairing, Sargent thought of the congestion as a subject that showed the British and Americans together, as long as it "could be prevented from looking like going to the Derby."[2] But, for an unknown reason, he never painted the picture or anything else depicting the Anglo-American alliance. Later, he returned to 27th Division headquarters and sketched O'Ryan.[3]

On 3 September, the Americans received withdrawal orders and moved back from the Canal and Dickebusch sectors during the next two days. The British 41st Division relieved the 27th, and the British 35th Division took the sector vacated by the 30th. Relieving the New Yorkers was not a smooth process. When the order reached the 53rd Brigade, it was so far forward that it took the men quite a while to reach the light railways that would carry them to the rear. After reaching the rear, the brigade found that the 41st Division was in the midst of moving forward, and considerable congestion ensued. Then the men of the 27th Division, looking forward to warm beds and clean uniforms, found that billeting and bathing facilities were hard to come by. O'Ryan later wrote that provisions had been made for his men, "but the lack of time and other circumstances prevented it being done to the fullest extent."[4] For the men of the 30th Division, it was also a "rather a hard trip, but the men stood it well," remembered Colonel Pratt. "The cars were dirty and those for the 1st Battalion had manure in them when they were backed on the siding. Our men had to clean them out and then buy straw to put on the bottom of the cars. I may be mistaken, but the trains the British use for a trip like this are better and cleaner cars. We seem to be the 'Goats.'"[5]

After the divisions left the front, rumors spread about where they were headed next. Speculation in the 30th Division was that it would join the rest of the American Army. But a fourteen-hour train ride on 6 September took the division to the rear in St. Pol in France, a town of 30,000 that the British used as a rest and training area—nowhere near the main body of the AEF. The 27th Division had left Belgium the night before and arrived several hours later in France at Beauquesne, where billets were arranged throughout the village. For the first time in a month, the Americans were out of reach from the German artillery, and the men could relax without fear of shellfire.[6]

While the recent operation was still fresh, the battalion and company commanders wrote after-action reports. Only those written by the 30th Division line officers remain in both their original form and printed versions in the division history.[7] For the most part, they are very detailed and provide a window into the chaotic American experience of being in the line for the first time. In one report, a lieutenant in the 119th Infantry complained that his platoon's ammunition supply was defective and that for twenty-four hours he had no reserve rounds.[8] Another officer told how the supply of water that reached the front lines during the nights of 2–3 September was not enough for one platoon, and "this shortage, which seems to exist in all parts of the line, is the greatest hardship the men have to bear."[9] These were annoying problems that had to be corrected. Other mistakes were not so insignificant and showed the weaknesses in the division's officer corps.

When one platoon reached its objective, for instance, the platoon commander could not communicate with his left flank because he did not have a telephone, a lamp, pigeons, or even a signalman. "Liaison was poor," he complained. "I had no ground flares, no panels, and no other means of getting in touch with aeroplanes."[10] Lt. F. J. Dietrele's concerns are echoed in many of the reports, in which officers told of poor liaison and suggested that further training in this area was essential. Liaison should not have been such an issue since II Corps made it a priority during the first phase of training by setting up liaison schools in each village.[11]

Such mishaps by the doughboys were also noted by the opposing German troops. In a report dated 3 September, the commander of the German 8th Infantry Division, Major General Hamann, remarked: "Withdrawal of our line confronted the American troops with a task to which they were by no means equal."[12] When the 27th Division moved out of its quiet sector to pursue the Germans, Hamann wrote: "The inexperienced troops do not yet know how to utilize the terrain in movement, work their way forward during an attack, or choose the correct formation in the event the enemy opens artillery fire."[13] His comments were similar to those of a soldier from the German 93rd Regiment who had been captured and interrogated days before by the 27th Division.

Hamann's belief that the 53rd Brigade withdrew from the line on 2 September because of exhaustion was incorrect. The withdrawal on that date was planned; the relief orders were sent on 31 August by the British 41st Division.[14] After the war, Hamann was more complimentary toward the New Yorkers. O'Ryan wrote him to gather information for *The Story of the 27th*, and the German officer responded that "reports reaching me from all sources, particularly from our artillery observation posts, were that your infantry was unusually energetic in their attack."[15]

The energy that Hamann witnessed was almost certainly the result of experiencing combat for the first time. Lieutenant Gow of the 107th Infantry recognized this and had even greater respect for the British after the fighting began. "I can understand now why the men who had been instructors could not describe an attack if they were asked about it," he wrote his family. "The thing is so tremendous that ones mind simply cannot grasp it. It just can't be done."[16]

Enlisted men also had plenty to say about the Ypres-Lys Offensive, and they wrote such thoughts in letters they sent home and in personal diaries and memoirs. The sound of battle created a lasting memory for many soldiers, and one from Tennessee described the constant firing of machine guns as the sound of "popcorn popping."[17] Another wrote how it seemed to him that the Germans knew the location of every trench, since they harassed the Americans during the day with artillery fire. At night, German planes bombed the front and rear, and the "artificial camouflage provided what little deception was practiced upon the enemy."[18]

The historian of Company K of the 117th Infantry recalled that "the night of the big barrage on Kemmel Hill was a night of discomfort and nervousness" among the men in his unit. Nerves were frayed, and Private Stewart saw a sergeant in his company advance cautiously with his rifle toward a noise in the rear that he insisted was caused by German soldiers conducting a raid. Moments later, he realized that it was a trench rat retreating to its hole.[19] After the men of Company K had participated in combat, they "were happier than we had been for many months, for the first battle experiences had been met with all the credit that was to have been expected, and we had not quailed at the smell of gunpowder."[20]

The bravery of the American soldiers made a great impression on the British. Before the 27th Division returned to New York, the British Second Army's General Plumer told O'Ryan that "the wonderful spirit that animated all ranks and the gallantry displayed in the minor engagements they took part in with us foreshadowed the successes they would achieve later."[21]

Once the 27th and 30th were in the rear again, they returned to training. This meant drilling twice a day and attacking imaginary enemy strongpoints, such as machine-gun nests.[22] This would have been training Period C, but with approval from the British, Read had sent a memo to the AEF Training Section on 9 August that recommended that structured training cease. At the time, this made sense for two reasons. First, the corps was in the process of losing three divisions. Second, the two remaining divisions were about to enter the line. AEF headquarters approved the recommendation and reminded Read that further training "will strongly emphasize the attack—to which should be devoted the greater part of all exercises, from those for the platoon to the division."[23]

Besides training, there was time for recreation. In St. Pol, civilians treated the doughboys warmly, prompting one soldier in the 30th Division to describe the town as "the most beautiful and comfortable area in which he was ever billeted."[24] The division reciprocated the hospitality by spending freely on beer and wine in the local cafés.[25] At Beauquesne, Scottish comedian and singer Harry Lauder visited the New Yorkers. He lunched with O'Ryan and his staff and later in the day sat down at a small portable piano and entertained members of the division. A member of the audience recalled that "Mr. Lauder was a little put out because there was not a larger crowd present to hear him. He said, 'I am here. Where is the crowd? Go get them.' He refused to begin, but wanted to wait and see if more would not come in. He finally began and was splendid at his trade. Our men had only just reached camp, were tired and sleepy and just did not want to come out. I did not blame them. All who did come had a fine time."[26] Lauder ended his performance on a somber note, telling the audience about the death of his son, an officer in the British army killed on the Somme, and how much he hated the Germans and the way they conducted the war.[27]

During the middle of September, the 27th and 30th were introduced to the tactic of advancing the infantry with support from tanks. The British conducted the training at their tank center near St. Pol. The effectiveness of cooperation between tanks and infantry depended upon how well ground troops had trained and other factors such as terrain and weather. Although some British officers continued to question the usefulness of the tactic, even after tanks were used in the Hamel operation in July, it was now an integral part of BEF doctrine and would remain so for the rest of the war. Rawlinson's Fourth Army used tanks successfully, particularly during the attack on Amiens, where 324 heavy tanks and 96 Whippets took part.[28] The downside was that this attack overstretched the Tank Corps, and production at home could not keep up with demand.

British staff officers hinted at the reason they were anxious to train the Americans with tanks. O'Ryan revealed in his history of the 27th Division that it was "intimated that in the near future, the division might be called upon to carry out a mission of great importance, which would require its use of what was popularly known as a 'shock division.'"[29] The mission involving the Americans would be against the Hindenburg Line, and the operation, which was in the early stages of planning, would include a significant number of tanks. An American tank battalion, the 301st, which had been training in Stanford, England, under British direction since early July with the new Mark V tanks, would support the 27th Division.[30] The 30th Division would be supported by a British tank unit (4th Tank Brigade). "Although not appreciated at the time," as the historian of the 119th Infantry wrote, the training with tanks "proved of inestimable value in the subsequent operations of the regiment."[31]

On 8 September, Haig asked his army commanders for recommendations about future operations. Although his query was vague, he wanted to know how their forces could contribute to a general Allied attack against the Hindenburg Line. General Foch had conceived the idea of a large-scale operation in July, and the plan presented to the Allied commanders on the 24th of that month sought to reduce the salient the Germans had created with their spring and summer offensives. Foch hoped that his offensive would remove the threats to the important Paris-Nancy and Paris-Amiens railway communications.

The Hindenburg Line, which the Germans called the Siegfried Line, or Siegfriedstellung, came into existence in the winter of 1916–1917, shortly after Field Marshal Paul von Hindenburg and First Quartermaster-General Eric Ludendorff took command of the OHL.[32] It was built by the forced labor of prisoners of war and conscripted French citizens and consisted of three trench systems protected by heavy barbed-wire entanglements. To strengthen their trench systems, the Germans constructed concrete machine-gun emplacements, concrete observation posts with concrete shelters, and dugouts that were wired for electric lights in some cases.[33] The high command of the German army believed the line was impregnable and that it would keep the enemy from Germany's borders.[34]

Byng responded to Haig the following day by suggesting an immediate attack against the German defenses before they had a chance to rebuild their forces. Awaiting reports from Gen. Sir Henry Horne, commander of the British Army, and Sir Henry Rawlinson of the Fourth Army, Haig traveled on 11 September to London for a meeting at the War Office "to explain how greatly the situation in the field had changed to the advantage of the Allies." During an interview with Secretary of State for War Lord Milner, he stressed that in the last month, his army had taken 77,000 prisoners and 800 guns. He argued that the German army was near collapse and was suffering from morale and disciplinary problems in many of its divisions.[35] What Haig sought from Milner were men to exploit this favorable condition. He requested home defense and reserve troops from England and aeroplanes and more ammunition for his army in France.

Milner agreed and promised to try to help.[36] But the secretary of state for war apparently was less enthusiastic about Haig's request than he admitted. Two weeks after a conversation with the BEF commander, Sir Henry Wilson told Milner that he thought Haig "ridiculously optimistic." He was concerned that Haig might embark on another battle on the scale of the Battle of Passchendaele.[37]

When Haig returned from London, he heard from his First and Fourth Army commanders. Horne wanted to cooperate with the Third Army by driving toward Cambrai and crossing the Canal du Nord. Rawlinson's plan was more ambitious. He wanted to seize the outer defenses of the Hindenburg Line and was anxious to attack this position as soon as possible because his intelligence staff reported that only three of the nine German divisions opposing the Fourth Army were highly rated, and the other six were rated average.[38] The three top-rated divisions had served in defensive positions for most of 1918; the other divisions were just as Haig had reported to Milner—under-strength with low morale. Fourth Army intelligence estimated that six more divisions were within a 72-hour march of reinforcing the lines.[39] Rawlinson's chief of staff calculated an attack that "if carried out at an early date would deny the enemy any opportunity of reorganizing his troops, improving his defenses, or becoming familiar with the scheme of his defenses."[40] The ground on which Rawlinson wanted to attack included the old British trench lines that the Germans were now using as a forward defense.[41]

Rawlinson's proposal had an important advantage. At his disposal was a defense plan captured from a German headquarters on 8 August. It revealed the extensive features of the Hindenburg Line, with detailed information about lines between the Oise River and Bellicourt. The plan provided every battery position, barrage line, and observation post, as well as infantry and artillery headquarters.[42] But Rawlinson had an even greater resource at his disposal for the battle plan—the 27th and 30th Divisions.

15

PRELUDE TO THE
BIG BATTLE

The two American divisions serving with the British lay at the very center of the Fourth Army's plan for an attack on the Hindenburg Line. Fourth Army commander Rawlinson, who now had a clear understanding of how the defenses were laid out by the Germans on the Hindenburg Line, said that the purpose of the operation was to complete the demoralization of the enemy by destroying his defenses, including wire and dugouts. The objective was to break through the Hindenburg Line in the Nauroy-Gouy sector south of Cambrai and cross the St. Quentin Canal. To meet this objective, Rawlinson needed fresh troops, and the 27th and 30th Divisions fitted perfectly into this plan.

Rawlinson ordered Lieutenant General Monash of the AIF to submit a proposal for a joint operation with his corps and the American divisions under tactical command of the Fourth Army. The Australian commander was pleased to have the Americans: "My experience of the quality of the American troops, both at the battle of Hamel and on the Chipilly Spur, had been eminently satisfactory. It was true that this new American Corps had no previous battle service, but measures were possible to supply them with any technical guidance that they might lack."[1] This statement did not mention the fact that a brigade from both the 27th and 30th Divisions had recently spent three weeks in Belgium and engaged the enemy during a three-day operation. But that operation was far from the scale and complexity of what he was planning for this attack. AIF historian C. E. W. Bean was correct when he noted that "the task thus allotted to the Americans by Monash was at least as great as any that he had ever set for Australian divisions, if not greater."[2]

Monash was happy to provide relief for the tired Australian divisions that took the line since 8 August. The constant fighting had driven two of his battalions to mutiny. On 14 September, the 59th Battalion, with only a short rest, was ordered back into the line after a week of continuous fighting. The men refused to move to the front, and it had taken the coaxing of officers to get them to obey.[3] A week later, a similar incident occurred when 119 men from the 1st Battalion refused to obey an order to go forward.[4]

Read was not told that something was in the planning stages until 19 September, when he received a telephone message from Lt. Col. W. G. S. Dobbie of the Operations Section at British General Headquarters. That is when he learned that the 27th and 30th Divisions were being transferred to the Fourth Army. Later in the day, Colonel Bacon paid a visit to Read and confirmed what he already suspected—that his troops would play a major role in the upcoming operation. Read visited Fourth Army headquarters the following day and learned the details of the operation. Ready or not, his troops were about to enter their first major battle.[5]

Monash's plan for the Hindenburg Line operation considered almost every conceivable scenario. He reasoned that because the line consisted of prepared defenses, a canal crossing would be risky. Instead, Monash proposed piercing the line only at the tunnel sector, where tanks could be used. To soften the defenses, he wanted a heavy preliminary bombardment that lasted two days.

The Fourth Army's operation plan seemed simple. Supported on its right by the French First army, it was to attack the Hindenburg defenses on the southern end of the line between St. Quentin and Vendhuile. This portion of the attack was to occur on two fronts—the British IX Corps on the south and the Australians and Americans on the north. British III Corps was assigned to the left but would not take part in the assault. It was to secure the left flank of the

Australians and Americans and mop up the ground west of the canal once the first objective was achieved. Air support would play a part before and during the operation. The RAF's 5th Brigade, which included 17 squadrons, or 337 aeroplanes, would supply crucial reconnaissance and observation.[6]

The American jump-off line faced the outer defenses of the Hindenburg system west of the Bellicourt tunnel entrance. Terrain sloped toward the east, rising at Bony. There was very little natural cover because any trees and hedges had been destroyed during the course of the war. But one obstacle stood in the way: the St. Quentin-Cambrai Tunnel. Although it is credited to Napoleon, it was originally conceived at the beginning of the eighteenth century by a military engineer named Devic. He developed a project to cross the Catelet plateau by means of an underground canal. Construction began in 1769 but was suspended six years later due to a lack of funding and little faith by the local government that such a project could be completed. In 1808, Napoleon examined the site and after consulting with the Institut National de France, he ordered that Devic's work be resumed. Soldiers, laborers, and prisoners completed the St. Quentin Canal. Despite setbacks caused by cave-ins, leakages, and rudimentary tools, it was finished in 1809.[7]

The Germans were using this extraordinary tunnel as a near-impregnable position. It is about 6,000 yards long, and below the surface it is between fifteen and twenty yards deep. The top of the tunnel is ten yards wide, and it is eighteen yards wide at the water level. The Germans used the blocks in the center and at each end as machine-gun emplacements. Inside the tunnel, the Germans placed numerous barges for quartering troops. In addition to the north and south entrances to the tunnel, there were numerous underground passages that connected with all parts of the main Hindenburg Line. Water flowed in a north-to-south direction.[8]

Three American regiments from each division were to be used in the attack. Each objective was identified by color on the operation maps. The outpost line was blue, the main trench system at the tunnel was green, and the Beaurevoir Line was red. On the right of the line, the 60th Brigade (119th and 120th Infantries) of the 30th Division was to move ahead 4,500 yards on a frontage of 3,000 yards toward Bellicourt. Two battalions from each regiment would advance

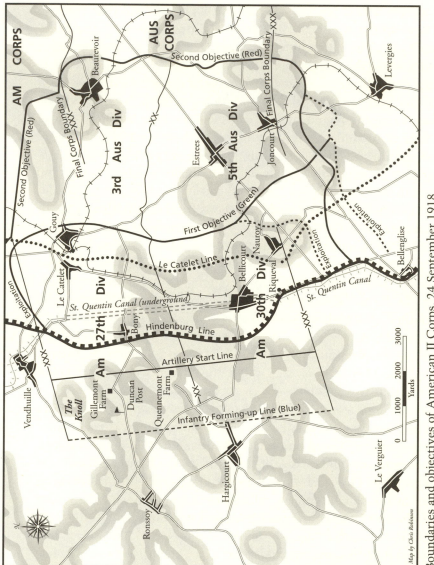

AM CORPS

AUS CORPS

Beaurevoir

Second Objective (Red)

Levergies

Final Corps Boundary XXX

3rd Aus Div

Second Objective (Red)

Estrees

5th Aus Div

Final Corps Boundary XXX

Joncourt

First Objective (Green)

Gouy

Nauroy

Bellenglise

Le Catelet

Le Catelet Line

Bellicourt

Exploitation

Exploitation

St. Quentin Canal (underground)

30th Div

Riqueval

St. Quentin Canal

27th Div

Bony

Hindenburg Line

XXX

Exploitation

Vendhuille

Artillery Start Line

Am

Am

XXX

The Knoll

Gillemont Farm

Duncan Post

Quennemont Farm

XX

0   1000   2000   3000

Yards

Infantry Forming-up Line (Blue)

Hargicourt

Le Verguier

Ronssoy

Boundaries and objectives of American II Corps, 24 September 1918

Map by Chris Robinson

118

750 yards, while the other two battalions were to follow for mopping-up duties. The 59th Brigade, with the 118th Infantry in the lead, would form the south defensive flank. It was to proceed 2,000 yards east of the tunnel, where the 5th Australian Division would pass through and beyond the Americans to secure the final objective, the Beaurevoir Line.[9] The 117th Infantry Regiment was to follow the 120th Infantry across the tunnel, then deploy south after the barrage. It would continue southward to protect the flanks of the 5th Australian Division. One company of the 120th Infantry Regiment, supported by a section of machine guns, was to seize and hold the southern exit of the tunnel at Riqueval. From this point, the 30th Division would pause and consolidate, then continue to the next objective, a strongpoint that stretched from Cabaret Farm to the north to Nauroy to the south.[10]

On the left of the line, two battalions from the 107th and 108th Infantries of the 27th Division were to advance toward Le Catelet with two other battalions following to support and mop up. One battalion of the 106th Infantry would follow in the rear of the attacking line of the 107th Infantry and assist in mopping up the tunnel and exits. Then the 105th Infantry was to follow in rear of the 106th, cross the tunnel, change direction to the left, then deploy and halt in rear of the 107th. After halting on the Green Line, the 107th and 108th would be leapfrogged by the 3rd Australian Division, following through the 27th Division sector. The Australians would then exploit the situation and attack east to the Red Line.

At the same time, the 105th Infantry, supported by three batteries of British field artillery and one company of tanks, was to advance north beyond the Green Line to its objective, the Red Line. The regiment was to consolidate on this line and establish contact with the 3rd Australian Division on its right and the British 18th Division on its left at the canal. Monash calculated that the Green Line would be reached by 10 A.M., and the Green and Red lines by 2 P.M.[11]

On 18 September, Monash submitted this plan to Rawlinson, who approved it with some modifications at a Fourth Army conference the following day. The first day's objective, which Monash thought would be the Beaurevoir Line, was to be attacked only if there was success in penetrating the main Hindenburg Line and the La Catelet Line, its support. The most significant change Rawlinson made was the addition of the British 46th Division, which was now attached to IX Corps. He also increased the heavy tanks to 162 and added Whippets and armored cars. Monash was in full agreement with the latter addition, but he was opposed to including IX Corps in the operation plan because it would broaden the area of attack. Rawlinson overruled him.[12]

Lt. Gen. Sir Walter Braithwaite, the IX Corps commander, had offered the 46th Division to Rawlinson for the difficult task of crossing the canal at Bellenglise, south of Bellicourt. He and his staff devised an elaborate scheme to cross the canal, where the water was six feet deep in some places. The plan was to use 3,000 lifebelts and light rafts, ladders, collapsible boats, and heaving lines. A few days before the attack, Braithwaite rehearsed his men on the banks of the Somme to acquaint them with the difficulties of the upcoming task.[13]

Haig read the final plan of operation and signed off on it with the realization that there were both political and military implications. Sir Henry Wilson had warned him about "incurring heavy losses in attacks on the Hindenburg Line, as opposed to losses from driving the enemy back to that line." He made sure Haig understood that "the War Cabinet would become anxious if we received heavy punishment."[14] Haig lamented in his diary: "The Cabinet is ready to meddle and interfere in my plans in an underhanded way, but does not dare openly say that it means to take the responsibility for any failure, though it is ready to take credit for every success. If my attack is successful, I will remain on as C. in C. If we fail, or our losses are excessive, I can hope for no mercy."[15]

The Fourth Army operation, set for 29 September, was part of a more general Allied attack. The AEF First Army and the French were to attack on 26 September between the Meuse River and Verdun, in the general direction of Sedan and Mézières. The following day, the British First and Third Armies would attack on the Cambrai front in the direction of Valenciennes and Maubeuge. On 28 September, the British Second Army, the Belgian army, and the French in Flanders were to attack on the Ypres front toward Ghent.[16]

For the attack on the Hindenburg Line to be a success, the Fourth Army would first have to occupy the outer German defenses, including the Knoll, a crop-laden crest the Germans had named Sappenberg, and Gillemont and Quennemont Farms. The two farms and the Knoll

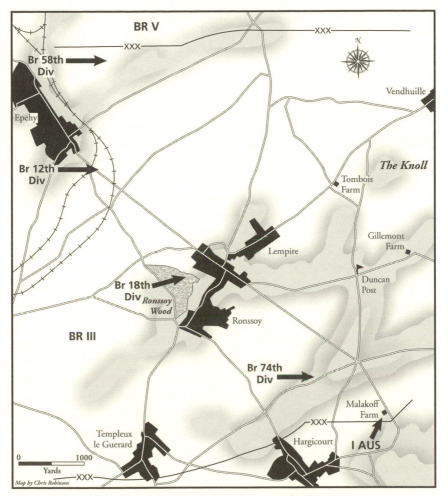

Operations of the British III Corps, 19–22 September 1918

were heavily fortified with field guns, machine guns, anti-tank rifles, and infantry.[17] If this objective was taken, it would become the jump-off point for the main attack by the Americans. As Rawlinson's chief of staff recognized, if the Germans held these three defensive points, "it would be very difficult to move our artillery sufficiently far forward for it to be able to support our attacking troops with an efficient barrage behind the main Hindenburg Line."[18]

The villages of Bellicourt and Bony are most associated with the attack in the American sector. Both date to around 1100, although no one is really sure because records are spotty. Roman ruins from the third century that were found in the forests near the villages suggest much earlier inhabitants. In the twelfth century, a monastery was established nearby that became a place of pilgrimages for hundreds of years afterward.

In 1917, as the Germans fell back and began constructing what became the Hindenburg Line, they forced themselves on the surrounding French villages. Written accounts suggest that Bony suffered the worst fate under German occupation. The testimony of one of its residents, Désiré Martin, backs up this statement. He was only 16 years old when the German army forced him and other villagers into slave labor to feed its troops at the front.

Martin was conscripted in Horse Column No. 102, and under the watchful eye of a German noncommissioned officer, he transported requisitioned provisions such as straw, oats, potatoes, and fodder in a wagon pulled by two horses. Martin's "service" with the German army ended abruptly when one of his horses developed colic. He kept this fact from the German authorities, and the animal died a few days later. The angry German veterinary officer at Bony accused him of deliberately denying the animal possible life-saving treatment, and as punishment young Désiré was banished from the village and taken to a military prison in Pommereuil Nord, a nearby commune in the Pas-de-Calais region. There he spent his days harvesting crops for the army and his nights sleeping in a tin hut that was either too hot or too cold, depending on the weather. He was fed mostly "soup," a concoction of water, rutabagas, and sauerkraut. Eventually Martin and two comrades escaped and found their way to Belgium, then on to Holland, where they remained until after the armistice.[19]

Other Bony citizens demonstrated their discontent, and as a result on 11 October 1916, with no warning, the Germans told the entire village to evacuate the following morning. This was a retaliatory measure because the locals had refused to cooperate in working to construct the defenses. That night villagers frantically gathered papers, valuable objects, linens, and food. The Germans even confiscated a stock of foodstuff that the Commission for Relief in Belgium had earmarked for the village.[20] Each evacuee was only allowed twenty-five kilos in baggage (a little over fifty-five pounds).

From Bony the villagers were led on foot to Epehy, about six kilometers away, where they were placed on cattle trucks and taken to Cambrai and then Caudry, another ten kilometers from Bony. They remained there for six months with most barely surviving on the one franc per day the Commission for Relief in Belgium gave each evacuee, which was not enough to buy meat, egg, milk, and butter that were a part of the daily staple. Some Bony villagers were sent to the village of Posix, which had even less food. The luckier ones were taken to Switzerland.

The Germans also occupied Bellicourt, and they evacuated its residents as well. On 10 March 1917, the Germans ordered the mayor to tell the villagers to kill all dogs so they wouldn't be able to sound the alarm if Allied troops approached. Two days later, three-quarters of the residents were notified to assemble in the village square and bring only twenty-five kilos of baggage and a knapsack for provisions. Women, children, and the elderly traveled in carts, while the healthy men followed on foot and pushed wheelbarrows. The following day the other quarter of the village residents were ordered to evacuate in the same way. They were driven in cattle trucks to Hautrage, Belgium, where they stayed for the remainder of the war with the assistance of the Commission for Relief in Belgium. Meanwhile, the Germans confiscated farms such as Guillemot and Quennemont and incorporated them into the Hindenburg Line defenses.

With the labor pool now banished from the villages, the Germans brought in Russian prisoners of war from the Eastern Front to do the work. As a young girl, Mademoiselle Lamont witnessed the poor treatment of the POWs outside her village. "They were working on the trenches and dying of hunger," she wrote after the war. "We used to see them picking up grains of wheat to eat."[21] Désiré Martin and Mademoiselle Lamont did not return to their villages for two years.

16

THE AMERICANS
MOVE FORWARD

As the Americans continued to train in St. Pol and Beauquesne, there was much action at the front. On 18 September, British artillery erupted against the German outpost line; a few hours later, the infantry advanced. This preliminary operation, led by British III, IV, and IX Corps, encountered strong defenses, including a line of villages and trenches well fortified with dugouts. In the III Corps sector, the attack was made against a fresh German division that had entered the line the previous evening, but by the end of the day the British had made few gains. Rawlinson was initially optimistic about the operation, as reflected in his diary entries for the 18th: "IX Corps got on well, but had hard fighting. Very important success as we can now take the Hindenburg Line." He remained positive the next day: "All looks hopeful. III Corps made some progress, but IV Corps did not get on."[1]

His optimism diminished when the fighting stalled, and on 21 September, Rawlinson ordered another attack by III Corps (British 12th, 18th, 58th, and 74th Divisions) to capture the outpost line with assistance from the 1st Australian Division on the right. The 74th Division objective was Quennemont Farm, Quennet Copse, and Gillemont Farm, while the 18th Division was ordered to seize the Knoll. The 12th Division was to strike at Braeton Post and Little Priel Farm, and the 58th Division was tasked with taking the trench system north of there.[2] Eleven tanks from the British 2nd Tank Battalion provided support. This attack started at 5:40 A.M., with the divisions advancing under a creeping barrage. Elements of the 74th Division in the north went as far as Quennemont and Gillemont Farms, but the Germans were waiting for them. The enemy laid down a protective barrage on its front lines but, miraculously, the British and Australians went on until several belts of wire stopped them cold. Men bunched up and sought protection in shellholes. Forward troops were isolated and support companies were caught in the cross-fire of machine guns. They made several attempts to advance, but they were stopped, and casualties mounted.

South of the line, the 18th Division advanced with one battalion from the 1st Australian Division and made it as far as Duncan and Doleful posts but could not make it to the Knoll. The division hung on to its position until relief from the Americans came on 26 September.[3] At this point in the war, the 18th was a very different division than the one Lt. Gen. Sir Ivor Maxse had formerly commanded. It was now composed mostly of conscripts, and the average company strength was down to about seventy men. Although the 18th Division had fought well thus far in the campaign, it was worn out and depleted.[4] The division's historian correctly called the results of the 21 September attack "a tragic business."[5] Both the 12th and 58th Divisions were also prevented from reaching their objectives as the fighting continued all day and into 22 September.[6]

Rawlinson's diary entry for the 21st recorded despair. "They [III Corps] were pushed back by the counterattack," he wrote, "and did not hold on well. They are very tired."[7] He had little confidence in the corps from the outset, and his frustration was directed mostly at the corps commander, Lt. Gen. Sir Richard Butler. A few days after the Amiens attack of 8 August, Rawlinson placed Butler on sick leave because of recurring insomnia. Butler returned to duty on 12 September, but Rawlinson was still unsure about his abilities after a visit to III Corps headquarters four days later. His diary for 16 September indicates such apprehension: "I am pretty sure the Australians and IX Corps will do their jobs, but I am not so confident about III Corps," he wrote.[8] Rawlinson also predicted that there might be trouble with Butler's portion of the outpost line attack because he had little control over his division commanders. He "has not the practical experience to make decisions," Rawlinson claimed, and he planned "to talk seriously with Butler, for it will be his fault."[9]

Despite the problems with III Corps, there were two bright spots in the preliminary operation. In the center, the Australian Corps over-ran German positions on the ridge, which included three former British lines. By the end of the day, it overlooked the Hindenburg Line from the tunnel north of Bellicourt to the canal south of Bellenglise. To the south of this position, the British 1st and 6th divisions of IX Corps encountered heavy machine-gun fire, preventing the infantry from coordinating its operations with the French. Yet they still secured a reasonably good jump-off position for the main attack, which the Americans would spearhead.[10]

On 20 September, the 27th and 30th Divisions transferred to the Fourth Army to operate with the Australian Corps in the proposed operation.[11] The two divisions moved to the area of Tincourt by British bus and truck; it took them about seven hours to reach their new station. Only days before, Tincourt had been in German possession. When they arrived, the doughboys found "there were no shelters of any kind available, but everyone was so tired, they simply laid down under some trees, wrapped blankets about themselves, and went to sleep."[12]

Tincourt was so close to the front, according to one of the 117th Infantry historians, that the men could see "the flash of guns are at no great distance," and "we all realized that our days in the rest area were over for the time being."[13] With the operation just days away, the past two weeks in the rear must have seemed a lifetime ago. Pvt. Harry T. Mitchell from the 107th Infantry recalled that "'resting' did not mean all the word implied," although he added that "as hard as we worked, we thoroughly enjoyed our stay in Beauqesne." His unit had entrained at Tincourt on the 23rd and afterward hiked to a valley near Haut Allains, where they set up camp.[14] There, the 107th spent the next six days preparing for an operation that over 300 officers and men would not survive.

A few days later, Mitchell and the rest of the 27th Division relieved the British 18th and 74th Divisions in the sector southwest of Guoy, while at the same time the 30th Division relieved the 1st Australian Division in the Nauroy sector directly west of Bellicourt. Both divisions entered the line with far less than the full AEF-established strength of 28,000 per division. Neither had received replacements since arriving in France. The 27th reported 16,136 men, and the 30th was a little better with 19,059.[15] There were three main reasons why the II Corps divisions were below strength. First, they did not have their field artillery regiments and ammunition trains, which included about 7,000 officers and men. Second, casualties as a result of training and operations had thinned the ranks; and third, illness from the first wave of the influenza outbreak that hit the Western Front around 15 September had left the divisions depleted.[16]

Still another factor affected the divisions. Many officers missed the operation because of the poor decision at AEF headquarters to begin an officers' school at Langres, near Pershing's headquarters at Chaumont, on 27 September. The 27th Division was ordered to send twenty-nine officers, while the 30th Division was ordered to send more than 100 of its officers.[17] Such thoughtlessness by Pershing's staff also affected the AEF First Army divisions that were about to attack in the Meuse-Argonne operation. Despite being under strength, the two II Corps divisions were still more than twice the size of the British and Australian divisions and four times the strength of the German divisions opposing them.[18]

For the Hindenburg Line operation, Read turned over tactical command to Monash, moved his headquarters close to him, and allowed the Australian commander full access to 27th and 30th divisional staffs. This was logical because neither Read nor any of his staff had experience directing a large-scale operation. Monash could not have been happier with the agreement. "I am bound to say that the arrangement caused me no anxiety or difficulty," recalled the Australian commander. "General Read and his staff most readily adapted themselves to the situation."[19] Although the orders and reports generated by Read's staff indicated that II Corps was "affiliated" with the Australian Corps, in reality, the Americans were serving under the Australians.[20]

Before he relinquished command to Monash, Read met with his two division commanders. O'Ryan, who had suspected that his division was training for a major operation, was now convinced "from the intensive character of the special training of the officers and men that the division was to take some important role of an offensive nature."[21] His suspicions were realized on 23 September, when Read outlined the upcoming operation to O'Ryan and Lewis. Read told them the most difficult part of the operation would be on the northern end of the tunnel because the British were having trouble with the enemy outpost line in this sector. He asked O'Ryan and Lewis their views about which division should be assigned to this sector, and both said they had no preference. For no apparent reason, Read decided to select the 27th Division; O'Ryan claimed that it was because of "its training and experience."[22] (This comment was probably prejudiced, since Lewis's division had the same amount of experience as the New Yorkers and more men.) O'Ryan told his troops that they might have to undertake a preliminary operation to gain a more suitable jump-off point, since the British III Corps attacks were not going well.[23]

On the eve of its first major operation, II Corps was on its own and received no instructions from AEF headquarters for the upcoming attack. Because the attack on the Hindenburg Line was part of a large Allied effort between the Meuse and Yser rivers, Pershing was occupied with planning and organizing his phase of the operation and seemed to have overlooked the divisions that were serving with the British. On 12 September, ten days before the American First Army attacked the St. Mihiel salient south of Verdun, seven American and two French divisions pushed the withdrawing Germans from the salient. The cost was high for both sides. American casualties numbered 7,000, and the Germans lost 2,300 killed and wounded, 15,000 prisoners, and 460 guns.[24] From here, First Army had the difficult task of shifting divisions to the northwest to the Meuse-Argonne region. Pershing certainly knew of the II Corps situation because Haig sent Bacon to Pershing's headquarters on 22 September "to find out how the latter's arrangements were getting on, and to acquaint him with what I am proposing to do with the two American divisions still with the British Army."[25] But Pershing sent no words of encouragement to Read, and there is no evidence that he followed the operation as it took place.

It was not clear how well the Americans would perform in their first big operation. The after-action reports for the Ypres-Lys Offensive showed that many officers encountered difficulty during combat. Major General Lewis expressed his apprehension in a memorandum to his 59th Brigade commander. "From numerous observations," he told Tyson, "I am convinced that the organizations of the command are not receiving the maximum and desirable amount of observation, and inspection by the commanders of the higher units. While, of course, I do not intend to dictate specifically how you and the members of your staff shall employ your time, I do desire to make the following remarks for your consideration."[26]

Lewis continued that he had "seldom seen a regimental commander supervising instruction, and, too often, the battalion commanders are content to stand around without actively engaging in the instruction, or correcting things that are obvious to a very cursory observation." He then told Tyson to "have frequent conferences with your field officers for the purpose of instructing them in these matters, and to learn what corrective steps are being taken by them."[27] His comments seem to have helped Tyson's brigade, since it fought well in both the upcoming operation and the next one at the Selle River.

To assist the Americans with operational planning, Monash created an Australian mission under the direction of Maj. Gen. Ewen George Sinclair-MacLagan. Eighty-three officers and 127 non-commissioned officers from the 1st and 4th Australian Divisions served as advisors to the 27th and 30th Divisions. Each was carefully selected to "ensure that the best experience of the Australian Corps was made available to the Americans in France." Sinclair-MacLagan, a career British officer, had served in Australia. When the war began, he received command of the 3rd Brigade of the 1st Australian Division, and, in 1917, he had commanded the 4th Australian Division, which fought well at the Third Battle of Ypres and the battles at Villers-Bretonneux and Hamel. These experiences gave Sinclair-MacLagan great authority to advise the Americans.[28]

Brig. Gen. C. H. Brand was assigned as liaison officer to the 27th Division, and Brig. Gen. I. G. Mace served in a similar capacity with the 30th. They worked with their American counterparts as far down as the battalion level to familiarize them with technical terms and matters regarding supplies, equipment, and tactics.[29] Monash later wrote that "it was only because of the creation of this Australian Mission to the Americans, and Sinclair-MacLagan's tact, industry, and judgment controlling it, that the combined action of the two corps in the great battle of the closing days of September proved as successful as it did."[30]

Monash organized meetings at his headquarters to further acquaint the Americans with the operation. The first was on 25 September. Read, his division commanders and their staffs, and the Australian mission attended. Monash was well prepared, having presented the key points in preceding days. Besides detailing the order of events for the attack, he outlined seven key points, from A to G: working as a team, strictly limiting prescribed objectives, following field orders, paying attention to detail, sending back information (both positive and negative), keeping men fit, and thinking ahead.[31] He used maps, diagrams, and a blackboard to stress teamwork: "One job for each man," he told his audience.[32] Regiments should attack with two battalions and use a third to mop up. Monash carefully stressed the latter point, mentioning his experience of watching attack troops pass over Germans hidden in dugouts, who then came up afterward and fired into the backs of the advancing troops.[33]

When the meeting ended, a tired Monash returned to his headquarters. It had lasted three hours, and he later wrote that he had spent most of the time explaining the intricacies of the attack and responding to a "rain of questions." But he had "no doubt that the American generals became fully informed as to the tasks and duties allotted to them, and fully understood them."[34]

O'Ryan's recollection of events differed significantly. "There were no more than five or six questions asked in all by the American officers present. General Monash's conversation and explanations were so lengthy and detailed that there did not seem to be necessity to ask many questions."[35] O'Ryan was concerned about the complexity of the preliminary and main attacks. Monash had asked him during the meeting to assign one of his regiments for a possible preliminary attack. O'Ryan selected the 106th Infantry. When O'Ryan asked why the regiment would have to attack on a front of 4,000 yards without support from other regiments, Monash replied that he wanted to keep the rest of the division out of the preliminary operation so it would be fresh for the main attack. As a compromise, the 105th Infantry could be used in limited support.[36]

O'Ryan was puzzled by the main attack battle plan, which called for the 105th Infantry, after following the 108th Infantry, to maneuver and change direction to the left and attack. From there, it would pass north through Vendhuile to relieve pressure on the British units attacking on that front. He wanted to know if this was practical. Monash's response was short: "The plan will be carried out in this manner."[37] Questions such as these might have been an indication that the plans for the operation were too complicated for the Americans. Regardless of how long the meeting lasted or how many questions were raised, a battle of this caliber was new to the Americans, and they needed Monash's guidance every step of the way.

There was much concern at II Corps headquarters about the preliminary attack. In the previous days, as the British preliminary attack was winding down, Simonds had met with Monash to express concern over British III Corps's failure to capture the outpost line in the northern sector. Monash tried to appease Simonds and told him "there will be a little operation tonight, and we will take it over." However, the following day, Simonds was told: "Sorry, but III Corps did not get there last night, and I think the 27th Division will have to have a preliminary operation."[38]

All this was an unsettling beginning for the first major battle for American II Corps, and O'Ryan's 27th Division would find itself in the midst of it. Monash, one must conclude, had not measured the situation with his usual care. The corps commander of the splendid Australian divisions often attempted too much, as the near-mutiny of men in two battalions had shown. He had too much to do, and a three-hour lecture to Americans was indeed a poor idea, particularly since he ignored O'Ryan's resulting concerns. The preparation for what (as O'Ryan well knew) would be a complicated—probably too complicated—battle was foreboding in its lack of clarity at the top, under Monash's direction. It remained to be seen how the Americans, in particular O'Ryan's division, would perform.

Both American divisions had their baptism of fire, and now, in the last days of September 1918, were to enter into the most important experience of their association with British forces on the Western Front. They were to spearhead an attack that, if successful, might bring an end to the war. Here in the British sector, led by an

Australian general, in the midst of Australian units, the divisions were equal in strength to four British or Dominion divisions and would lead the way against a strong German position. But despite its strength in numbers, the American II Corps was deficient in tactical experience and would pay a heavy price.

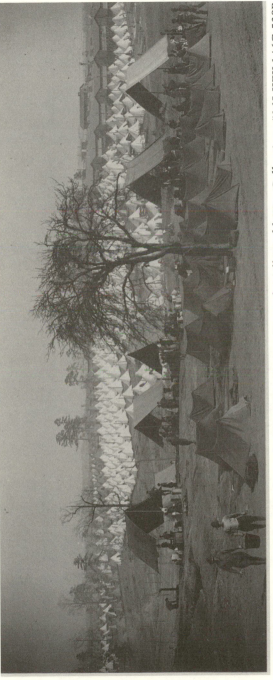

Enlisted men's tents, Camp Wadsworth. War Department General Staff World War Collection, #165-WW-146C-530B-059, RG 165-WW, NARA.

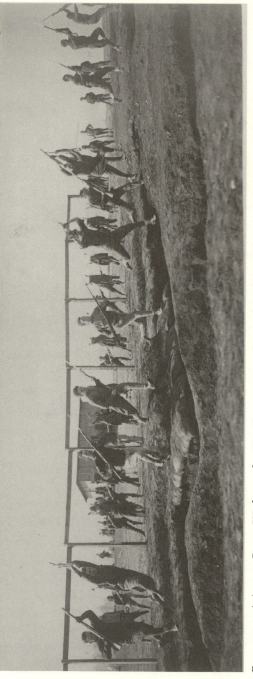

Bayonet training at Camp Wadsworth. War Department General Staff World War Collection, #165-WW-146C-006, RG 165-WW, NARA.

Writing to the folks back in New York. War Department General Staff World War Collection, #165-WW-471A-044, RG 165-WW, NARA.

Hospital ward at Camp Wadsworth, South Carolina. U.S. Army Signal Corps, #SC-4700, RG111, NARA.

Gen. Sir Henry Rawlinson, British Fourth Army commander. U.S. Army Signal Corps, #SC-59-BO, RG111, NARA.

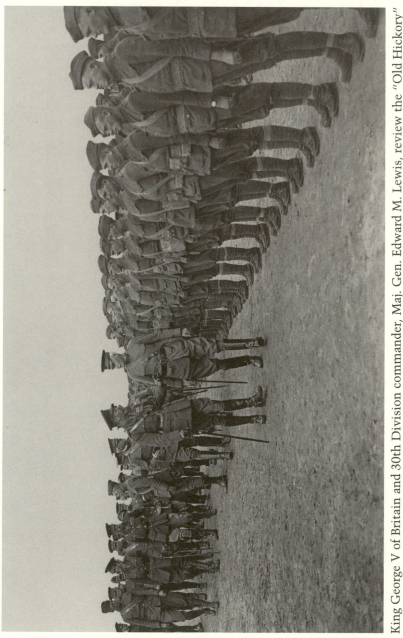

King George V of Britain and 30th Division commander, Maj. Gen. Edward M. Lewis, review the "Old Hickory" Division in the British Second Army Area, Belgium. U.S. Army Signal Corps, #SC-1560, RG111, NARA.

The devastated village of Bellicourt, France, in early October 1918 after continuous shelling during the Somme Campaign. U.S. Army Signal Corps, #SC-1703-BO, RG111, NARA.

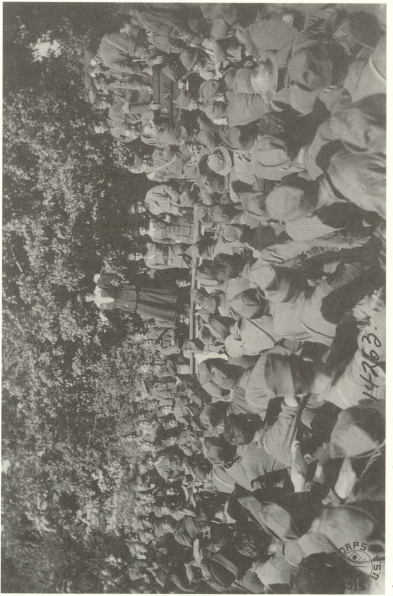

Elsie Janis entertains homesick American troops near the Ypres front in July 1918. U.S. Army Signal Corps, #SC-14263, RG111, NARA.

Col. George S. Simonds, American II Corps chief of staff, 19 July 1918.
U.S. Army Signal Corps, #SC-17224, RG111, NARA.

Maj. Gen. Edward M. Lewis, American 30th Division commander, 30 July 1918, at 30th Division Headquarters, Watou, Belgium. U.S. Army Signal Corps, #SC-17851, RG111, NARA.

American and British troops take a break from training with a friendly game of cards near Calais, France, 18 May 1918. U.S. Army Signal Corps, #SC-363-BO, RG111, NARA.

A German prisoner (right) and his American captor (left), 29 September 1918. The German soldier was operating a machine gun while wearing a Red Cross armband when he was taken captive near Bellicourt. In the background are British and American soldiers. U.S. Army Signal Corps, #SC-1792-BO, RG111, NARA.

A doughboy of 30th Division takes aim with his machine gun in the Ypres-Lys Campaign near Watou, Belgium, in August 1918. U.S. Army Signal Corps, #SC-18706, RG111, NARA.

Doughboys of 119th Infantry entering the trenches near Ypres, Belgium, in July 1918. U.S. Army Signal Corps, #SC-18707, RG111, NARA.

Doughboys of the 107th Infantry train with British tanks in preparation for the upcoming attack on the Hindenburg Line, 13 September 1918. U.S. Army Signal Corps, #SC-24514, RG111, NARA.

A doughboy leads a British supply tank toward the Cambrai–St. Quentin front, 29 September 1918, during the attack on the Hindenburg Line. U.S. Army Signal Corps, #SC-24062, RG111, NARA.

A section of the St. Quentin Canal that flows by Riqueval, France. 1 October 1918. U.S. Army Signal Corps, #SC-24541, RG111, NARA.

An Australian soldier on horseback precedes an American tank into Bellicourt after the attack on the Hindenburg Line, 3 October 1918. U.S. Army Signal Corps, #SC-25978, RG111, NARA.

A burial party from the 106th Infantry near Duncan Post, 3 October 1918. U.S. Army Signal Corps, #SC-29571, RG111, NARA.

BEF commander Field Marshal Sir Douglas Haig and Lt. Col. Robert Bacon, the American liaison to the BEF, finish lunch during their visit to the battlefield near the St. Quentin Canal in October 1918. U.S. Army Signal Corps, #SC-28260, RG111, NARA.

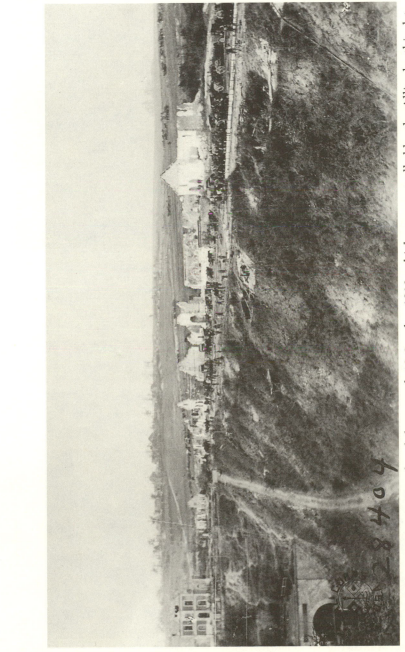

A view of the St. Quentin Canal and the tunnel, 10 October 1918, which was controlled by the Allies by this date. The village of Bellicourt, France, is in the background. U.S. Army Signal Corps, #SC-28404, RG111, NARA.

A traffic jam in front of 30th Division caused by Australian, American, and British transport units attempting to deliver material to the battle lines at Montbrehain, 14 October 1918. U.S. Army Signal Corps, #SC-29688, RG111, NARA.

British artillery supporting the American attack at Vaux-Andigny, France, 17 October 1918. U.S. Army Signal Corps, #SC-33383, RG111, NARA.

Exhausted British Tommies rest in a trench at Molain, France, 17 October 1918. U.S. Army Signal Corps, #SC-33375, RG111, NARA.

A busy point near Busigny, France, as a British tank passes by German wounded escorted from the front by American soldiers, 17 October 1918. U.S. Army Signal Corps, #SC-33379, RG111, NARA.

Souvenir hunters from the 107th Infantry show off their war trophies, 26 October 1918. U.S. Army Signal Corps, #SC-30049, RG111, NARA.

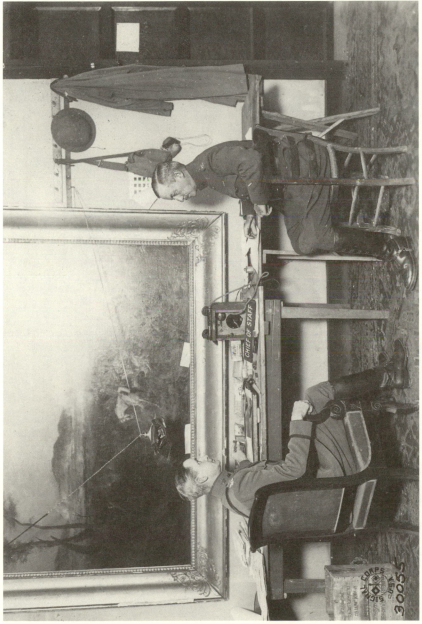

Maj. Gen. John F. O'Ryan and his chief of staff, Col. Stanley Ford, confer at 27th Division headquarters, 18 October 1918. U.S. Army Signal Corps, #SC-30055, RG111, NARA.

Reaction to the news of the armistice near 27th Division headquarters in Corbie, France, 11 November 1918. U.S. Army Signal Corps, #SC-32396, RG111, NARA.

Somme American Cemetery, Bony, France.

The Somme American Cemetery in Bony, France. U.S. Army Signal Corps, #SC-97417, RG111, NARA.

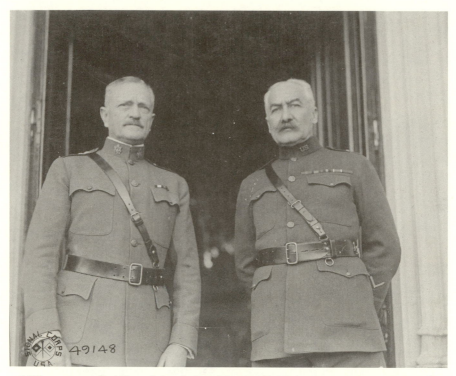

AEF commander Gen. John J. Pershing with Maj. Gen. George W. Read, the American II Corps commander, 22 January 1919, Bonnetable, Sarthe, France. U.S. Army Signal Corps, #SC-49148, RG111, NARA.

17

THE AMERICANS
ENTER THE LINE

As dawn broke on 25 September, the 27th Division had replaced the British 18th and 74th divisions in the Gouy sector, and the previous night, the 30th Division had relieved the 1st Australian Division in the Nauroy sector. Hostile shelling had slowed relief in the 30th Division sector, and it was not completed until 2 A.M. on the 25th. On the way to the front, the Americans passed through the heart of the Somme Valley—what Brigadier General Tyson called that "terrible battlefield that is the abomination of desolation."[1] They were then crowded into the trenches constructed to accommodate Australian and British units. An average Australian or British battalion now numbered around 500 officers and men. The American equivalent, a regiment, was more than twice that strength.[2]

In a trench held by Company F of the 118th Infantry, the Germans greeted the new occupants with a raid that was foiled by the alert Americans, resulting in small losses to both sides.[3] A German soldier captured that morning confessed that air reconnaissance had observed the relief the night before, but his unit was not aware that the Americans had taken over.[4] During the next two days, the Germans continued to harass the American line with raids and aircraft patrols, which were followed by intense shelling.[5] The Germans clearly

159

knew that the 27th and 30th were in the line, but whether or not they expected a major attack is unclear.[6] British and Australian planes patrolling the German lines took reconnaissance photographs that did not reveal new defensive earthworks.[7] Some German POWs interrogated by American intelligence officers indicated they expected an attack, while others said that their forces were caught by surprise.

One of them professed to know that an attack was imminent "because they had shot down a British airplane carrying the plan of attack." As a result, the German regiment "received a fresh draft" on 28 September.[8] However, a German soldier who was captured by the 107th Infantry on 29 September said that "the attack was a complete surprise." He also claimed to "not know who was on the line when the attack began."[9] Further proof that the Germans were likely surprised by the attack comes from Sgt. E. G. Graham of the 118th Infantry. During burial detail on 1 October, Graham found a dead German under an army straw tick who was wearing only his underwear and socks.[10] Evidently he had not had time to dress.

Because the British were unable to entirely secure the outpost line, the two American divisions were charged with carrying out this task on 26–27 September. On the north end of the line, the 27th Division was assigned the more difficult job, using the 106th Infantry to advance 1,000 yards on a long front of 4,000 yards to secure a jump-off line for the main attack. In the 30th Division sector, the 118th Infantry had an easier undertaking. Because the British had already taken the portion of the outpost line opposite the division (except in a few places), the regiment was to make a much shorter advance on a 1,200-yard front to straighten the line in preparation for the main attack. The flanks of the attackers were to be protected by a smokescreen fired from one field artillery brigade on each side. Maps used for the preliminary operation identified the start line in brown and the objective lines in green. Tanks from the British 4th Tank Battalion were to support the 106th Infantry, and the British 1st Tank Battalion was to advance with the 118th Infantry. Both regiments would move forward from a taped line and receive assistance from a creeping barrage. The 106th was formed on the left of the jump-off line, and the 118th was formed on the right.[11]

Since the element of surprise was gone, British and Australian artillery units preceded the preliminary operation with intense bombardment of the German defenses, firing 750,000 shells. The unique aspect was detonation of mustard gas for eight hours. This was the first time the British used this particular type of gas, although the Germans first used gas at the Second Battle of Ypres on 22 April 1915, and the British speedily followed suit. The British had more than 26,000 18-pounders and 6,200 6-inch mustard howitzer rounds in their arsenal. Rawlinson ordered the gassing to start at 10 A.M. on 26 September and to continue until 6 P.M. The targets were the German artillery and centers of communication.[12]

To manage the expected high casualties, medical units readied themselves for the operation. Like the infantry and machine-gun units they were to support, the two sanitary trains (102nd and 105th), each comprised of two field ambulance companies and two field hospitals, had no large-scale operational experience. During the Ypres-Lys Offensive, the 27th and 30th Divisions relied heavily on British ambulances and field hospitals for assistance. For the battles at the Hindenburg Line, British and Australian medical units would again cooperate with the Americans by providing dressing stations, ambulance posts, and rest stations for doughboys who were only slightly wounded.[13]

Besides relying on the British and Australians for medical personnel and artillery, the two American divisions also had to rely on them for auxiliary labor and administration units.[14] But one crucial area, traffic control and road clearance, was undertaken by the II Corps Military Police Company. Formed on 10 September from detachments of seventy noncommissioned officers and men transferred from the 27th and 30th Divisions, it was primarily tasked with rounding up stragglers. Also, when villages such as Bellicourt and Bony were captured, the military police were responsible for assisting refugees and other inhabitants.[15] Each division still had a military police unit to maintain order in its sector. The 102nd Military Police of the 27th Division appeared to have the most experienced commander, Maj. Harry T. Shanton. Before joining the army, he was the transportation manager of Buffalo Bill's Wild West Show.[16]

Monash held another conference on 26 September with the American division and brigade commanders, the Australian division commanders and staffs, and officers from supporting units. As the artillery bombardment could be heard in the background, Monash went over the operation plan and answered last-minute questions from the nervous Americans. The conference lasted over two and a half hours, and, according to Monash, "No one present will soon forget the tense interest and confident expectancy that characterized that meeting."[17] Field Marshal Haig arrived before the conference ended, and Monash persuaded him to greet the senior officers and say a few words of encouragement.[18] There was not much he could say to them that they didn't already know. So Haig confidently predicted a positive outcome and told the assembled officers that "the biggest battle of the war started this morning, and the enemy will be attacked by 100 divisions in the next three days."[19]

General Read was not in attendance but knew about the situation at hand. Although he had relinquished tactical command to Monash, he was still very active in organizing his corps for its first major operation. Between 21 and 24 September, he issued three detailed field orders.[20] Each summarized the movements and reproduced battle plans as prepared by Monash's staff. The third order, #16, was the most detailed. It provided the general plan for the preliminary operations and main attack, and instructed unit commanders on how to deal with liaison, how to assemble, and what to expect of road conditions.[21] Once the fighting commenced, the field orders would be of limited use since conditions would change rapidly. Read was doing his best to prepare the corps, but it would be up to the division and brigade commanders to conduct the battle at the front.

Right on schedule, the 118th Infantry commenced the preliminary operation at 9:30 P.M. on 26 September. It started out well, and by 10:55, the regiment's 1st and 3rd Battalions had established a new line 500 yards in advance of the jump-off point.[22] The straightening of the line continued the next day in conjunction with the preliminary attack of the 27th Division.

At 3:30 A.M. on 27 September, the 106th Infantry headed toward the starting line while shells fell all around. Because the troops had to move rapidly against heavy German machine-gun fire, each man was ordered to leave his overcoat, blanket, and field kit at company headquarters and instead carried a raincoat, rations, fighting equipment, and five grenades.[23] Twelve tanks supported the 106th Infantry, while two companies (K and M) of the 105th Infantry were on its left flank. The officers and men were well aware of the complexity

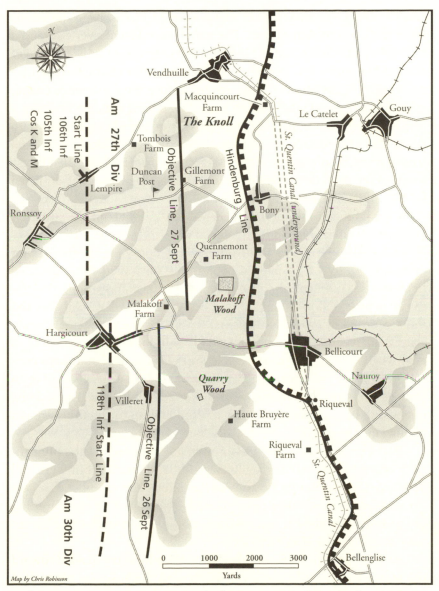

Preliminary operation against Hindenburg Line, 26–27 September 1918

of the attack. In previous days, Major General O'Ryan lectured the company commanders about their task, and his words of wisdom were passed on to the lower ranks. He emphasized that they were not to be taken prisoner but were to "fight to the finish."[24] If captured, a soldier was to give only the following information: "I left my billet in a rear area two or three days ago, at which time I heard that the rest of the division was going south. How far south I do not know, but believe the move was made by rail. Since that time, I have seen no other unit of the division in this area, only British troops."[25]

The 106th Infantry jumped off at 5:30 A.M. and at first moved forward unimpeded toward the objective line with protection by a creeping barrage and coverage from the 105th and 106th Machine-Gun Battalions and tanks.[26] A short time later, signal flares and wounded men returning from the front indicated that some of the regiment had reached the outpost line. But the good news was premature.[27] As planned, Company M of the 105th advanced to the outpost line to mop up. There, it found the situation far from at hand. Instead of mopping up, the unit became engaged in a heavy fight. During the attack, it lost two of its lieutenants. One of them, Lieutenant Rudin, was "in the van of his men and pointing the way with an uplifted arm" when he was hit by machine-gun fire.[28] Other officers were wounded, and as the morning progressed, all order broke down. Messages from the front were sent to 53rd Brigade headquarters, but they told little news of what was happening. One of the early telephone messages O'Ryan received vaguely summed up the chaos: "Situation around the Knoll very obscure."[29]

As elements of the 105th and 106th Infantry tried to advance, the enemy filtered down through ravines and communication trenches into deep dugouts that were still intact even after days of artillery fire. When the Americans passed over the dugouts, the German troops came above ground and fired at them, inflicting heavy casualties.[30] The resistance the doughboys encountered at the German outpost line was at least as intense as what had earlier prevented British III Corps from taking this same position.

Further confirmation that all was not going well came at 1:25 P.M. in a message from the 106th Infantry, which said that its right battalion had been attacked and that "the situation is not clear."[31] At the same time, an Australian air patrol reported that fighting was still going on around the Knoll but could not give an accurate assessment due to poor visibility. However, an American officer who reported to O'Ryan's headquarters five hours later contradicted the information. He had come from the front shortly before and was sure that the Knoll and the Gillemont and Quennemont Farms "were in our hands, with only pockets of the enemy remaining to be mopped up."[32] It became evident a short time later that this officer was wrong.

That same morning of 27 September, while elements of the 27th Division were in the midst of a difficult fight, the 30th Division's 118th Infantry renewed the attempt to adjust its line. Early reports from the 3rd Battalion indicated that it had gained all objectives by 10:15 A.M. The reports said that the 1st Battalion was in the process of extending the divisional line to include Malakoff Wood but had to withdraw after German machine-gun fire became too heavy, at a cost of many casualties. The fire came from Quennemont Farm on the left, where the 106th Infantry was in trouble, thus preventing the troops of the 30th Division from advancing farther.[33] As the 118th was fighting to consolidate its line, a message came at 6 P.M. from the 106th Infantry headquarters, stating what was already obvious: "The whole front is practically the same as the jumping-off point this AM."[34] This message had actually been sent much earlier, but transmission was a problem throughout the day. A frustrated battalion commander in the 106th Infantry reported: "All our communications are down, and we can't use anything but runners." He blamed the problem on shelling that had severed the wires.[35]

As night fell on 27 September, the 105th and 106th withdrew to a line that was only a short distance in front of where they had jumped off that morning. But most disturbing was that an unknown number of troops from both regiments were still holding their forward positions around the Knoll and the farms, and this would have a major impact on the main operation. Despite the heavy losses, the gains were minimal. Casualties from the two days of fighting were 17 officers and 300 men killed, with more than twice those numbers wounded and missing.[36] Most were from the 106th Regiment. Nearly all company officers were killed or wounded.

German troops picked apart the New York soldiers with such ease that it reminded one historian of Pickett's charge at Gettysburg, when advancing Confederates were struck down by Union artillery fire.[37] A German Second Army report corroborates the chaos of the American attack. Its 84th Schleswig-Holstein Infantry Regiment encountered some doughboys near Lempire, who were initially "in assembled formation, but then took to flight, streaming to the rear in the fire of our artillery."[38] Our troops "victoriously repulsed all enemy attacks," the Germans claimed. The German counterattacks were "executed against its right and center. The main line of resistance is everywhere in our possession unchanged."[39]

After the attack, the 53rd Brigade commander gave his account of the day's action. He blamed his brigade's failure on the "very great shortage of officers." Even more detrimental to the attack, Brigadier General Blanding pointed out, was that the officers available had little time to study and disseminate their orders, maps, and serial photographs of the ground on which they were to advance. He was also critical of the support provided by the tanks. His brigade had minimal training with the machines in early September, and this became evident during the fighting. They had no effect on German machine guns and artillery.[40]

Meanwhile, the Germans were expecting the 118th Infantry to continue its advance on 28 September. With reconnaissance from their planes, they placed artillery fire and increased machine-gun fire on positions that contained concentrations of Americans.[41] But the 118th did not advance that day. Instead, it waited for relief from the units of the 60th Brigade. For the regiment, the fighting was over, and it moved to reserve its strength for the next day's main operation. During its period in the line, the 118th suffered ten killed and more than 100 wounded.[42]

That night and into the early morning of 28 September, the 54th Brigade (107th and 108th Infantries) relieved the 105th and 106th Infantries. Patrols from the 2nd Battalion of the 108th Infantry were sent forward to gain contact with missing troops. During the afternoon of the 28th, the patrols found one officer and seven men of the 106th Infantry. They also found several German strongpoints. After they sent the British artillery the coordinates, its guns shelled the area but did minimal damage because the Germans hung on to most of the outpost line.

It was unclear how many soldiers from the 27th Division were still at the outpost line and what part, if any, of the ground was in

American possession. Australian aircraft flew patrols over the front and "verified some American troops on the desired line, but could get no flares to answer signals." German machine guns fired at the airmen, offering further proof that the ground was not under Allied control.[43] At II Corps headquarters, Major General Read was shaken by the perilous situation and called a conference early on 28 September. Staff officers from the 27th Division, Australian Corps, and Fourth Army were present.

First on the agenda was the idea of adjusting the artillery fire to a line closer to the Americans so that troops might advance under its protection from the start. But according to Brig. Gen. K. K. Knapp, in command of the artillery that was supporting II Corps, this was impractical due to a lack of time. Changing the barrage schedule by bringing it farther back would put Americans near the Knoll and the farms at risk.[44] Knapp was well liked and trusted by the II Corps officers, and they felt that he "made every effort to give our men all possible advantage of artillery protection."[45] The idea of postponing the operation was also suggested to Monash, and, according to one of his biographers, he thought it was the better solution. However, Rawlinson overruled him. The Fourth Army commander said that a delay would mean changing the arrangements on other fronts where troops were set to attack the next day.[46]

It now made sense for the lead regiments of the 27th Division to form up as close as possible to the barrage line for the attack an hour earlier, then try to fight their way forward by the original start time without artillery support.[47] This was a difficult solution for all parties involved, made even more difficult by the fact that it was British artillery supporting American ground troops. If the 27th Division had its own artillery, the decision might have been much simpler. O'Ryan later justified the resolution: "The 53rd Brigade, which was gallantly holding its gains, was entitled to every consideration, even though some sacrifice was involved. To voluntarily assume the risk of destroying those because of a decision to increase the security of the 54th Brigade, no matter how logical it might be in the tactical sense, would be repulsive to the mass of the officers and men of the division, and destructive of morale."[48]

With the next day's attack moved up one hour, tension remained high at II Corps headquarters. To reassure Read about the operation,

Haig paid him a visit. He found the II Corps commander "very anxious." Haig referred to him as "a good honest fellow" and told Read not to worry about the next day's events because "the reality was much simpler than his imagination pictured it to his mind." No one knows if Haig really believed this, but his words may have been some comfort.[49]

Rawlinson also thought the next day's attack would be successful. He wrote in his diary: "I feel pretty happy about the prospects as a whole, for even if the Americans are inexperienced, they are keen as mustard and splendid men."[50] Monash did not share this optimism. He had little faith in the 27th and 30th Divisions, according to C. E. W. Bean. As the official correspondent with the AIF, Bean, who was on a first-name basis with the Australian Corps commander, visited his headquarters the night of the 28th. "He [Monash] was very insistent on the fact that he doubted whether the Americans would succeed in carrying out their objectives." Monash's attitude that evening left Bean with the feeling that "John was hedging against a possible defeat, in which case he would be able to throw the blame onto the Americans."[51]

18

MAIN OPERATION

29 September 1918

With the attack set to start on schedule, the units in the line from the preliminary attack were ordered into reserve and replaced by the fresh regiments. This meant that in the 27th Division sector, the 54th Brigade took over the line from the 105th and 106th Infantries of the 53rd Brigade. The 108th Infantry Regiment was on its right and the 107th Infantry Regiment on its left. In the 30th Division sector, the 60th Brigade relieved the 117th and 118th Infantries of the 59th Brigade; the 120th Infantry was on the right and the 119th Infantry on the left. That night, the engineer units laid the jump-off lines. Two men and an officer from each company crawled out of the trenches and moved forward with rolls of white tape, which they laid on the ground, parallel to the trenches. The commander of the 105th Engineers described the process: "This tape is done on the night before the attack is to commence, and consists of putting a line of white tape (one inch wide) along the whole front of our position just in advance of the front line trench, the object being to give the attacking troops a definite line to form on and to advance uniformly behind the barrage. Outposts will be sent out in advance of laying this line to prevent the enemy from surprising the taping party. These outposts stay out until just before the attack and then they are called in."[1]

Additionally, the engineers conducted road and water reconnaissance and searched for enemy traps and mines, all under the constant threat of machine-gun and shrapnel fire. The Germans observed the process and responded with a heavy barrage that caused a considerable number of casualties among the engineers working on the road.[2] At the same time, the tanks turned on their engines and rumbled forward under the cover of aircraft flying over the line to drown out the noise.[3]

In the rear, the infantry and machine-gun troops prepared for a Sunday morning they would not soon forget. To ease their jittery nerves, a soldier in the 27th Division remembered how "the British had given us a big half tumbler of rum before the charge, and Thank God for that."[4] Paul Maze, a French artist serving as an interpreter on Rawlinson's staff, wandered through the 27th Division line during its preparation for the assault. To his surprise, the men seemed relaxed and "settled down to their job with great spirit."[5] But this was not true of all doughboys. Sergeant Melvin remembered being in the trenches in front of Bellicourt on 28 September when an officer told him that his unit would go over the top the next morning at 5:54 A.M. They would know it was time to start when a big shell was fired way back behind the line. "We had to lie there all night and worry about that," Melvin later wrote. "It is impossible to describe the feelings a man has with that in front of him. I always said I knew how a man felt who was condemned to die, for we all thought it was our last night. We thought of our families and the ones we loved."[6] Another doughboy recalled that after the jump-off, "the trip over the top was terrifying, yet exhilarating, but I believe most of the boys were in a trance. I know I was. I had gone to confession and communion."[7]

Men from both divisions were certainly well equipped for the operation. Each carried 220 rounds of ammunition and two Mills grenades, and the regiments had 600 smoke bombs and 2,500 red ground flares for distribution as needed.[8] The night before the jump-off, a hot food ration was served to the troops on the firing lines. This included fresh meat, which the men savored; it could not be enjoyed as a field ration because it was too hard to eat on the battlefield.[9]

At 4:50 A.M., the New Yorkers commenced the attack against the Hindenburg Line with the 107th Infantry heading toward Gillemont Farm. On its left, the 108th Infantry advanced in the direction of Quennemont Farm. The BEF meteorologist predicted fog and a light wind with limited visibility for 29 September, and his prediction was correct. As the attack started on schedule that morning, visibility was almost nonexistent.[10] First reports received at division headquarters indicated that the attack was "going well." At 8:10, the 108th was reported to have crossed the Hindenburg Line and was on its way to the tunnel. An hour later, the situation changed drastically. Regimental messages stated that its 3rd Battalion had suffered heavy casualties from machine-gun fire at Gillemont Farm but still continued to advance. At 10:05, reports came from the 107th Infantry that casualties were heavy, especially among officers, and that one battalion had fallen back.

Almost two years after the Hindenburg Line operation, the U.S. Army Chief of Staff requested that O'Ryan provide a detailed observation of his division's battlefield performance. His report provides insight into the 107th Infantry's tactics during this phase of the battle. The Germans counterattacked against the Americans in an attempt to demoralize the regiment by inflicting heavy casualties. The massed troops that attacked over the open ground were protected by artillery and mortar fire. The rolling terrain and the manmade features of the ground provided cover. The 107th was able to counter the attacks "with disciplined resolution and expertness in the use of the rifle." But the Americans were forced to take cover in trenches and shell holes because of their heavy losses.

Unbeknown to the attackers, the Germans had changed tactics and employed expert bombers who worked their way down the approach trenches. They were supplied by specially trained men who passed bombs along to them. Each group was supported, at a distance of several hundred yards, by a group of rifle grenadiers, who were also supplied with rifle grenades, and light mortar groups. Field artillery also provided cover. The supporting fire was effective because each bombing group carried a red rag on a stick that it kept in sight at a prescribed distance behind it. The American troops of II Corps were trained in mobile open warfare in the United States, but the British Army indoctrinated them to use the more static set-piece attack that required less movement. To counter the tactics of the Germans, O'Ryan thought, a unit's men should enter a battle without any fixed idea that it was to be a set-piece action or open warfare, or with their minds committed to any classification of combat. Instead, men should go into battle with the knowledge that their training supplied them with a military team capable of successfully meeting any phase of combat.[11]

Meanwhile, throughout the 27th Division sector, the tanks that were supposed to support the infantry were, once again, of little use. Because of the fog and smoke from the artillery, tank drivers could not see the infantry, and many lost their way almost immediately after leaving the tape.[12] Seven tanks did come within 100 yards of Gillemont Farm, but they were destroyed by anti-tank guns once they became visible through the mist.[13]

Despite setbacks, it appeared that O'Ryan's troops had reached their objectives. But they took heavy losses while mopping up. Patrols sent forward were subject to sniper and machine-gun fire. "It was a slaughter; we ran into a trap," remembered Cpl. Norman Stone. "It was the saddest thing I ever encountered. The machine-gun fire was thicker than flies in summer."[14]

As the Australians came up to what was left of the 108th Infantry to leapfrog the Americans, they found leaderless battalions. On the right flank, the 2nd Battalion was mopping up Quennemont Farm. The 3rd Battalion had parts of two companies on the Hindenburg Line south of Bony, but its left flank was held up at Gillemont Farm. Meanwhile, the 3rd Battalion of the 107th Infantry and a combined battalion of the 106th Infantry were holding a position on the western edge of Gillemont Farm. Mixed organizations of the 106th and 107th Infantries intermingled and held trenches around the Knoll and to the rear of this position.

A few hours after the jump-off, much of the two brigades of the 27th Division were depleted by heavy casualties.[15] Many Americans lay dead or wounded throughout the battlefield. To one New York soldier, "they'd just become figures going down, like pins in a bowling alley."[16] The Germans were also taking significant casualties, and the German Second Army issued orders to withdraw from the front to the rear of the canal.[17] The 107th Infantry was in the thick of the fight, and although it could not break through the line, the regiment was able to hold on until it was joined by the 3rd Australian Division, which was following closely behind. The Australians had jumped off four hours later to give the Americans time to capture Le Catelet Line, where it would leapfrog over them and continue the advance. But as they approached the start line, the Australians immediately encountered heavy fire—and many dead Americans.[18] The large numbers of Germans who survived the artillery bombardment had no intention of surrendering and were overwhelming the Americans, and now the Australians.

Reports from the 3rd Australian Division indicated that "many Americans were leaderless near Gillemont Trench and Willow Trench."[19] Still, the Allies counterattacked and captured Quennemont Farm. In the midst of the battle, the Australians provided great assistance to the inexperienced Americans. Lt. Col. Harry Murray, commanding the 4th Australian Machine-Gun Battalion, accompanied officers of the three machine-gun battalions in the 27th Division sector. "Mad Harry" carried out liaison duty and helped the inexperienced Americans when the Germans counterattacked. For his great service, O'Ryan recommended him for the Distinguished Service Medal, which he received two weeks after the armistice.[20]

At 27th Division headquarters, O'Ryan had difficulty keeping abreast of the fighting. As was the case in the preliminary operation, he received a flow of contradicting messages. Those sent early from the brigade headquarters indicated success in reaching the objective, but only a few minutes later, word came that the lead regiments were under machine-gun fire and were bogged down. Aircraft observed the situation, but poor visibility obscured reporting. At 10 A.M., O'Ryan received a first-hand account from a wounded officer of the 107th Infantry Regiment that the "casualties, especially the officers, were heavy."[21] One officer recalled what it felt like to be shot. "There is a sharp pain when you are hit, and a shock that leaves you faint. This lasts about 15 minutes, then the pain is gone, but a raging thirst sets in. I guess I smoked at least a dozen cigarettes in about 20 minutes."[22]

By 11 A.M., the leading brigades of the 3rd Australian Division moved forward to eventually pass through the Americans. At noon, the Australians reached the line of the 108th Infantry near Gillemont Farm. As the afternoon progressed, the Australians extended their lines farther west to overlap the 107th Infantry. Neither this American regiment nor the Australians could advance any farther because of enfilading and cross fire from Bony, Gillemont Farm, and the hill slopes east of the canal and north of Gouy.

According to the plan of operations, the 105th Infantry, located on the extreme left, was required to cross the tunnel and turn to the north along the east bank of the canal to seize Le Catelet and Gouy. Here it was to be leapfrogged by the 3rd Australian Division, which was following behind the 107th. But when the latter failed to advance because of heavy fire at the Knoll, the 53rd Brigade commander ordered the 105th to take up a defensive position and hold it against counterattacks. With the British 18th Division, it captured the Knoll and Macquincourt Trench, but neither the Americans nor British could advance, and they were driven back to Tombois Road. The 105th commander, Col. James M. Andrews, blamed the failure to proceed beyond the Knoll on "the smoke barrage laid down by the Allied artillery, which proved very confusing to our troops; the direction of the march was hard to maintain, and due to some as yet unexplained phenomena, our marching compasses were so unstable as to be practically useless."[23]

Monash followed the progress of the battle through a steady stream of messages sent by Maj. Gen. Sir John Gellibrand, commander of the 3rd Australian Division. At 2:20 in the afternoon, Gellibrand relayed a report from an Australian liaison officer with the 105th Infantry that its headquarters was at Duncan Post, to the rear of Gillemont Farm. All of the regiment's battalions had been committed, "but headquarters does not know where they are."[24] Two hours later, Gellibrand presented Monash with a much clearer picture of the situation: "As soon as troops advanced," he wrote, "the enemy opened fire at close range with machine guns and artillery. The center battalion is now trying to reach Gillemont Farm, and the left battalion is pushing forward, but the enemy is in strength opposite them with good observation."[25]

At 2 P.M., the few American officers still left were ordered to organize and command detachments that had been pushed back to the left regimental sector. Three hours later, O'Ryan issued an order to the commanding generals of his two brigades "to secure the left flank of our advances and prepare a defensive line of support for the

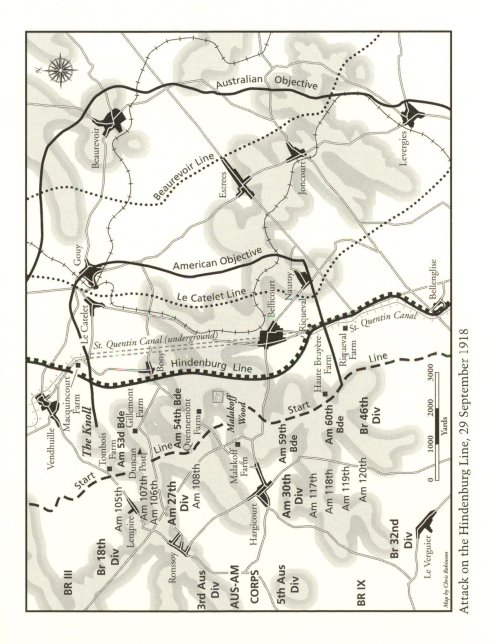

Attack on the Hindenburg Line, 29 September 1918

Map by Chris Robinson

Australian Objective

Beaurevoir

Beaurevoir Line

Estrees

Levergies

Joncourt

Gouy

American Objective

Nauroy

Bellenglise

Le Catelet Line

Bellicourt

Le Catelet

Riqueval

St. Quentin Canal

St. Quentin Canal (underground)

Riqueval Farm

Bony

Hindenburg Line

Haute Bruyère Farm

Line

Macquincourt Farm

Vendhuille

The Knoll

Tombois Farm

Am 53d Bde

Gillemont Farm

Am 54th Bde

Quennemont Farm

Malakoff Wood

Am 60th Bde

Br 46th Div

Start

Duncan Post

Am 107th Post

Line

Am 108th

Am 59th Bde

3000

2000

1000

0

Yards

Start

Am 105th

Lempire

Am 106th

Am 27th Div

Malakoff Farm

Am 30th Div

Am 117th

Am 118th

Am 119th

Am 120th

Ronssoy

Hargicourt

Br 32nd Div

Le Verguier

BR III

Br 18th Div

3rd Aus Div

AUS-AM CORPS

5th Aus Div

BR IX

Australian Division now attacking in the general line. Gather all stragglers and available men, and connect with the British 18th Division in the north and the 3rd Australian Division in the south."[26]

Following O'Ryan's order, both brigade commanders formed a defensive line in support of the Australians attacking near the Knoll, Bony, and Gillemont Farm. The commander of the 54th Brigade was to take charge of the left regimental sector, and the commander of the 53rd Brigade was ordered to do the same in the right regimental sector. With no other infantry to send forward, O'Ryan sent three companies of the 102nd Engineers to occupy a reserve position north of Ronssoy. He notified the 53rd Brigade commander that it is "not the idea that you should put them in the line, but they are to be used as reserve and kept in a secure place, where they may be available for such use, in case of necessity."[27]

In the early morning of 1 October, the 27th Division withdrew and marched in the direction of Peronne for a much-needed rest. The operation was over for the New Yorkers. In two days of hard fighting, the division lost 26 officers and 648 men.[28] The 107th Infantry had the greatest number of losses, with 349 officers and men killed. It was the highest number of casualties for an American unit on a single day in the entire war.[29] Among them was Cpl. Alexander Kim of Company L, one of the few Chinese-Americans serving with the AEF. He was shot through the head in front of Gillemont Farm.[30] A survivor of the battle, Pvt. John Bowman of the 108th Infantry, which also took its share of casualties, summed up the operation when he said, "We've had our real touch of war, and it has been awful."[31]

Burial parties were sent out to collect the dead or mark their temporary graves. Also, Lieutenant Colonel Murray, in command of the 4th Australian Machine-Gun Battalion, made a reconnaissance of the battlefield east and northeast of Duncan Post on 30 September and witnessed the carnage resulting from heavy machine-gun fire directed at the 27th Division as it left the trenches the previous day. Even though the division did not meet all of its objectives, Murray was impressed by the fact that all of the dead New Yorkers he encountered were facing forward, an indication that none of the Americans retreated when the fire grew intense. This touched him enough to write O'Ryan: "I am convinced that the officers and men of the 27th Division did all that was humanly possible for brave men to do, and their gallantry in this action must stand out through all time in American history."[32] O'Ryan may have been in no mood to receive accolades from the Australian. It had been reported to him that "the bodies of our dead were looted, with money, valuables, and letters and diaries taken," he wrote in his official report. In one case, the ring finger of a soldier was cut off. It was believed to have been done by the Australian troops, but this could not be proven.[33] There was no investigation of this matter by the Americans or the Australians, and it did not go any farther than the mention O'Ryan made in his report to Read.

Besides the killed and wounded, one officer and thirty-three men of 27th Division were taken prisoner. Among the American POWs was Pvt. James F. Walker of the 106th Infantry, who was captured along with three other soldiers from his company as they hid from machine-gun fire in a shell hole. At first, their captors treated the prisoners like "civilized human beings," but once they were behind the lines, it was a different story. The Americans were "cuffed and shoved about," fed only a slice of sour black bread "as thick as tissue paper," and given a bowl of coffee made from burned barley. While the fighting continued, the Germans kept the POWs in a cage, then took them across the border to Belgium and finally to Germany. There, Walker was held with other Americans until after the armistice.[34]

German prisoners were a common sight behind the American lines, and the surrendered enemy men and officers were handled in an efficient manner. Those captured by the 27th Division were sent to a POW cage operated by the 102nd Military Police at Ronssoy. Mounted men from the unit were charged with taking the prisoners from the infantry and escorting them to the cage. Guards were posted at all times to ensure that the prisoners were not interfered with or robbed of their possessions.

In their search for stragglers, the military police found that 150 men had been separated from their units. But traffic problems were the main issue the MPs faced, and these reached a climax as the infantry and support units headed toward the jump-off line. "Every available man worked night and day" to keep the lines moving, claimed a private in the 102nd. "So great was the demand for help," Pvt. Charles L. Campbell recalled, that "mechanics, wagoners, horses-shoers and cooks were used. Splintered vehicles and dead horses that blocked the way" complicated their job. Such work was also dangerous. A bomb dropped by a German aeroplane killed one soldier while he directed traffic.[35]

19

ATTACK BY 30TH DIVISION

To the south, in the 30th Division sector, the advance was more successful. The attack started at 5:30 A.M., also under a screen of mist and low clouds that mixed with smoke from the barrage. But in this case the poor conditions actually gave the attackers an advantage. While the fog and smoke clouds "hindered the maintenance of order and cohesion," as the historians of the 30th Division recognize, "they were of tremendous assistance in blinding the enemy's machine guns and field artillery."[1]

But it was the deafening noise that most remember from this operation. The division's commanding officer, Maj. Gen. Edward M. Lewis, recalled vividly that "four minutes after the starting signal, the air was a hell of torturing sound . . . the scream of bursting shrapnel, the whistle of bullets, the splintering explosions of grenades, the staccato bark of countless machine guns . . . that all helped to build up a direful symphony of battle."[2]

Men from the two lead regiments mingled as they headed in the direction of the defending Germans, who could barely see what was coming toward them. On the right of the line, the 120th Infantry crossed the canal and continued eastward until 11 A.M., when it met severe resistance and could not advance farther. Still, it managed to

179

capture Nauroy and occupy the Le Catelet-Nauroy Line. Elements of the regiment had gone eastward beyond Nauroy but could not make contact with the 119th Infantry on their left and had to pull back. A battalion of the 117th was then ordered to advance through Bellicourt to support the 119th on its left.

With help from the 117th, the 119th Infantry encountered less resistance, and a field message received at 30th Division headquarters said that it had broken through the Hindenburg Line at 7:30 A.M. The 119th's success may have been influenced by an informal order from its tough-talking colonel, who instructed his men "to break that line, or not a one of us comes back."[3] Its 1st Battalion took the north portion of Bellicourt, and companies advanced as far as Nauroy.[4] But it could not hold on. Lewis received reports that the 119th had run into trouble northeast of Bellicourt. He responded by ordering the 117th regimental commander to "rush" his reserve battalion to join the attack. At 12:55 P.M., Lewis stressed the severity of the situation to his 59th Brigade commander, Brig. Gen. Lawrence D. Tyson: "The trouble seems to be around Bellicourt. Have that battalion (reserve) go over there and go through it, and help in the attack that is developing. The 46th Division may want to ask assistance of the 117th to go down a little further than their boundary if necessary. . . . The definite task of that battalion is to mop up Bellicourt and go through it, and assist in the attack to the northeast. The information we have is that machine guns are firing from Bellicourt and along the ridge to the southeast."[5]

Lewis then notified the 119th Infantry commander of his order to send the reserve battalion of the 117th to his assistance and told him that "the best information we have from some of our units and the Australians is that parties of the enemy have been shifting in from the north on the 27th Division front." A half hour later, Lewis received a report that "Bellicourt is now mopped up."[6]

East of the 30th Division sector, the British 46th Division attack across the canal near Bellinglise went well and would turn out to be the success story of the day. It was led by the 137th Brigade. Some of its men crossed in light portable belts, lifebelts, or on planks when bridges were unavailable. The 1/6th North Staffords captured Riqueval Bridge before the Germans had a chance to destroy it with demolition charges. A considerable artillery fire aided the attack, and again the fog enabled the British to catch the German sector by surprise. Casualties for the 46th were light with the exception of the 138th Brigade, which took heavy fire from the German positions to the west, where the Americans and Australians were having trouble.[7]

During the early afternoon, the 8th Brigade of the 5th Australian Division passed through the 120th Infantry and, after mopping up in and around Bellicourt, continued attacking toward the east. The 120th was ordered into support positions, but some of its men lost contact with the regiment and continued to fight with the Australians. One of the Australian liaison officers, Brig. Gen. H. A. Goodard, said that the Americans "were like lost sheep, not knowing where to go or when to go."[8] By late afternoon, mixed American and Australian units were unable to make any significant advances, so the two brigades from the 30th Division reinforced the flanks and dug in for the night. Following the 120th was the 117th Infantry (less one battalion that was held in reserve and sent to assist the 119th Infantry), which proceeded across the canal tunnel, changed direction, and attacked to the south and southwest to protect the 30th Division's right flank. By noon, the right flank of the 117th had contact with the British 46th Division, and its left flank had come into contact with the advance line of the 120th Infantry near Nauroy.[9]

Command of the forward area passed to the 5th Australian Division at 1:05 A.M. on 30 September. The division, with Americans still intermingled, had attacked the previous day at 6 A.M. with the 3rd Australian Division, which had leapfrogged the 27th Division on the left. By noon of that day, the fighting had died down, and the 30th Division units retired from the line.[10] In the late morning of 30 September, Lewis issued a stern order to his brigade commanders: "It is absolutely essential that the division be organized today and fed tonight." He warned that this "can only be done through personal reconnaissance. . . . Waiting for tardy reports and map references is a waste of time. Checking on the ground is the only satisfactory way."[11]

Maj. Gen. Sir I. G. MacKay, who was on the staff of the Australian mission during the planning of the operation, provided much-needed assistance to the 30th Division as it consolidated its lines for a withdrawal. He wrote a series of instructions for Lewis on reorganizing and controlling units and employing staffs. Then he went forward to the 59th and 60th Brigade headquarters to provide commanding

officers with these instructions. Later, he assisted Lewis in the withdrawal of the 30th Division from the line on the night of 1–2 October.[12]

After almost two days of heavy fighting, the 30th Division
advanced 3,000 yards on a front of 3,750 yards and took 47 German
officers and 1,432 men as prisoners.[13] The accomplishment was
achieved at a high cost. More than 500 men died after three days of
fighting, and another 2,000 were wounded. Private Edgar Blanchard of
Company G of the 120th Infantry was one of the lucky ones who
survived without "a scratch," although he did get some close calls
like a "hole shot through his helmet." He told his mother in North
Carolina that "we went through the drive with 198 men in my company, and when we came out, we did not have but 53."[14] A battalion
commander of the same regiment wrote home of the similar fate of
his men. "We went into the fight with 22 officers and 800 men,"
Major Hobbs told a family member, but "I now have 11 officers and
200 men."[15]

Despite the heavy casualties and the loss of order in some instances,
the attack in this sector can be considered successful. Much of the
success of the American 30th Division came from the work the
British artillery began the day before the attack and continued until
the jump-off. With trench bombardment, counter-battery fire, and a
barrage that cut the wire, the artillery caught the Germans in their
dugouts and caused numerous casualties among their units. German
prisoners captured by units of the 30th Division substantiated this
fact by telling their interrogators that the barrage caused heavy casualties.[16] While there was much for the division to be proud of, it
would still need to prove itself in the coming weeks.

20

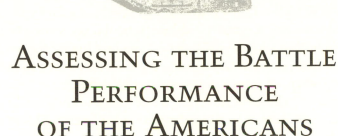

ASSESSING THE BATTLE PERFORMANCE OF THE AMERICANS

Back home, families in the Carolinas, Tennessee, and New York were unaware that their sons were entering into a dangerous operation, because strict censorship of letters prevented soldiers from discussing battles. But news of the operation to break the Hindenburg Line and its outcome was swiftly reported by Philip Gibbs, a veteran British reporter whom the *New York Times* hired as a special correspondent to cover the British sector. His stories were syndicated and picked up by newspapers in New York, Knoxville, Raleigh, and Columbia just days after the fact. He was especially fond of the American soldiers, and his coverage of their operations was more than fair.[1] Col. Robert Bacon, who was still the American liaison officer at British headquarters, was also closely following the recent fighting. He wrote in his diary on 2 October 1918 that he was "brimful of the events of the last three days of glorious contact with our 27th and 30th Divisions." Yet he also noted how difficult it was to speak of the recent fighting "without great sobs in my heart and in my voice, for many are the homes that are already desolate. America is paying the great price."[2]

Charles H. Brent, the AEF chief of chaplains, was an eyewitness to II Corps' great battle. He was likely present to visit with the forty

chaplains attached to the 27th and 30th Divisions, who were preparing
to identify and bury the dead after the fighting. When the Americans
jumped off, Brent slept safely in his car, which was parked on the slope
of a hill below Templeux-le-Guèrard near the Australian Tank Corps
headquarters. "Bombing and shelling where?" his diary records. "My
car was near fresh shell holes and fairly safe in that you don't often
find shells where ones have already landed." Conditions changed
the next day. "Two shells have burst in the dressing station, and an
Australian padre had his face blown to pieces."[3]

With the American phase of the operation completed, assessment of the Americans' performance was beginning to form. Gen.
Sir Henry Rawlinson had much to say. At Fourth Army headquarters,
he followed events on 29 September through the constant stream of
field messages. Late in the day, he reluctantly concluded that II Corps
was in trouble. "The Americans appear to be in a state of hopeless
confusion and will not, I fear, be able to function as a corps, so I am
contemplating replacing them. . . . I fear their casualties have been
heavy, but it is their own fault."[4] Although he was correct about the
heavy casualties, the Americans maintained order among the chaos.

Rawlinson was also quick to place blame on the Americans for
not accomplishing their objectives on the first day. He recorded in
his diary: "My heaviest losses in this battle have been the American
Corps. They were too keen to get on, as gallant new troops always
are, and did not pay enough attention to mopping up, with the result
that the Germans came out of the dugouts, after they had passed,
and cut them off."[5] Although there is some truth in this statement,
Rawlinson failed to recognize that even though not all of the objectives had been met, the Germans facing the Fourth Army were soundly
defeated. Not surprisingly, the self-assured army commander didn't
consider that his battle plan was faulty in that he was asking too much
of the inexperienced American divisions in such a difficult operation.

Monash's comments are also no surprise. In his memoirs, he
defined mopping up to mean "killing or disarming of all enemy
found in hiding, the picketing of the entrances and exits of all dugouts,
and laying siege to them until their occupants surrendered."[6] He
surmised that "American Infantry had either not been sufficiently
tutored in this important matter, or the need of it had not penetrated
their understanding."[7] This is simply not true. Examination of the

message logs from the 107th Infantry shows that the Americans had indeed mopped up, but they had encountered an enemy in great numbers, who counterattacked with the skill and determination of an experienced army.

The reality is that Monash designed a difficult battle plan, and the consensus of his biographers is that this operation was far from his best effort. One suggests that in preparing for this offensive, "Monash was not at his best. . . . His plan for capturing the Hindenburg Line was deeply flawed."[8] Monash should not have used the Americans to spearhead an operation of this nature, especially after the failure of III Corps to secure the jump-off line in the 27th Division sector. Rawlinson should have ordered Monash to use American II Corps as a reserve, but he failed to do so, and the Americans were cast into an operation that had little chance for success. The fact that Monash had to convene several meetings, some of considerable duration, and form a mission to assist the Americans demonstrated the complexity of the battle plan.

Despite his criticism of the Americans, Monash found space in his book to praise them. They "showed a fine spirit, a keen desire to learn, magnificent individual bravery, and splendid comradeship," he wrote.[9] Bean also supported the Americans in a lecture he gave in 1940. He stressed the strong relations between the two allies and made it clear that "if Australian or other divisions had been faced with the same task at the same stage of their training, they probably would have failed just as completely."[10]

Other Australians offered their own assessments of the American performance. "As individuals, the Americans were not to be blamed," recalled one Australian officer, who observed the doughboys. "But their behavior under fire showed clearly that in modern warfare, it was of little avail to launch an attack with men untrained in war, even though the bravery of the individual may not be questioned."[11] Maj. Gen. C. H. Brand, one of the Australian advisors to the 27th Division, thought the task the Americans undertook "would have sorely tried any veteran division."[12]

Since most of the criticism of the American battle performance was directed at the 27th Division and, in some cases, its 108th Infantry, O'Ryan took it upon himself to defend his officers and men. The farmers and horsemen from upstate New York followed the other regiments on the morning of the 29th, with orders to clear pockets of resistance, but they were unable to accomplish the mission. O'Ryan wrote in the history of the 27th Division that "very careful consideration had been given to this regiment [108th] regarding the problem of adequate mopping up."[13] Furthermore:

> The personnel of the regiment were highly trained, well disciplined, and intelligent. They thoroughly understood the importance of mopping up. The difficulties and importance of the task had been impressed upon then by the experience of the 106th Infantry two days before. Nevertheless, so complex was the enemy's defensive system, and so resourceful and determined were the enemy machine gunners that had been placed at isolated posts, that a number of these machine-gunners succeeded in evading detection and destruction during the earliest phases of the attack.[14]

O'Ryan continued his argument ten years later in a letter to the American Battle Monuments Commission about another of his regiments. They had queried him during the writing of the *27th Division Summary of Operations in the World War*, an early draft of which claimed that on 27 September, "all assaulting units had failed to mop up and round themselves under fire from the rear as well as the front." In a five-page rebuttal, O'Ryan claimed that even though the 106th Infantry was fired on from the rear in the progress of their advance, "it was not due to any general failure to mop up." He explained that the units of his division had been "warned of the importance of thorough mopping up." But the enemy had prepared a defensive system with a "view to concealing combat detachments until after the attackers' mopping-up parties believed their work to be completed."[15]

Evidence from several sources supports O'Ryan's claims. An Australian artillery officer assigned as liaison officer to the 105th Infantry recalled that "most of the enemy machine-gunners appeared well sheltered behind the tall weeds east of the canal, which afforded them excellent cover. They could not be noticed unless moving about."[16] Furthermore, an inspection of the tunnel by three American engineers in December 1918 found conclusive evidence that the preliminary barrage by the British on 26 September was only moderately effective, particularly in the 27th Division sector. After examining the northern entrance to the St. Quentin Canal and surrounding dugouts, the engineers discovered only one machine-gun post destroyed along the Hindenburg Line from Bony to Bellicourt. All others were still intact.[17] Even a report of artillery for the Fourth Army stated that "provided he was with secure shell cover, the enemy's losses in killed from the bombardment were probably not great."[18]

Other Americans who investigated the tunnel at Bellicourt discovered that the Germans had also used graveyards as dugouts after blowing open the graves and tossing the bodies aside.[19] Rawlinson, who was so critical, inspected the German defenses around Gillemont Farm on 5 October and admitted in his diary that it was a "most interesting defense . . . and it is clear why it gave so much trouble."[20]

Although the German defenses were strong, the Americans clearly exhibited a lack of combat experience. As in the Ypres-Lys Offensive, communications were a problem. Signal wires were shelled and cut by the tanks, and the two field signal battalions suffered heavy casualties. Another predicament was the number of troops assigned to units. Because so much equipment was carried onto the battlefield, large parties were needed, and they became easy targets for German artillery.[21] The pigeons that were used elsewhere on the Western Front were not delivered until the night of 29 September, too late for use in this operation.[22]

Tanks, which had showed great promise prior to this operation, largely failed in their mission to support the infantry. Within the 27th Division sector, twenty-three tanks were assigned to sustain the attack on its front, but British mines left over from previous operations destroyed two of the tanks and sixteen were lost to artillery fire. Strangely, the British had supplied the American engineers with intelligence reports about German anti-tank mines, along with diagrams and instructions on how to dismantle them. But, for some unexplained reason, the British failed to instruct their allies about their own unexploded munitions, and the Americans suffered as a result.[23] Tanks that avoided contact with mines or a direct hit often outran the infantry they were supposed to support. A commander in the American 301st Tank Battalion recognized this fact in the "lessons and suggestions" portion of his report. "There was a marked tendency on the part of some tank commanders to get too far ahead of the infantry and, consequently, lose touch," wrote to 1st Lieutenant Reynell. He stressed that "if infantry cannot get forward owing to opposition, the first duty of the tank is to overcome the opposition. To do this, it will often be necessary for tanks to come back to their infantry and lead them forward again."[24]

Also, mechanical defects plagued some of the tanks during the fighting and they had to be abandoned in enemy territory. On at least one occasion, crews removed machine guns from the tank and went forward on foot. The greatest casualties to tanks were caused by direct hits from artillery fire. Several tank commanders in the 27th Division sector reported evidence that German infantry machine gunners had devised a signaling system to point out the locations of tanks to the artillery.[25] Tanks supporting the 30th Division on the southern end of the line did much better. Eight tanks of the 1st British Tank Battalion reached the Hindenburg Line and were able to crush wire and take out machine-gun nests east of Bellicourt and north of Nauroy. Their success was no doubt the result of battlefield experience. Unlike the men of the 301st Tank Battalion, the British 1st Tank Battalion had been engaged in heavy combat before the Hindenburg Line operation, especially in March and April at Villers-Bretonneux.[26]

Even though the errors of the 27th Division receive the most attention in this operation, it was not alone in its mistakes. The 30th Division achieved its objective on 29 September, but it also made mistakes. The division's G-3 (Operations), Maj. W. F. L. Hartigan, wrote a report three days after the battle that outlined the division's deficiencies, such as the "loss of direction" of men who became confused in the mist and smoke barrage and were left leaderless by noncommissioned officers who failed to carry compasses and "assume charge of stragglers." Company officers and noncommissioned officers, according to Hartigan, "were not sufficiently informed of the general plan, and of their own objective and mission, in particular." He concluded: "As long as they are allowed to hold rank without performing the duties, we will have NCOs incapable of initiative or the exercise of command."[27] The historian of the British 18th Division echoed Hartigan's analysis. "The men of the American 30th

Division were magnificent," he thought, "but their staffs were lacking in experience."[28]

Read recorded a similar sentiment. He agreed with the Australians and British on the II Corps' performance and pointed out that the American "lack of experience was the chief failing of the regimental and higher command. While the staffs, as a rule, functioned efficiently and handled the tactical situations with skill, there was a tendency for them to lose the remarkably close touch with the combatant units that all British headquarters maintained." The men "learned along the lines from the experience with the British, and a remarkable improvement was noticeable toward the close of the operations."[29]

Read was correct; the attack on the Hindenburg Line was the greatest challenge the 27th and 30th Divisions had seen. Although the operation did not go entirely as planned and casualties were high, the Americans displayed much courage and a willingness to fight as equals among the British and Australian forces. After the action at the St. Quentin Canal, the officers and men of the two divisions were battle-hardened, well-disciplined veterans. The next operation would prove that they were also quick learners; the mistakes they made on 29 September were largely corrected.

21

BACK TO THE FRONT

II Corps had a brief respite of only five days before it was moved back to the front as part of the British Fourth Army. This gave brigade commanders little time to draw lessons from the recent Hindenburg Line attack, so it was not clear how the Americans would perform during the next attack. Although the 27th and 30th Divisions sustained heavy casualties in the fighting of 29–30 September, were below strength and had no possibility of receiving replacements, they were still larger than the depleted British divisions.[1] The Australian Corps, still attached to the Fourth Army, had been continuously in line since 8 August and was in dire need of a rest. The Americans were to replace it.

What the Americans and their allies did not realize was that the new attack, early in October, would mark the beginning of the end of the war. At that time, the main American force to the south was not getting far in the Meuse-Argonne operation, despite two general attacks on 4 and 14 October. But on the British front, the drive of former weeks continued, the line was moving, and German forces, under pressure everywhere, simply could not sustain the impact of repeated attacks.

After breaching the Hindenburg Line on 29 September, the Fourth Army continued to push forward. The Beaurevoir Line had not been taken, and Rawlinson was adamant that his army must complete the destruction of the final defenses the Germans had prepared just to his east. Once this was accomplished, he would push the Germans back across open country.

The next operation commenced on 30 September amid heavy rain. Although the weather was a hindrance to aerial artillery spotting, the British 1st and 32nd Divisions of IX Corps managed some progress that day and the next. The divisions conducted mostly small-scale and uncoordinated attacks, and on 1 October, they penetrated the Beaurevoir Line between Wiancourt and Sequehart. However, a German counterattack regained the line that night. A coordinated attack to the north that same day was more successful. Monash's tired corps pushed past the Bellicourt Tunnel entrance and took the Hindenburg support line at Le Catelet. This area had been loosely secured by mixed American and Australian troops on the night of 29 September but was now firmly in Allied hands.[2]

Rawlinson recognized that a full-scale assault was necessary to break the Beaurevoir Line. On 2 October, five divisions (British 1st, 32nd, 46th, and 50th and 2nd Australian) with support from eight brigades of artillery and twenty-two tanks were ordered to assault the last German-prepared defense the next day. At 6:30 A.M., the attacking divisions advanced 2,000 yards on a front of 10,000 yards and opened up part of the Beaurevoir Line until the German Second and Eighteenth Armies recaptured the villages of Beaurevoir and Montbrehain at the end of the day. It took three more days of fighting by the British 25th and 50th divisions and the 2nd Australian Division to retake the villages.[3] The Australian division was actually preparing to withdraw when Rawlinson ordered Monash to keep his troops at the front a day longer. The 6th Australian Brigade led the assault on Montbrehain on 4 October. Inadequate tank support slowed the attack; the machines joined the fight late. By then, the infantry was encountering German reinforcements, including fresh artillery.

Montbrehain was eventually taken at the cost of 300 Australian men and 40 officers.[4] Such losses this late in the war seemed

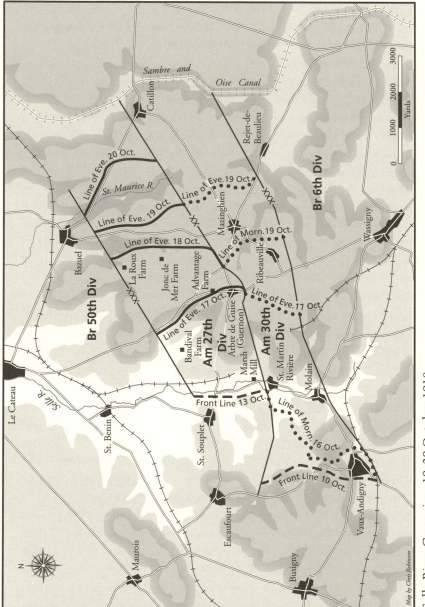

Sambre and Oise Canal

Carillon

Rejet-de-Beaulieu

Br 6th Div

Line of Eve. 20 Oct.

St. Maurice R.

Line of Eve.19 Oct.

Line of Eve. 19 Oct.

Mazinghien

XXX

Wassigny

Line of Eve. 18 Oct.

Line of Morn.19 Oct.

Bazuel

Br 50th Div

La Roux Farm

Jonc de Mer Farm

Advantage Farm

Ribeauville

Line of Eve. 17 Oct.

XXX

Line of Eve. 17 Oct.

Line of Eve. 17 Oct.

Bandival Farm

Am 27th Div

Arbre de Guise (Guernon)

Am 30th Div

St. Martin Rivière

Molain

Le Cateau

Selle R.

Marsh Mill

Front Line 13 Oct.

Line of Morn. 16 Oct.

St. Benin

St. Souplet

Escaufourt

Front Line 10 Oct.

Vaux-Andigny

Maurois

Busigny

N

Map by Chris Robinson

Selle River Campaign, 10–20 October 1918

3000

2000

1000

Yards

0

192

unnecessary to the Australian official historian, who argued that Rawlinson should have included the attack as part of his larger objective.[5] However, Monash and his division commanders considered the attack worth making and did not question Rawlinson's orders, so it is unfair to blame the consequences entirely on Rawlinson.[6]

With the Beaurevoir Line in Allied possession, the Fourth Army had an excellent vantage point from which it could launch further attacks against the retreating German forces. In his victory dispatch of 6 October, Haig expressed pleasure at the success: "The effect of the victory upon the subsequent course of the campaign was decisive. The threat to the enemy's communications was direct and instant, for nothing but the natural obstacles of a wooded and well-watered countryside lay between our armies and Maubeuge."[7]

Now that Montbrehain was no longer contested, Rawlinson ordered Monash's troops to withdraw from the line, and half of the American II Corps relieved the Australian Corps during the night of 5–6 October. Both brigades of the 27 Division were in reserve, and only the 30th Division was ordered to the front. The Australian artillery remained to support the Americans. The British issued rations because the Americans would be too far from the supply lines. The food was packed at the company base in sacks that had previously been oat sacks for horses. Among the contents were canned meats, coffee, sugar, bread, beans, jam, salt, cigarettes, and (on several occasions) the last copy of the Paris edition of London's *Daily Mail*. Each sack in the limbers had a tag tied to it with the number and name of the corporal commanding each squad.[8] Staples such as bacon, oatmeal, and potatoes were also issued to the doughboys, and unlike their initial experience with British food, the hungry soldiers did not complain about these rations.[9]

The 59th Brigade was placed on a front of 4,000 yards, with its 118th Infantry on the right and the 117th Infantry on the left, 1,200 yards to the rear. The 60th Brigade was in reserve, between Bellicourt and Villeret.[10] Before the 30th Division arrived at the front, Major General Read sent a request to AEF headquarters that all officers of the 27th and 30th divisions who were currently at schools return immediately to their units. "Considerable casualties and the fewness of replacements furnished," he wrote, "have reduced the number of officers for duty, with combatant units below what is considered prudent to lead into battle."[11] This was a desperate (but necessary) appeal since so many of his line officers became casualties during the Hindenburg Line attack and the platoons and companies were short of commanders. Pershing's staff did not send a formal response to Read, but the division strength reports for October indicate that the officers returned to their commands.

With the German army now forced into open country, the Fourth Army continued the pursuit, and the Americans spearheaded most of the attacks. Because the 117th occupied a sector too far behind the 118th, it had to straighten its line before the next attack. A minor action was planned for 7 October to make this correction. It was similar in scope to the preliminary operation the brigade conducted before the main Hindenburg Line attack.[12] At 5:15 A.M., a rolling barrage began the attack, but the artillery covered only a portion of the front. As a result, the British 25th and 50th divisions, which were protecting the American flanks, could not advance. This caused the 3rd Battalion of the 117th to run into stiff opposition. Company L took the brunt of casualties when machine-gun and shellfire poured in from the vicinity of Geneve, Bois de la Palette, and Ponchaux. It lost a captain and 1st lieutenant. "At the time the barrage lifted," the company commander recalled, "we were within 50 yards of the enemy's lines, at which point we were held up for ten minutes by heavy machine-gun fire."[13] It was also difficult for the troops to proceed on what barely could be called "roads." An engineer in the 30th Division remembered that one of them "was just a solid line of vehicles going to the front. My chauffer, who has driven on Fifth Avenue, stated that the road we were passing over was harder to drive than New York streets, and there seemed to be more vehicles."[14]

Four hours after the jump-off, Major General Lewis halted the attack when the center companies of the 3rd Battalion established liaison with the 118th and stopped near Mannions. Although the battalion had advanced only 500 yards and taken heavy casualties, it captured 150 prisoners of the German 20th Division. Lewis blamed the losses on failure of the barrage and lack of preparation time. His division had been in line less than a day, and it appeared that not all officers knew the battle plan. This problem continually haunted the 30th Division until it was withdrawn. But there was a more serious reason for the high casualties. During the fighting, Companies G and H of the 117th were told falsely that the 3rd Battalion of their regiment had been annihilated when the Germans counterattacked. They were rushed forward to repel what turned out to be a nonexistent attack and suffered from intense shellfire moving in and out of the line.[15]

When word of this mishap reached corps headquarters, Read instructed Lewis to publish a Fourth Army telegram that warned British troops about listening to rumors of peace talks: "There are indications that the attention of officers and men is in danger of being diverted by insidious rumors from their single task of defeating the enemy," it cautioned. The message made clear that an "army will concentrate its entire energy on bringing the operations in the field to a successful and decisive conclusion."[16] Most likely the warning had an impact on the Americans since there were no further incidences of rumors affecting the next series of operations.

On the afternoon of 7 October, the Fourth Army issued an order for the 30th Division to attack again the next day. The 118th would lead the assault, and one battalion of the 117th would support it. It first required an advance of 3,000 yards on a line running northwest from Brancourt. After securing this line, the barrage would halt for thirty minutes, then the support battalion would pass through and exploit the second objective, requiring a push of 3,000 yards to the northeast toward the village of Premont. Instructions were issued for mopping-up parties to help secure the village. The Americans were supported on their right by the British 6th Division and on the left by the British 25th and 66th divisions. This operation was more complex than a mere straightening of the line, made even more difficult because Read's staff did not distribute orders to 30th Division headquarters until late evening. Again, Lewis had no time to instruct brigade commanders before the attack was due to start.

In the hours preceding the jump-off, the Fourth Army artillery pounded the Germans with 350,000 shells. On 8 October at 5:10 A.M., the infantry moved forward under a barrage and with support from a battalion of heavy tanks and two companies of Whippets. Machine-gun fire from the numerous emplacements around the west of Brancourt-le-Grand raked the lead elements, preventing progress. Troops from the 6th Division were held up and could not protect the American flanks. Fortunately, two hours later resistance lightened when the

Germans retreated, fighting a rearguard action. On the right flank, Company C of the 120th Infantry was pulled from reserve and was able to advance enough to fill a gap that developed between the 118th Infantry and the 6th Division. By 7:50 A.M., the 2nd Battalion of the 118th reached its first objective at Brancourt, and by 1:30 P.M., the regiment's 1st Battalion entered the village. There the elements of the 118th mopped up and then consolidated a line and dug in for the night. On this day, the action of three men of the 30th Division earned the Medal of Honor. In one instance, Sgt. Gary Evans Foster accompanied an officer to attack a machine-gun nest in a sunken road near Montbrehain. When the officer was wounded, Foster single-handedly killed several of the Germans with hand grenades and his pistol, and then brought eighteen back as prisoners.[17]

That evening, Read again notified the 30th Division there was no time to rest and that it would resume the attack at 5:20 A.M. in the direction of St. Souplet. This time, to prevent any confusion about the attack, a conference was convened at 60th Brigade headquarters to ensure that all subordinate commanders received and understood the latest orders. Officers were told that the first objective was a line running north from Bohain to west of Busigny. It required elements of the 59th Brigade to advance from 4,000 to 5,000 yards. The second object was to be taken by the 60th Brigade, after passing through the 59th and advancing 2,000 yards farther to the northeast.

The eventual object was to secure the Selle River and the high ground from St. Benin to Molain. Such an attack, the American officers were told, would not be easy as it necessitated advancing a great distance through several villages, farms, and woods that probably contained enemy units. Despite Read's best efforts to see that his men were prepared for the next attack, the orders again arrived late at the 119th regimental headquarters, around 3:30 A.M. on 9 October. The runner sent to deliver the orders from this command post to the battalion commanders and front-line troops did not reach them until 4:30 A.M. The barrage was ordered to commence half an hour later, but the order was changed to 5:30 A.M. As the 119th Infantry historian suggests, the difference of a thirty minute delay "might have caused disastrous results."[18]

A similar situation occurred within the 117th Infantry sector. The regiment was ordered to assault Busigny with the 2nd Battalion

in the lead, the 1st Battalion in support, and the 3rd Battalion in
reserve. But it received the instructions late, and when they finally
arrived, they were incomplete and inaccurate. The regimental commander found that an error had been made in defining boundaries,
most importantly the line of departure. It was believed to be three
miles away, but the exact location was unknown. An attempt was
made to reach 2nd Battalion headquarters to warn of the situation,
but a message sent by telegram wire failed. Therefore, when the
time to start the attack arrived, the lead battalion was not in place.
The 1st Battalion commander took the initiative and commenced with
two battalions moving forward. This resulted in the 117th forming
a defensive flank to the right, while its left moved forward to join
the 119th Infantry. The regiment managed to reach the western bank
of the Selle River but could not cross on account of heavy fire on
the right flank.[19]

Eventually the fire from German machine guns died down, and
the 119th Infantry advanced 4,000 yards on the left of the sector
and captured St. Benin, St. Souplet, and Escaufort. On the right, the
120th Infantry met strong resistance and suffered heavy casualties
from fire coming from the direction of Vaux Andigny and from the
high ground to the south and southeast. Most of it came from the
right where the British 25th Division was held up and remained
some distance to the rear. By the day's end, the Americans had liberated
three villages and more than 700 French civilians and had taken a
large number of machine guns, field pieces, and ammunition.[20]

That evening, news of the 30th Division's advances reached Col.
Robert Bacon, still the American liaison at Montreuil, prompting
him to write of "the wonderful events of the last few days that are
almost too much to comprehend."[21] His enthusiasm was well founded,
but there was much fight left in the German forces, as Americans
would learn over the next several days.

Following instructions from Rawlinson on the evening of 9 October, Read ordered the 30th Division to advance the next morning to
the line of Le Cateau-St. Souplet-Andigny, parallel to the Selle. The
terrain surrounding the Selle formed an obstacle that the Germans
used to great advantage. Although the river was between fifteen and
eighteen feet wide, it was not more than four feet deep. The Germans
dammed it at St. Souplet, St. Benin, and at the southern exit at Le

Cateau. The only place it could be crossed without much difficulty was south of St. Souplet. Otherwise a bridge was needed.[22] East of the Selle, as the Fourth Army historian describes it, "the slopes became more abrupt, small streams ran in the valleys, and there were large tracts of woodland. . . . The pasture between these tracts was divided into many small enclosures bounded by high, thick hedges, which, while constituting a serious obstacle to an infantry advance, at the same time afforded it excellent cover from view except at short ranges."[23]

This next attack commenced at 5:30 A.M. on 10 October. The objective of the 60th Brigade was the river and the high ground beyond, from St Benin to Molain. The 119th Infantry took the lead, and the brigade captured St. Souplet and St. Benin (the latter with the British) and established its line on the western bank of the Selle. Fire from the high ground to the east prevented the brigade from crossing the river. On the right of the line, the 120th Infantry encountered heavy fire when taking Vaux-Andigny and could not take its main objectives, the village of Molain and the Selle. The 118th Infantry, which was in reserve, followed the 120th. It covered the exposed right flank of the 120th and then closed a gap that developed between the American regiments and the British 25th Division. Even though they were making a determined stand, the Germans were clearly in retreat, as congestion of their transports on the roads and railroads indicated. The Americans also witnessed the Germans destroying their supply dumps—a good sign indeed.

To keep up the pressure, Rawlinson again requested that the Americans continue the advance, and on the morning of 11 October, the 118th was ordered to pass through the 120th and attempt to reach the river. It was to be supported by the 119th Infantry, which would attack from its position along the west side of the Selle but not cross until the 118th reached its objective.

The attack started when three battalions of the 118th and one from the 120th advanced to the river and captured La Haie Manneresse and Vaux-Andigny. But enemy resistance prevented the Americans on the right from advancing farther because the British 25th Division, which was covering their flank, was held up in the Bois de Riquerval. The Germans, no longer in retreat, prepared to make a stand east of the Selle.

22

A CHANGE IN THE LINE

During the lull in the fighting, Read ordered the 30th Division to retire for much-needed rest and resupply. Despite the communication problems, the division fought well. However, it suffered a significant number of casualties—more than 300 killed and about three times that many wounded.[1] During the evening of 11 October, the 27th Division relieved the 30th. The New Yorkers were rested after the Hindenburg Line attack and resupplied with the few articles of clothing that remained in the depots. After continuous fighting, uniforms were in bad shape, and the II Corps quartermaster had not received any new shipments in weeks. Again the British came to the rescue and equipped some Americans with tunics and trousers.[2]

O'Ryan's two brigades left the reserve area in Tincourt and marched east; the 54th halted at Brancourt and the 53rd at Bellicourt.[3] The 54th and the 2nd Battalion of the 105th replaced the 60th Brigade on the night of 11–12 October, and the 53rd Brigade was in reserve at Busigny. The move to the front lacked secrecy. On the 13th, the Germans shelled Busigny, striking the courtyard of the chateau where O'Ryan made his headquarters. Fragments struck Maj. Chester H. King, commander of the 104th Machine-Gun Battalion, and forced him to evacuate. Other shells seriously wounded several dispatch riders at the division's message center. German shells also found their way to the 106th Infantry regimental headquarters, almost killing several of its staff officers.[4]

On 14 October, the 27th was ordered to reduce its front. It was to be replaced by the British 6th Division on the southern end of the line, and the British 50th Division would take over a portion of the line to the north. The 27th still occupied a front of 4,200 yards and was prepared for an upcoming attack. Plans were helped by the possession of a captured German map showing that the enemy intended to construct two temporary defenses. They were noted as Hermann Stellung I and II. The first line was to run east of the Selle River from St. Souplet north to Le Cateau, while the other was to be constructed east of the Sambre and Oise Canal. British air reconnaissance on 14 October photographed the country as far as the town of Maubeuge, which is situated on both banks of the Sambre, but the images did not reveal the Hermann lines. They did show newly dug trenches between Vaux-Andigny and Le Cateau that were protected by wire, as well as a number of rifle pits in pairs on the high ground between the Selle River and the Sambre and Oise Canal.[5]

Before the reduction in the 27th Division sector took place, O'Ryan ordered a detachment from the 54th Brigade to conduct a raid in German territory. His purpose was not only to identify German units opposing the Americans but also to ascertain if any obstacles had been put in place between his front and the Selle. This was no ordinary trench raid. O'Ryan wanted to give the Germans the impression of a large-scale attack. He arranged for the Australian artillery to place a barrage on a front of 1,500 yards that covered the German trenches opposing the 108th Infantry at St. Souplet. The barrage first covered the flanks, then rested for three minutes. The barrage would then cover the middle sector about 200 yards wide, then fire continuously on the German front-line trenches. After O'Ryan worked out the details with 54th Brigade commander Brig. Gen. William Pierce, twenty-one men from the 108th went forward at 4 P.M. in broad daylight. The raiding party waded across the Selle at a point that was three feet deep and captured two noncommissioned officers and twenty-one enlisted men, while only two men in the raiding party were slightly wounded. After the prisoners were interrogated, it was determined they were from the German 204th Division and had been instructed to hold the line at all costs.[6]

This raid and others like it, along with air reconnaissance, provided the Allies with valuable information about the German units, especially regarding their front and their defensive positions. Although not nearly as elaborate as the Hindenburg Line, the front had many trenches and strongpoints. The line stretched from the eastern bank of the Selle as far south as St. Souplet, then it crossed to the west bank of the river and continued south through the village of Molain. A high railway embankment paralleled the river a few yards east, from north of Le Cateau to a point east of St. Souplet. To the east of the river the Germans positioned themselves on a low ridge as well as on another ridge 2,500 yards to the east that dominated Catillon and the valley of the Sambre and Oise Canal.

To dislodge the Germans, Rawlinson planned the largest attack since 29 September, which would begin on 17 October. The day before, 16 October, the 30th Division reentered the line between the 27th Division and the British IX Corps. Rawlinson tasked the two American divisions with crossing the headwaters of the Selle between Molain and St. Souplet, where they would capture the hamlet of Arbre de Guise (Guernon) and the villages of Mazinghien and Ribeauville.

The plans called for the 27th Division's brigades to attack side by side on a 2,000 yard front and then expand to 2,800 yards at the objective line. The 53rd Brigade was to attack on the right, with the 105th Infantry in the lead and the 106th in support, and the 54th Brigade was to attack on the left, with the 108th Infantry in the lead and the 107th in support. In the first phase, one battalion each of the 105th and 108th Infantries was to wade across the Selle and advance up to 3,000 yards, overrunning the rail embankment and reaching the line of the Le Cateau–Arbre de Guise road. After pausing, the lead battalions were to proceed to the second-phase line 1,600 yards farther, where they would dig in and consolidate. One battalion from each regiment would follow the lead battalion to mop up bypassed German units and positions. Another battalion from the 105th Infantry would attack the villages of Arbre de Guise (Guernon) and Advantage Farm near the second-phase line. In the 53rd Brigade sector, a third battalion of the 105th Infantry would push on to the third objective, 1,800 yards in advance. In the 54th Brigade, the 107th Infantry was to pass through the 108th and proceed to this line. Patrol elements were then to advance to the exploitation line, another 1,800 yards, near the canal and the village of Catillon.[7] Artillery support for the 27th Division would come from the 4th Australian Division.[8]

The 30th Division would attack with its two brigades. Its 59th Brigade had the task of capturing the villages of Molain and St. Martin Rivière, then advancing to the first objective, which was a line running northeast through the western outskirts of Ribeauville. It would halt for three hours there while the 60th Brigade was to pass through on to the second objective, a north-south line through La Haie Tonnoile Farm. After this second objective was reached, patrols were to push out to the line of the Sambre and Oise Canal near Catillon. The 5th Australian Division, with five brigades of light and one brigade of heavy artillery, was designated to support the 30th Division.

To assist the infantry, ten tanks were allotted to the 27th Division and twelve to the 30th from the 301st Tank Battalion. Tanks were becoming scarce at this point in the war, and since 30 September, the 301st had attempted to rebuild what it possessed after losing half of its forty tanks during the Hindenburg Line attack. The commander of the 301st, Maj. Ralph I. Sasse, noted in his history of the unit that the infantry troops his battalion was to support were skeptical about using tanks with infantry since so many of the machines proved to be a failure during the attack on the St. Quentin Canal. Some of this skepticism might have been avoided if the tanks had been able to train with the infantry prior to the 29 September jump-off, but frantic efforts to move the infantry into line did not allow for such exercises. Only some elements of the 30th Division witnessed a tank exercise in mid-September. Instead of providing more training, Sasse ordered his company and platoon commanders to work with the infantry to ensure that the maneuvers orders were understood, and this was done only to a small degree.[9]

Everything possible was used to assist the infantry. In the battle plan, two aero squadrons from the Australian Flying Corps, the 35th and 3rd, would play a major role in the attack.[10] Not only would the squadrons fly contact patrols to verify the progress of the infantry, but a patrol from each squadron would watch for any counterattacks. If one was spotted, "this plane will drop white parachute lights immediately over the counterattack troops. All troops should be warned to keep a sharp lookout for this signal."[11] Aircraft were to drop phosphorus bombs throughout the attack until the advance element reached the second-phase line in order to create an additional smokescreen and blind German observation posts on key high ground. Two other squadrons would also carry out a noise plan to conceal the movement of the tanks to the front on the morning of the attack—a tactic that proved beneficial during the Hamel operation in July and the Amiens operation in August. Also, one squadron of the British 20th Hussars was assigned to both the 27th and 30th Divisions for patrol and messenger service.

Rawlinson scheduled the attack for 17 October, with the 30th Division on the right of the line and the 27th Division to the left. He did not expect the Americans to advance beyond the first objective that day, but emphasized that every effort should be made to exploit success since German resistance might collapse at any time. A preliminary bombardment commenced at 8 A.M. on 16 October, followed by the attack the next morning. It started poorly on the right of the 27th Division sector. The 53rd Brigade led the assault, with the 1st Battalion of the 105th Infantry and the 106th in support. When the barrage opened at 5:20 A.M., German artillery responded with a counter-barrage that struck the assembled troops, and the 1st Battalion took heavy casualties, including a company commander, before it could advance. As was the case with the Hindenburg Line attack, officers were among the early casualties, causing great confusion in the ranks. In the rear, the 2nd Battalion lost two company commanders as it advanced to assist the 1st Battalion.[12] Support from the 3rd Battalion was of little use since casualties were high. It was also disorganized from heavy shelling and gas concentration during the march to the assembly area. The 106th Infantry also had to cross a trench system on the west side of the Selle opposite Marsh Mill, 1,000 yards south of St. Souplet. The trenches, which were constructed early in the war by the Germans for training, contained a considerable number of craters that became obstacles.[13]

Also at 5:20 A.M., the 107th Infantry advanced from its jump-off point west of St. Souplet in the direction of the Selle. In the van was its machine-gun company, which was attached to the 1st Battalion and had orders to maintain contact with the British 150th Brigade on its left and protect the flank if necessary.[14] This was a difficult assignment since the company, like the entire regiment, was badly depleted after taking heavy losses in the attack against the Hindenburg Line two weeks earlier. The company commander reported an effective fighting strength on 15 October of three officers and fifty-one men—less than one-third its original size.[15] One of the three officers was Lt. Kenneth Gow. Shortly after the barrage commenced, he went ahead of his unit to scout for suitable roads to transport the machine-gun carts. Gow only made it a short distance when fragments from a German shell pierced his face and neck. He died instantly.[16] A letter he wrote to his family in the days before the attack advised his parents not to mourn in the event of his death, but to accept that they had "given a son to a great cause."[17]

On the 27th Division's left, the 108th Infantry also encountered problems. The 1st Battalion led the attack with the 3rd Battalion in support to mop up. Initially, the assault hit resistance from machine-gun elements in front of the railway embankment, but the 1st Battalion was able to overrun the line. However, it could not keep up with the creeping barrage. An attempt to reorganize the regiment at the railway after the battalions were intermingled was difficult because of heavy fog. The 108th pushed on and, by 6:30 A.M., overran Bandival Farm.[18] Support from the tanks again proved disappointing as they had difficulty crossing the river, and those that did cross became disabled. On this day, the British 66th Division took Le Cateau Station and 400 prisoners.[19] This is the same division that trained the 27th Division back in June and July.

About midnight, the 27th Division ordered its forward units to the ridge 1,500 yards to the east of their current positions. The division continued to patrol aggressively and support attempts by the 30th Division to move forward on the right until it was relieved on 20 October.[20] During the two-day battle, the 27th Division attacked and defeated most of the German 204th Infantry Division, advancing 5,500 yards through the German defenses. It suffered more than fifty casualties.

The 27th Division engineer detachments took severe casualties. O'Ryan claimed that they suffered from what he later called "The Psychological Effect of Certain Physical Features of Terrain." The engineers accompanied the leading waves of infantry with ropes and a portable foot bridge. When they encountered a sunken road that ran parallel to St. Souplet several hundred yards from the start line, these detachments, encumbered with the bridge material, stopped instead of going beyond the start line into the open. Because of the fog and uneven terrain, they could not tell how much farther to advance. When the barrage fell, the engineers had farther to go than the distance prescribed for them; they were delayed and caught by the enemy counterbarrage. As a result, they suffered casualties that otherwise would not have occurred. O'Ryan believed that the men were psychologically paralyzed by the unusual terrain. Whether or not this is true, fifteen engineers were killed in action on 17 October, and more than three times that many were wounded.[21]

In the 30th Division sector, the attack commenced at 5:20 A.M. on 17 October, with the 59th Brigade in front and the 60th in reserve. They held a front of 2,000 yards; each regiment had a battalion in front, one in support, and a third in reserve. The 113th and 115th Battalions provided machine-gun fire, which raked St. Martin Rivière, Molain, and connecting roads. On their right were the British 46th and 6th Divisions. Facing them were three German divisions: the 15th Reserve, the 24th Infantry, and the 3rd Naval. The attackers jumped off in a thick fog, which made the situation difficult for even the most experienced British commanders, as evidenced by the actions of the British 139th Brigade of the 46th Division. It attacked on a front with one battalion, the 8/Sherwood Foresters, in the lead. Although the battalion initially caught the Germans by surprise and took many prisoners, it suddenly lost direction in the mist and split apart. The left element of the battalion headed east toward Andigny Farm, which created a gap at Regincourt on the high ground. When the mist cleared, German machine-gun fire opened up from this area and to the northwest, inflicting heavy casualties.

Along the river, the German defenses were minimal, but they still posed a threat. There were trenches and wire near Le Cateau, and as the 59th Brigade attempted to cross the Selle, it was held back by enemy fire and fog that caused the lead battalion to lose its way, reminiscent of what had happened during the attack of 29 September. Another reason the brigade did not reach the objective was because it fell behind the barrage. Lead troops of the brigade finally reached a road running southwest from Arbre de Guise and dug in. That night, the 60th Brigade relieved the 59th, which passed into division reserve.

The Americans did not expect stiff resistance from the Germans or a heavily reinforced front. Prisoners taken by the 30th Division troops claimed that they were fighting a rearguard action, but the intensity of fighting by the Germans indicated a more organized defensive stand. By the afternoon, the attack died down and the troops dug in.

The attack resumed early the next morning, but the 60th Brigade advanced only a few hundred yards before falling back to its original position along the road south of Arbre de Guise, where it remained throughout the day. After dusk, the lead regiment, the 119th Infantry, advanced and, this time, moved forward 2,000 yards to capture Ribeauville unopposed. The 119th Infantry attempted to take the village earlier and found it abandoned by the Germans.

One troublesome obstacle that delayed the American advance was the ridge overlooking Catillon, a village that provided approaches to the Sambre and Oise Canal. The ridge was not taken, mostly because of the failure of the British 6th Division to support the right flank of the Americans; this did not go unnoticed at 30th Division headquarters. Its chief of staff, Col. John K. Herr, recalled years later how he contacted the commander of the 6th Division to coordinate the jump-off on 16 October. His counterpart responded that the 6th would not jump off despite orders to do so. When Herr asked why, he was told, "There is no use in concealing from you the truth; we just can't do it. We can make a bluff at starting off and open up with artillery fire, but we simply cannot make a real attack."[22] Yet the British 16th and 18th Brigades did get as far as their intermediate objective on 17 October.[23]

Herr relayed this conversation to the 30th Division's commander, Major General Lewis, who informed II Corps headquarters that the right flank of his division was now going to be exposed. But Read took a passive approach to the situation and refused to take the matter up with Rawlinson. The corps commander referred to such matters as "soldier's talk" in his final report. Instead, he told Simonds to suggest that the 30th Division form a defensive flank on its right to make up for the loss of the British 6th Division. Lewis recognized that this solution was not acceptable since a flank would not protect against enfilade fire from the German artillery and machine guns. The matter ended there, and the attack ensued with the inevitable result.

When the attack commenced on 9 October, the 6th Division failed to advance abreast of the 118th Infantry, thus exposing the regiment to German fire from Bohain.[24]

The following day, the 60th Brigade advanced at 5:15 A.M. with support from two battalions of the 59th. With little trouble, the 119th Infantry passed through Mazinghien and established a line on the eastern outskirts of the village. The 120th Infantry had a more difficult time, and it made several attempts before passing north of Mazinghien. All the while, casualties were mounting. One of them, Pvt. Judson W. Dennis, was killed by machine-gun fire near Busigny on 17 October 1918. A letter to his family arrived that very day with news that he had survived the Hindenburg Line attack—one of the few times they heard from him since he left for France that summer.[25]

Those who were severely wounded and needed treatment beyond what the field hospitals could provide were transported back to England and treated at Tottenham in North London, a complex of hospitals. The locals were fascinated by the sight of the American soldiers. At St. Anne's hospital in 1918, "the Yanks would come out of the ward," one resident of the area recalled, "and get on the fence and as we came down the road, they'd say 'there son, go get us a bottle of beer.' They would give us a tener [sic]for going—they didn't know the money."[26]

On the battlefield, the Americans were amazed by what the Germans left behind as they retreated. Colonel Pratt inspected the ground held by the enemy and wrote that "the most interesting things captured in this dump were the 3,000 sets of armor for machine gun men, and two types of clubs that were used by the Germans, probably in close combat."[27] Pratt also recorded a disturbing find compliments of the German army: "Today Company A, which was working on the mines in Booby Traps, found what was thought to be a mine in the church at St. Martin Reviere. 300 pounds of Perdite was removed from the church steeple. It was afterwards discovered that this charge of explosive was connected by wires and explosive caps with the front part of the church, and so arranged that when anybody knelt at the altar, the Perdite would be exploded.[28]"

On the night of 17 October, Rawlinson issued orders to relieve the II Corps, and its front was taken over by the British IV Corps a few days later. The British 1st Division took over the 30th Division sector, and the British 6th Division relieved the 27th. Although it was not known at the time, the war was over for II Corps. Its 27th Division moved to Corbie, and the 30th went to Querrieu for training. One unit, the 1st Battalion of the 105th Engineers, remained in line at Montbrehain with the Fourth Army until 4 November. There it helped repair the light railways from this village to Bohain. They were back in the valley of the Somme, far from the fighting and out of harm's way.

23

REFLECTIONS ON THE SELLE OPERATION

For the hard-fighting Americans in II Corps, the war effectively was over. But they had made their contribution. During the Selle River Campaign, they contributed a good deal more than usual. Considering that the two divisions of the corps were essentially new to combat, they had done extraordinarily well compared to their British and Australian counterparts. The American infantry and machine-gun units received good instruction from the British and Dominion forces, and were able to apply what they had learned in this final operation. This was done against a German opponent that was far from collapsing. A historian of the operation writes that the Germans "fought hard and skillfully used defense in-depth doctrine. Their position and intervention units were well organized, and the position divisions were relatively strong in manpower."[1] This was true even when the Germans were surrendering at alarming rates.

Even the American tanks proved successful in this operation by knocking out some of the German machine-gun nests. But many also lost their way in the mist and smoke. In one instance, a lieutenant had the added difficulty of trying to operate with a broken compass, and, as a result, he crossed the Selle three times, believing he was crossing different streams.[2]

The Selle River Campaign is largely ignored when considering the final campaigns of the war. But Field Marshal Sir Douglas Haig acknowledged its importance and sent Read a congratulatory message on 20 October. He told the American corps commander that "all ranks of the 27th and 30th American Divisions under your command displayed an energy, courage, and determination in attack that proved irresistible. . . . You have earned the lasting esteem and admiration of your British comrades in arms, whose successes you have so nobly shared."[3] Haig was correct. The Americans had fought well and provided a valuable contribution to this phase of the Fourth Army attacks. The British had every reason to admire their doughboy comrades.

Still, the achievements of American II Corps are overshadowed by the large-scale Meuse-Argonne operation.[4] In *My Experiences in the World War*, Pershing devotes less than a page to the Selle River Campaign, and most of that consists of Haig's congratulatory message.[5] It is doubtful that Pershing followed much of II Corps' progress in mid-October since he was busy reorganizing the main body of the AEF.

Out of line for the last time, the 27th and 30th resumed their training. With training came inspection by American and British officers and subsequent reports. The first was actually an ongoing inspection by the II Corps acting inspector general, who compiled his notes while the divisions were still in combat at the Selle. Brig. Gen. George D. Moore offered an analysis of the training from the first period in June to the Hindenburg Line attack. His criticism of the men in II Corps, especially in battle, stated the obvious: liaison was poor, staff work was faulty.[6] He also noted the lack of discipline and the fact that it was taking its toll on the Americans, especially in the 27th Division. Since its formation at Camp Wadsworth in 1917, there had been incidents and infractions. After arriving in France, the division became more disciplined, but later, it began to show signs of wear. Its soldiers committed mostly minor infractions, such as straggling and wearing uniforms incorrectly.

While in the rear, the doughboys explored the battered cities and villages that were no longer under German occupation. The city of Amiens was of particular interest, and on 2 November 1918, members of the 30th Division attended a mass at its cathedral to remember the dead Americans, British, and Australians.[7]

Also during this period out of line, the two division commanders in II Corps received a form letter from General Pershing about the state of the American army in France. It was sent to each AEF division commander with his name typed in the salutation to give the document a personal touch. The observations were made while he was in command of the First Army. Pershing sent these letters instead of publishing the message in orders, which "are too often considered perfunctory."[8]

Copies sent to O'Ryan and Lewis were, at this juncture, of little value. The eleven points addressed in the document covered everything from liaison and plans of attack to staff efficiency, straggling, and the personality of officers. Pershing encouraged commanders to make sure older officers and their staffs were alert and "well toward the front to direct correct tactical dispositions and see that there is no hesitation, and that important ground once taken is strongly held." Most important, he said, each "division commander should impress his own personality upon the division, and see his officers frequently."[9]

During the second week of November, the 27th and 30th divisions were visited by Brig. Gen. W. J. Dugan, who was attached to Ivor Maxse's training branch. He carefully observed the Americans over the course of three days. Although his comments were of limited value to the divisional commanders because the armistice was signed one day after he filed his report, they are insightful and worth noting. His main observation was that the "system of training is indifferent" and that the "officers and men don't strike one as being very keen on training."[10] He suggested that this was due to the fact that training started too early, and too many hours were devoted to each subject. Dugan concluded that senior officers lacked imagination in preparing interesting training programs and didn't think that the staff work was running on smooth lines. "The work of reconstruction is causing a good deal of floundering, chiefly due to want of experience and the absence of a sound working system throughout all units."[11]

Of greater significance to the divisions was the news of the armistice. It was mostly anticlimactic for the two American divisions. In fact, they were not aware that an armistice had been signed on the morning of 11 November until later in the day. O'Ryan was alerted later that day by two Australian soldiers who passed him on the street outside his headquarters and asked, "Why in the hell don't you celebrate?" The 27th Division commander observed that at that moment, among the Americans, there was "not a ripple of excitement. Everything went on as usual."[12] But that night, the soldiers did celebrate, and they were allowed to imbibe liquor, which O'Ryan normally forbade. A witness to the celebration said that "soldiers were parading up and down the streets, yelling and hollering like a bunch of cowboys just after a range drive."[13] In the 30th Division rest area, there were no reports of wild celebrations. Rather, the men talked of going home. Some of Read's staff officers had a more festive attitude about the historic event and flocked to Amiens, where they were joined by their British, Canadian, Australian, and French counterparts. The city was packed with jubilant soldiers, and, according to two American officers, "tables in the Amiens restaurants and cafes were as hard to procure that night as on Broadway on New Year's Eve."[14] With this revelry, the war was officially over for the 27th and 30th Divisions.

24

BROTHERS IN ARMS

There were several advantages of placing American divisions under British command. The first, undoubtedly, involved supplying the divisions. Even though Pershing established a comprehensive Service of Supply with base sections throughout France, his First Army divisions at the front suffered from a lack of fresh food and replacement clothing, as well as inadequate equipment. The American supply lines, almost all of which traveled by rail from the Bordeaux area on France's southwest coast, were long. Their carrying capacity was limited. That fact forced Pershing to make a choice between delivering food or delivering ammunition during periods of heavy fighting. Ammunition took priority; the men sometimes went on iron rations. The 27th and 30th divisions also occasionally had problems distributing food, but when this occurred, the British came to their aid. They were better fed by the British than were their American counterparts at St. Mihiel and in the Meuse-Argonne because the British supply lines running between Amiens to the south and Hazebrouck in the north had no trouble.

Another advantage of being under British command was that despite being organized as a corps, American II Corps remained essentially a skeleton organization, and therefore it was not necessary to

take key officers from the two divisions and place them in corps
staff positions. The British handled the higher command and much
of the tactics that otherwise would have fallen to American staff
officers, who were in short supply. But the main advantage was that
American division commanders and their subordinates were dealing
with experienced British staff officers who were more than willing
to share the lessons they had learned over the previous three years.

When training the Americans, the British stressed aggressive
trench fighting with bayonets and grenades.[1] The British officers also
emphasized the role of chain of command in preventive measures.
For example, officers were encouraged to check soldiers' feet for
trench foot and to ensure that they had proper clothing and equipment to prevent injuries related to cold weather that might keep
soldiers out of line unnecessarily.[2]

The 27th and 30th Divisions were each about the size of a British
corps. Pershing purposely organized large divisions for two reasons.
First, there was a shortage of trained officers that he could choose
from to command his divisions, and, second, American military
leaders were convinced that large divisions could continue in battle
for longer periods, thus lessening the need for rotations.[3] Both factors
became significant for American II Corps since its two divisions suffered
high casualty rates and received no replacements while in line.

Essentially, the two divisions were amalgamated into the BEF,
a situation that Pershing attempted to discourage early on but did
nothing to prevent after he organized the First Army. In the instance
of the 27th and 30th Divisions, Haig won the battle with Pershing
about the use of American troops. He had complete access to 50,000
eager (but inexperienced) doughboys to amalgamate with his Fourth
Army. Haig was patient with Pershing and better understood the
importance of the Anglo-American relations than his American counterpart. This was reflected in a congratulatory letter he wrote to the
27th Division before it left France. He told the New Yorkers: "In the
greater knowledge and understanding borne of perils and hardships
shared together, we have learnt, at last, to look beyond old jealousies
and past quarrels to the essential qualities that unite the great English-
speaking nations. . . . I feel confident that the new era opened on the
battlefields of the Old World will see the sympathy and friendship

now established between our two nations constantly deepened and strengthened."[4]

Pershing, on the other hand, refused to recognize the usefulness of the relationship. In his memoirs, he wrote: "Except for the details of trench warfare, training under the French and British was of little value."[5] Perhaps the tense conferences with Haig and Robertson still weighed heavily on his mind. What he failed to understand was that by allowing the British to use the 27th and 30th at the front, he helped hasten the end of the war. Even though the divisions did not reach all of their objectives and suffered high casualties during the Hindenburg Line attack, the operation might have been scaled down if it had not been for the fresh American troops.

Although tense moments over the amalgamation issue occurred, Pershing and Haig enjoyed a warm personal relationship. The American ambassador in charge of Pershing's headquarters personnel, Lloyd C. Griscom, described the two leaders as "of the same type—self-contained, direct, honest, and incapable of intrigue. They had great respect for each other, but when they met for a conference, the very similarity of their reserved characteristics prevented them from indulging in an open, free, and frank discussion."[6]

It is quite clear that Pershing had little interest in the 27th and 30th Divisions after they remained behind with the British as the American II Corps. If he did have any concerns about the performance of the two divisions in the British sector, they were laid to rest by Lt. Gen. Claude William Jacob of British II Corps.[7] The divisions under his command helped train cadres of the 27th and 30th while they were at the Ypres front in late August. He told Pershing when they met on 22 November during a parade for the king and queen of Belgium: "The Allies pushed the Germans just to the crest of the hill, and it took just a little added push by the Americans to put them over."[8] Jacob did not mention that the Germans who had occupied Mt. Kemmel had mostly abandoned their position before the Americans took over the front. Still, the British general's encouraging words must have pleased Pershing, since he made a special note of the conversation in his diary.

Pershing also wanted to know what his division and brigade commanders thought of their experiences with the British and Australians and ordered his operations officer to send questionnaires to them on 10 December 1918. Officers were to address three major issues: the part American units played compared with that of the foreign unit, the efficiency of American troops as compared with those with whom they served, and any difficulties due to a difference in language.[9] All ten divisions that served at some point, with the British, as well as the divisions that served with the French, were surveyed and given only ten days to report back to the operations office. Each report was to be marked "Strictly Confidential" and would have limited distribution.[10] The actual memorandum ordering the report was marked "Secret," and it is doubtful that anyone outside of the AEF or War Department ever saw the reports. Unfortunately, Haig did not place a similar demand on his general officers, and we have less input from the British about their relationship with the Americans. Only the diaries and letters excerpted in this book hint at how some British officers and men regarded the doughboys. But we are fortunate to have the comments from the II Corps general officers, which are revealing but not altogether surprising.

Within the 27th Division, O'Ryan saw the relationship as valuable. "We trained about one month with the British, and the British officers assigned to each regiment helped us wonderfully in all the little things that we wanted to pick up on," he wrote. "We were trained in field exercises and on a larger scale in war than we had ever been trained before, as the British had large training grounds about 20 miles south of Calais, as well as every sort and kind of school."[11] O'Ryan did disclose one interesting fact: the men in his division had no particular affection for the British since many of the New Yorkers were of German American and Irish American blood and would have preferred to serve with the French. The British officers and men recognized the hostility and made a special effort to be cordial to the Americans, and over time, a bond developed between the allies.[12]

The comments from the 30th Division commander were also encouraging. Lewis recognized that "the fraternization of Australians and Americans was more marked than that of the English and Australians, or the English and Americans." He also remarked that the "relations of officers in this division were uniformly pleasant, even cordial, including those between the British and Australians."

His 60th Brigade commander, Brig. Gen. Samson L. Faison, had mixed reviews of the alliance: "The relations that prevailed between troops of this brigade and the British infantry were good, while the relations with both the Scotch infantry and English artillery were the best. Yet, Tommy considered himself a superior soldier to the American and took no pains to conceal it. In fact, he took every opportunity to impress upon the mind of the American soldier that such was the case. Our soldiers resented any such attitude and denied that it was based on fact."[13]

Brig. Gen. Lawrence D. Tyson, in charge of the 59th Brigade, thought the British were wonderful: "Their officers are splendid and tireless, and uniformly courteous and helpful, and they seemed to have the greatest admiration for the Americans, and we saw no spirit of jealousy or pettiness in our contact with them. They were thorough, very fine, and I am glad, indeed, that we had the opportunity of serving with them; it has been great for America. It would have been better, perhaps, if there had been more Americans to serve with them, which may have eradicated any feeling that may have been in the hearts of the two nations against each other."[14]

Beside the responses to the questionnaires, Maj. Gen. George W. Read's final report also sheds light on the relationship. "From the time II Corps was assigned to the British Fourth Army until it was transferred to the British Third Army, after the signing of the armistice," Read wrote, "relations between the corps and army were always excellent. . . . The amalgamation was complete and founded on a spirit of mutual esteem and profound good will. . . . All officers at both headquarters seemed determined that good feelings and cooperation should surmount every natural difficulty, and the relations, at no time, were other than most satisfactory."[15] Read is the only American officer in the AEF who actually used the word amalgamation.

Read's chief of staff was less enthusiastic about serving with the British. This comes as no surprise, since Col. George S. Simonds wanted II Corps transferred from the British in August 1918. He was more vocal about the coalition than other officers because he had worked with the British long before the first American divisions arrived in this sector. "The problems with them [the British] are far more numerous and complex than to be expected," Simonds surmised. "Although they are of our language, race, and, to a considerable

extent, our ideas and ideals, their methods of procedure are certainly
different than ours. Furthermore, the general run of their enlisted
men . . . is inferior in intelligence, initiative, and adaptability to
American soldiers."[16]

Simonds also wrote about the British officers he encountered.
Overall, "the type officer of this class is a man of character and always
a gentleman," he observed. "His word, once given, can always be
relied upon. He is a man of positive opinions and wants to do things
his way. He is sometimes hard to convince, and sometimes presents
the attitude of not wanting to hear the other side. However, he does
listen to reason, and he does make concessions."[17]

Simonds was less impressed with Gen. Sir Herbert Plumer. He "is
a man of positive opinions, who wants to dominate things wherever
he happens to be," Simonds opined. "He gave me the impression that
his judgment might sometimes go wrong." Gen. Sir Henry Rawlinson
was more to his liking. He "has a nervous energy, more apparent
than in most British officers. He is a man of considerable tactical
ability. He keeps his finger on the pulse of his troops, clear down
into the ranks, and knows at all times the state of their supplies,
their casualty lists, health conditions, morale, etc. He always showed
the utmost consideration to his subordinates, consulted his corps
commanders freely, gave considerable weight to their opinions, and
gave them great latitude in their operations." Rawlinson's chief of
staff, Maj. Gen. Sir Archibald Montgomery, impressed Simonds even
more. "He is a student of his profession—keen, alert, and of pleasing
personality; and, he was able to efficiently coordinate the work of
the staff."[18]

Early on, Simonds carried the brunt of II Corps responsibilities
until Read was appointed its commander, and one of his first concerns
was the British supply system. It was organized to accommodate
fewer men than an American division, and it was not clear how this
would impact the II Corps. This ultimately became the responsibility
of Col. Edward S. Walton, II Corps quartermaster. He concluded that
the supply question was worked out through trial and error and
praised the British in their efforts to accommodate the Americans.
"Although we had our troubles, of course," Walton wrote, "none of
them was caused by lack of cooperation."[19] Certainly II Corps in no

way had the logistical difficulties regarding supplies that other AEF divisions experienced.

In World War II, the amalgamation issue, essentially that of Allied cooperation, arose again. To better understand how this situation was handled in the past, the War Department ordered a study of the American and British relationship of 1917–1918. The purpose was to assist Gen. Dwight D. Eisenhower's buildup of a coalition of armies for the eventual invasion of France. Produced in 1942, the study was based primarily upon the questionnaires ordered by Pershing, and the conclusions were to be expected.

"In general, the American soldier considered the English enlisted man as difficult to make friends with, but a good fellow, and worth risking one's life for," the author of the study learned. "He was inclined to be condescending toward his American cousins, but they were fully prepared to take this out of him by whatever means necessary, after which perfect harmony prevailed."[20] A common issue the Americans reported in 1917–1918 was some difficulty in understanding the British. "A foreign language doesn't cause as much irritation as your own language spoken differently," remarked one AEF officer.[21] Despite such arrogance, the doughboys and Tommies were able to communicate on the battlefield, where it counted most.

25

BORROWED SOLDIERS

How do we gauge the contribution of American II Corps, particularly on the battlefield? After arriving in France on 31 May 1918, the 27th Division lost 1,829 officers and men killed in battle, and another 6,505 were wounded. The 30th Division did not fare much better after it arrived on 24 May. It lost 1,641 officers and men killed and sustained 6,774 wounded. Also, 229 of the 27th Division were taken prisoner, compared with 75 from the 30th Division. However, the two divisions captured a large number of the enemy. The 27th Division recorded 2,357 Germans passing through its POW cages, while the 30th Division claimed 3,848 prisoners. Such statistics are impressive, for the New York troops spent a mere fifty-seven days at the front and the southern soldiers only twelve more.

Both divisions had high casualty rates, but this was common throughout the AEF. Poor command from line officers is to blame, but inexperience within all ranks was another reason so many men did not return home. As the 27th and 30th Divisions remained at the front for longer periods, casualties decreased, despite a determined enemy that fought with skill to the very end. Both divisions can credit their later success on the battlefield to the tutoring they received from the British, even though Pershing did not want the Americans to receive formal training from their allies. "A fixed principle," General Read recalled, "was that in this training, no British advisor or instructor could at any time take command of one of our units."[1] While the British officers never actually took command of the American regiments during training or operations, their influence was apparent in almost every facet of how the doughboys distributed food and clothing, cared for the sick and wounded, and operated during the Hindenburg Line and Selle River operations.

The 27th and 30th Divisions did not have the problems Pershing's First Army encountered. His decision to commit 225,000 men to attack the St. Mihiel salient benefited from the fact that the German army, with only 25,000 men, had already begun to withdraw from the area. Then, a mere two weeks later, he shifted these same divisions fifty miles toward the Meuse River and ordered the tired officers and men to attack a position that the most experienced British and French units would have found difficult. This is not to say that II Corps did not encounter similar difficulty. Despite the best efforts of the British, the first two operational experiences of the 27th and 30th Divisions exposed a number of serious weaknesses that were inherent in the other AEF divisions. Liaison was poor and orders were not effectively transmitted to the unit commanders. This was, of course, due to the inexperience of officers at all levels, but these weaknesses were mostly corrected during the Selle River Campaign.

It cannot be overstated how unique these two divisions were among other National Guard units in the AEF. By the time of the armistice, the ranks of the 27th were still composed largely of New Yorkers, while the rolls of the 30th were filled primarily with men from North and South Carolina and Tennessee. The other National Guard divisions in France had lost much of their local composition through replacements. Despite prodding by Read, neither of the American II Corps divisions received any additional troops until after the fighting ceased—a further indication that Pershing placed little importance on this corps. He also left its officer corps intact, even though he consistently relieved ineffective officers in other AEF corps. The 30th Division, which followed command by five different generals, was led by Lewis, a Regular, for most of its service in France. Its counterpart, the 27th Division, was under the fine leadership of O'Ryan.

He had the distinction of being the only National Guard officer to command a division throughout the war.

A larger question is how the 27th and 30th Divisions compare to other AEF divisions, and to the Australian and British divisions with which they trained and served. The divisions of II Corps were largely left to their own devices and operated under the British in many ways. As a result, they were better fed and equipped than the remainder of the AEF. Also, the 27th and 30th Divisions had a clear advantage over other AEF divisions regarding training because of the British army and its experienced instructors.

On par with the II Corps divisions were two Regular Army divisions (1st and 2nd) and another National Guard division, the 26th. They were the earliest combat organizations to arrive in France. While most of the AEF received the bulk of its training in the United States, these three divisions mostly trained in France under the supervision of French instructors.[2] Perhaps it is no coincidence that the 1st, 2nd, and 26th served in all major operations and were considered the best of the American First Army. The 27th and 30th Divisions suffered about the same percentage of casualties as the remainder of the AEF and experienced difficulty with liaison during battle. Neither of the II Corps divisions received replacements, while the divisions of the American First Army were kept at full strength with drafted men. Discipline within the 27th and 30th was far superior to that of other American divisions. Both II Corps divisions had fewer court-martials and incidences of straggling than the rest of Pershing's doughboys.

The 27th and 30th Divisions were, of course, National Guard troops, while the Australian and British armies of 1918 were composed mostly of conscripts. But the Americans actually resembled the British army of 1914–1915. Because of their inexperience, they made numerous tactical errors and suffered unnecessary casualties in the same way the BEF took tremendous losses during the first two years of the war. Certainly the reason American II Corps was well disciplined directly correlates to its association with the British. American officers such as O'Ryan had visited the front in the British sector in 1917 to observe and were impressed with the high level of obedience the Tommies displayed.

The Americans were less impressed with the Australian troops. Monash's troops had a reputation for lack of discipline, and this was certainly true in comparison to the British troops. The Americans often witnessed Australian soldiers failing to salute superior officers. Even more startling was the claim by some doughboys that they had seen Australian soldiers rifling through the belongings of dead American troops. As at least one historian has argued, the problems of discipline were the result of overuse and a lack of replacements.[3] Yet, on the battlefield, the Australians were good role models for the Americans in their tenacity to continue fighting even after serving on the line for long periods, receiving replacements, and taking heavy casualties. In these respects, the Australians and the Americans were similar. In summary, it is difficult to make a direct comparison between the II Corps and the larger body of the AEF, or between the II Corps and the associated Australian and British units. Yet it can be said that the 27th and 30th divisions represented the U.S. army well during its association with the BEF. Indeed, Pershing made the correct decision to leave them with that army.

EPILOGUE

After the welcome-home parades, the divisions demobilized, and the men were sent home to get on with their lives. For many of them the war would become a distant memory and be overshadowed by the much larger world war twenty years later. Few would discuss their experiences in France and Belgium, so families and future generations could only guess at the horror of machine-gun and shellfire. But John F. O'Ryan could not forget. Almost two years after arriving home from France, he published *The Story of the 27th Division*. The book was a monumental achievement, comprising two volumes and more than 1,000 pages. He sent the book to family members, friends, and fellow army officers who inspired or assisted him during the writing.

Pershing was among the first to receive *The Story of the 27th Division*. O'Ryan had great admiration for his former commander-in-chief and wanted him to share in this accomplishment. The 27th Division commander also had an ulterior motive in sending Pershing the gift. He sheepishly asked the general of the armies to write a brief accolade that his publisher could use for publicity purposes. Pershing politely refused. In a letter written by an aide, he told the former division commander that he felt his history was one of the

224

best personal accounts of the war. If he wrote a few words for O'Ryan's book, however, then there would be an obligation to do so for other officers writing books.

Several years later, Pershing's main nemesis and sometime-friend during the war, Sir Douglas Haig, also received a copy of O'Ryan's work. Haig was more grateful for the present and, in turn, sent O'Ryan a map of the Hundred Days Campaign in which the 27th Division played a major part. He also wrote O'Ryan a thoughtful note:

> I feel it is a very high honor that you should present me with a copy of your own account of doings of your splendid division. I always remember with pleasure the occasion on which I first made your acquaintance in France when I inspected a number of machine-gun companies of your division, soon after you had arrived in the British area for training. I felt sure that you were a most workmanlike body of troops, and I was always afraid that you would be ordered away by higher authority to some other part of the front, when I was in sore need of fresh troops.[1]

Three weeks later Haig died unexpectedly on 29 February 1928 at the age of sixty-seven. His body lay in state in both London and Edinburgh, his place of birth and his home after the war. An estimated 25,000 people viewed his coffin each day in both cities. He was accorded a state funeral at Westminster Abbey. Neither O'Ryan nor Pershing attended.[2]

There are many unit histories involving the American II Corps divisions and their attached units, but none is as powerful as O'Ryan's. From 1919 to 1940, thirty unit histories associated with the two divisions were published, as well as a single-volume history of the 30th Division. *The Thirtieth Division in the World War* lacked the depth and insight of O'Ryan's work since it was written in the third person by two authors who had no direct affiliation with the division. With the exception of O'Ryan's book, those written by veterans for other veterans were destined to become souvenirs of their shared experience. There is no evidence that any of the unit histories, including O'Ryan's, were reviewed or excerpted in newspapers or periodicals. This is surprising in his case, since he was considered a prominent New Yorker before the war and served afterward for a short period as city police commissioner.

In the years following the war, associations affiliated with both divisions held reunions. Which division actually first broke the Hindenburg Line, the 27th or 30th, was hotly debated when the veterans from New York gathered with those from the south, as both wanted to claim this honor. A North Carolina newspaper reported: "Twenty-five thousand folders containing a facsimile of the official operations map of the 30th Division in France were put on sale by the Buncombe County Colonial Dames. The proceeds of the sale will be turned over to the association to help defray the expenses of its campaign combating that of the 27th New York Division, claiming credit for breaking the Hindenburg Line."[3] The 27th Division Association was the more active of the two organizations. During a four-week period in May and June 1930, it sponsored a "Back to the Front" reunion voyage to France, where the veterans revisited the sacred battlefields in the British sector.[4]

Official commemoration of both divisions was the responsibility of the federal government. The American Battle Monuments Commission (ABMC) dedicated the Somme American Cemetery and Memorial, near the village of Bony, in 1937. Named after the area near the Somme River where the two divisions fought, the cemetery holds the graves of more than 1,800 Americans. The legacy of the 27th and 30th is also commemorated three miles from the cemetery with a marker on the battlefield, also dedicated in 1937. The Bellicourt Monument stands atop the St. Quentin Canal Tunnel. It contains a map of the operation to break the Hindenburg Line and an orientation table showing the direction of the attack.[5] A further testament to the courage of the 27th and 30th is the Kemmel Monument near Vierstraat, Belgium. It was erected by the ABMC in 1929 and pays tribute to the first operation in which the two divisions participated. Thus, the contribution of the American II Corps during World War I is permanently enshrined on the former battlefields of the Western Front.

Memorializing the dead extended beyond the white headstones and well-manicured grounds of Bony Cemetery. For a price, mothers and widows had ample opportunity to keep alive the memory of their loved ones. Sarah Harris, whose son, Pvt. Ezra Harris in Company E of the107th Infantry, died during the 27 September preliminary attack, was solicited just months after his death. First, the Soldiers Record Publishing Company sent Ezra's grieving mother a form letter that requested a photograph of her son for inclusion in their three-volume state casualty list: *Soldiers of the Great War*. After publication she could purchase a set for "any sum you can send." Mrs. Harris apparently declined since Ezra's image is not included in the New York section. She probably didn't buy the volumes either. Then in the spring of 1920, she was contacted by the "Historical Committee of Company E, 107th Infantry, U.S.A." with an offer to buy a copy of its unit history. With a clever sales pitch, they assured her that "this announcement to you is not written in the cold spirit of selling you the book. . . .We are offering you something that you have wanted, and will prize and hand down to generations to come." Since the book was selling for only two dollars and fifty cents, the letter also suggested she "may want more than one copy."

At the end of 1923 she was encouraged to join the Gold Star Association, which had been loosely organized in the summer of 1918. One of its early goals was to send its members overseas to visit the graves of their lost sons at U.S. government expense. By sending in her membership application, Sarah Harris would help the "Association show the Government that the demand for a visit to the graves in France is universal and widespread." With or without her support, in 1928, the organization received a charter as the Gold Star Mothers Association and successfully lobbied Congress for funding to send widows and mothers to Europe during several pilgrimages from 1930 to 1933. Sarah Harris did not join them to see Ezra's grave. She died in 1925.[6]

Wealthy families from New York contributed enormous sums to help rebuild the nearby villages in honor of their fallen sons. Edith McCormick donated more than 30,000 francs toward a public school in the name of Lt. John McCormick. A graduate of Columbia University, her only son almost survived the war. Three days before the 107th Infantry was pulled from the line, McCormick returned from burial duty and fell asleep in a shell hole. A short time later he was stuck by a shell fragment. His mother also set up a scholarship at his alma mater.

In the once-tranquil villages where the Americans of the 27th and 30th Divisions shed their blood, the slow rebuilding process began

in 1919. The families of doughboys were generous in helping Bellicourt and Bony recover. This was particularly true of the latter village.
In 1922, an anonymous American family paid to have the bells replaced
in Bony's church, and the next year the Gold Star Association of
New York organized a fund-raiser to rebuild the village school that
was endorsed by Major Generals Lewis and O'Ryan. It was hoped
that the school would serve as a memorial building to "tell future
generations of French school children of what our soldier crusaders
did for France in the time of its great need, and enshrine our boys in
human hearts, a more desirable memorial than 'storied urn or animated
bust.'" The school was completed at a cost of almost $7,000 in 1924
and stands today as the Bony Town Hall.

The families of the two farms, Gillemont and Quennemont, were
not so fortunate. These farms saw more devastation than any land-
mark on the Hindenburg Line. Gillemont Farm and its adjoining
fields were owned by the St. Quentin Hospital and leased to the
Biziaux family. In early 1919, Emile Biziaux brought his family back
to what was left of the farm, which was largely destroyed. As they
worked to clear the fields of the remnants of war, Emile lost his life
when he dug up an undetonated shell. The Biziaux family managed
to keep the farm going until 1955, when the hospital sold it. Although
nothing is known of Quennemont Farm's prewar history, it was
completely destroyed during the conflict, and there was no attempt
to make it habitable afterward. The ground where it once stood will
be forever known as a tragic place of war.[7]

Appendix A

STAFF
American II Corps, 29 September 1918

Command and Staff

Maj. Gen. George W. Read, Corps Commander
Col. George S. Simonds, Chief of Staff
Lt. Col. Richard K. Hale, Assistant Chief of Staff, G-1
Lt. Col. Kerr T. Riggs, Assistant Chief of Staff, G-2
Col. Fred E. Buchan, Assistant Chief of Staff, G-3
Lt. Col. John P. Terrell, Assistant Chief of Staff, G-4

American 27th Division

Maj. Gen. John F. O'Ryan, Division Commander
Col. Stanley H. Ford, Chief of Staff
Brig. Gen. Albert H. Blanding, 53rd Infantry Brigade Commander
Brig. Gen. Palmer E. Pierce, 54th Infantry Brigade Commander

American 30th Division

Maj. Gen. Edward M. Lewis, Division Commander
Col. John K. Herr, Chief of Staff
Brig. Gen. Lawrence D. Tyson, 59th Infantry Brigade Commander
Brig. Gen. Samuel L. Faison, 60th Infantry Brigade Commander

Appendix B

ORDER OF BATTLE

American 27th and 30th Divisions, 10 August–1 September 1918

American 27th Division

53rd Infantry Brigade
    105th Infantry Regiment
    106th Infantry Regiment
    105th Machine-Gun Battalion

54th Infantry Brigade
    107th Infantry Regiment
    108th Infantry Regiment
    106th Machine-Gun Battalion

Divisional Troops
    104th Machine-Gun Battalion
    102nd Engineer Regiment
    102nd Field Signal Battalion
    Headquarters Troop

Trains
    102nd Train and Military Police
    102nd Supply Train

102nd Engineer Train
102nd Sanitary Train (Ambulance Companies and Field Hospitals, 105–108)

American 30th Division

59th Infantry Brigade
    117th Infantry Regiment
    118th Infantry Regiment
    114th Machine-Gun Battalion

60th Infantry Brigade
    119th Infantry Regiment
    120th Infantry Regiment
    115th Machine-Gun Battalion

Divisional Troops
    113th Machine-Gun Battalion
    105th Engineer Regiment
    105th Field Signal Battalion
    Headquarters Troop

Trains
    105th Train Headquarters and Military Police
    105th Supply Train
    105th Engineer Train
    105th Sanitary Train (Ambulance Companies and Field Hospitals 117–120)

Appendix C

ORDER OF BATTLE

Allied Army,
29 September 1918[1]

Australian Corps

2nd Australian Division

5th Australian Infantry Brigade
    17th Battalion
    18th Battalion
    19th Battalion
    20th Battalion

6th Australian Infantry Brigade
    21st Battalion
    22nd Battalion
    23rd Battalion
    24th Battalion

7th Australian Infantry Brigade
    25th Battalion
    26th Battalion
    27th Battalion
    28th Battalion

3rd Australian Division

9th Australian Infantry Brigade
    33rd Battalion
    34th Battalion
    35th Battalion

10th Australian Infantry Brigade
    37th Battalion
    38th Battalion
    39th Battalion
    40th Battalion

11th Australian Infantry Brigade
    41st Battalion
    42nd Battalion
    43rd Battalion
    44th Battalion

5th Australian Division

8th Australian Infantry Brigade
    29th Battalion
    30th Battalion
    31st Battalion
    32nd Battalion

14th Australian Infantry Brigade
    53rd Battalion
    54th Battalion
    55th Battalion
    56th Battalion

15th Australian Infantry Brigade
    57th Battalion
    58th Battalion
    59th Battalion
    60th Battalion

5th Cavalry Brigade

American II Corps

American 27th Division

53rd Infantry Brigade
    105th Infantry Regiment
        1st Battalion
        2nd Battalion
        3rd Battalion

    106th Infantry Regiment
        1st Battalion
        2nd Battalion
        3rd Battalion

    105th Machine Gun Battalion

54th Infantry Brigade
    107th Infantry Regiment
        1st Battalion
        2nd Battalion
        3rd Battalion

    108th Infantry Regiment
        1st Battalion
        2nd Battalion
        3rd Battalion

    106th Machine Gun Battalion

Divisional Troops
    104th Machine Gun Battalion

    102nd Engineers

    102nd Field Artillery Battalion

    301st Tank Battalion

American 30th Division

59th Infantry Brigade
    117th Infantry Regiment
        1st Battalion

2nd Battalion
3rd Battalion

118th Infantry Regiment
1st Battalion
2nd Battalion
3rd Battalion

114th Machine Gun Battalion

60th Infantry Brigade
119th Infantry Regiment
1st Battalion
2nd Battalion
3rd Battalion

120th Infantry Regiment
1st Battalion
2nd Battalion
3rd Battalion

115th Machine Gun Battalion

Divisional Troops
113th Machine Gun Battalion

105th Engineers

105th Field Signal Battalion

British 4th Tank Brigade

Australian and British Auxiliary Units Attached to II Corps

3rd Anti-Aircraft Search Light Section
British 1st Siege Company of Railway Engineers
British 182nd Tunneling Company
4th Australian Field Artillery Brigade
5th Australian Field Artillery Brigade
7th Australian Field Artillery Brigade
8th Australian Field Artillery Brigade
10th Australian Field Artillery Brigade
12th Australian Field Artillery Brigade

13th Australian Field Artillery Brigade
14th Australian Field Artillery Brigade
6th Army Brigade, Australian Field Artillery Brigade
3rd Squadron Australian Air Force
2nd Anti-Aircraft Batteries
5th Balloon Wing
20th Regiment Hussars

Appendix D

ORDER OF BATTLE

German Army,
29 September 1918, North to South

8th Division

153rd Infantry Regiment

54th Division

    84th Infantry Regiment
    27th Reserve Infantry Regiment
    90th Reserve Infantry Regiment

121st Division

    7th Reserve Infantry Regiment
    60th Infantry Regiment

185th Infantry Division

    65th Infantry Regiment
    161st Infantry Regiment
    28th Reserve Infantry Regiment

75th Reserve Division

    250th Reserve Infantry Regiment
    249th Reserve Infantry Regiment
    251st Reserve Infantry Regiment

Corps Units

65th Reserve Field Artillery Regiment
42nd Foot Artillery Regiment

Appendix E

COMPARATIVE STRENGTH OF AMERICAN AND BRITISH DIVISIONS, 1918

American Army[1]

> Division: 28,105 officers and men that contained two brigades of infantry and one brigade of artillery. It also contained engineer, machine gun, signal, medical, and transportation units and a headquarters.
>
> Brigade: 8,324 combatants
>
> Regiment: 3,770 combatants
>
> Battalion: 1,027 officers and men

British Army[2]

> Division: 12,000 to 15,000 infantry and staff that contained a pioneer (labor) unit and three brigades.
>
> Brigade: 3,000 to 5,000 infantry and staff
>
> Battalion: 1,000 to 1,600 infantry and staff

NOTES

PREFACE

1. The military units sent overseas by the U.S. government were designated as the American Expeditionary Forces (AEF) in 1917. The AEF is often cited incorrectly as the "American Expeditionary Force." The AEF consisted of American troops not only on the Western Front but also in Great Britain, Italy, Poland, and Russia, hence the use of the word "Forces."

2. Center of Military History, *Order of Battle of the United States Land Forces in the World War*, vol. 2, *Expeditionary Forces: Divisions* (Washington, D.C.: Government Printing Office, 1947), 127; and Shrader, "'Maconochie's Stew,'" 101.

3. The nickname of "Tommy" for a British soldier allegedly derives from the name Tommy Atkins, the name the Duke of Wellington entered in the first sample soldier's paybook. See Gilbert, *The First World War: A Complete History*, 86; and Haythornwaite, *The World War One Source Book*, 401.

4. The origin of the nickname "Doughboy" for an American soldier is uncertain. One definition claims that the term dates to the Civil War when the cavalry derided foot soldiers because their globular buttons resembled flour dumplings. In another version, Laurence Stallings claims that "there can be little dispute as to the derivation of the name. In Texas, U.S. Infantry along the Rio Grande were powdered white with the dust of adobe soil, and hence were called 'adobes' by mounted troops. It was a short step to 'dobies,' and then, by metathesis, the word was Doughboys." Stallings, *The Doughboys*, 15.

5. Cooke, "The American Soldier in France, 1917–1919," 250.

6. Terraine, *Douglas Haig: The Educated Soldier*, 473. Lloyd George made this comment after learning of the Allies' successful final assault to drive against the Beaurevoir Line on 5 October 1918. The pursuit to the Selle was in progress by 10 October 1918.

CHAPTER 1. ORGANIZING AN ARMY

1. "Report of the Secretary of War," in U.S. War Department, *Annual Reports of the War Department, 1917* (Washington, D.C.: War Department, 1918), 7.

2. Millett, "Over Where? The AEF and the American Strategy for Victory, 1917–1918," 235.

3. Mead, *The Doughboys*, 70–71.

4. "From a National Guardsman," 773.

5. Although the state units were officially designated as the National Guard, many of the Regulars still referred to them as the militia.

6. John J. Pershing to Joe Breckons, 23 May 1916, Box 34, Papers of John J. Pershing, 1882–1971, Library of Congress, Washington, D.C. (Hereafter Pershing Papers, LOC.) See also Smythe, *Guerrilla Warrior*, 261.

7. Maslowski and Millett, *For the Common Defense*, 247–249.

8. The General Staff was established in 1903. According to historian Russell F. Weigley, it undertook "the planning function, preparing war plans for all possible contingencies and assuring the availability of all needed materials." It was headed by the chief of staff. See Weigley, *History of the United States Army*, 316.

9. Cooper, "The National Guard Mobilizations of 1916 and 1917," 38–39.

10. Weigley, *History of the United States Army*, 320–321.

11. Clendenen, *Blood on the Border*, 286–287.

12. Cooper, "The National Guard Mobilizations of 1916 and 1917," 38–39.

13. Bullard, *Fighting Generals*, 290.

14. Ibid., 285.

15. Ibid., 289.

16. Roosevelt and Wood organized the 1st U.S. Volunteer Cavalry Regiment, also known as the Rough Riders, during the Spanish-American War.

17. John F. O'Ryan to Oswald Garrison Villard, 2 October 1916, Oswald Garrison Villard Papers, Houghton Library, Harvard University. "Kitchener's Mob" refers to the "new armies" of Field Marshal Lord Kitchener (see Chapter 3). See also Hall, *Kitchener's Mob*. Hall enlisted in the 9th Royal Fusiliers of the 36th Brigade, 12th British Division and served as a machine-gunner.

18. Doubler, *I Am the Guard*, 171–172.

19. Risch, *Quartermaster Support of the Army*, 605–608.

20. Ibid.

21. Ibid., 617–619.

CHAPTER 2. WANTED: AMERICAN TROOPS

1. Sheffield, *Forgotten Victory*, 95.
2. For a comprehensive study on the recruitment drive of 1914–1916, see Simkins, *Kitchener's Army*.
3. War Office, "General Staff Appreciations for the War Cabinet," January–March 1917, WO106/311, National Archives, Public Record Office, Kew, England.
4. Bridges, *Alarms and Excursions*, 180; and Smythe, *Pershing: General of the Armies*, 8.
5. Although Pershing was a major general, his appointment to command the AEF gave him the temporary rank of general. He was the highest-ranking officer in the U.S. army, even though he was not the most senior officer. That was actually Maj. Gen. Leonard Wood, who was not chosen to command the AEF for a variety of reasons. See Trask, *The AEF & Coalition Warmaking*, 11.
6. Frothingham, *The American Reinforcement in the World War*, xxx.
7. Coffman, *The War to End All Wars*, 19.
8. Maj. Paul H. Clark to the Commander-in-Chief, "Military Situations," 17 May 1918, Papers of General John J. Pershing, National Archives Gift Collection, Entry 22, RG 200, NARA. (Hereafter Pershing Papers, NARA.)
9. French, *The Strategy of the Lloyd George Coalition*, 58.
10. Harries and Harries, *The Last Days of Innocence*, 116–117.
11. Ibid.; and Pershing, *My Experiences in the Great War*, 1:187–190.
12. Pershing, *My Experiences in the Great War*, 1:144. For more detailed analysis, see Griffith, *Battle Tactics of the Western Front*.
13. Harries and Harries, *The Last Days of Innocence*, 116–117; and Woodward, *The Military Correspondence of Field Marshal Sir William Robertson CIGS*, 7.
14. Pershing stayed in Paris until 6 September 1917. Because there were too many social distractions and interruptions from visitors, he moved AEF headquarters to Chaumont, 150 miles east of Paris on the upper Marne. Smythe, *Pershing: General of the Armies*, 45.
15. Simkins, *The First World War*, 3:31.
16. Holmes, *The Western Front*, 143; and Simkins, *The First World War*, 3:32–33.
17. Bond and Cave, *Haig: A Reappraisal 70 Years On*, 16; and Terraine, *Ordeal of Victory*, 177–178.
18. Blake, *The Private Papers of Douglas Haig*, 245.
19. Pershing, *My Experiences in the Great War*, 1:111–116.
20. Ibid.

CHAPTER 3. AMALGAMATION

1. Nenninger, "American Military Effectiveness in the First World War," 137.

2. The Supreme War Council was formed on 7 November 1917 with a mission "to watch over the general conduct of the war" and coordinate military operations on the Western Front. The prime ministers of England, France, and Italy headed it. Because President Wilson was in America and unable to attend, Tasker Bliss, the soon-to-be-retired chief of staff, was appointed as the American representative. See Smythe, *Pershing: General of the Armies*, 60.

3. Ibid., 11.

4. Bruce, *A Fraternity of Arms*, 151.

5. Baker to Pershing, 24 December 1917, File #14903-19, Entry 11, RG 120, NARA.

6. Blake, *The Private Papers of Douglas Haig*, 272.

7. Pershing, *My Experiences in the Great War*, 1:315.

8. Pershing to Chief of Staff, 1 January 1918, File #14903-20, Entry 11, RG 120, NARA.

9. Ibid.

10. Reports of Commander-in-Chief to the Chief of Staff, AEF, 1 January and 3 January 1918, File #21, Entry 22, RG 120, NARA.

11. Smythe, *Pershing: General of the Armies*, 74–77.

12. Pershing, *My Experiences in the Great War*, 1:287–289. President Wilson sent his advisor Col. Edward House to Europe from 7 to 21 November 1917 to discuss issues such as finance, maritime transport, the future conduct of the war, food, petroleum, and munitions with Allied leaders. Ferrell, *Woodrow Wilson and World War I*, 120-121.

13. "Relations with the British," Reports of the Commander-in-Chief, 13 January 1918, Entry 22, RG 120, NARA.

14. David Lloyd George to Woodrow Wilson, 3 December 1917, in Link, *The Papers of Woodrow Wilson*, 44:128.

15. Esposito, "Woodrow Wilson and the Origins of the AEF," 127–129.

16. Pershing, *My Experiences in the Great War*, 1:105.

17. Trask, *The United States in the Supreme War Council*, 73–79.

18. "Agreement between the Commanders-in-Chief of the American and British Forces in France regarding the Training of the American Troops with British Troops," 31 January 1918, File #14903, Entry 11, RG 120, NARA.

19. Fowler, *British-American Relations, 1917–1918*, 130–135 and 145–153.

20. "Agreement between the Commanders-in-Chief of the American and British Forces in France."

21. Pershing to Haig, "Papers Relating to American Troops Serving with the British," 12 February 1918, File #284, Entry 267, RG 120, NARA.

22. Bruce, *A Fraternity of Arms*, 159–161.

CHAPTER 4. THE SUNNY SOUTH: TRAINING IN THE UNITED STATES

1. Center of Military History, *Order of Battle of the United States Land Forces in the World War*, vol. 3, Part III, *Directory of Troops* (Washington, D.C.: Government Printing Office, 1948), 677–678.

2. Denfeld, "World War I Mobilization Camps."

3. Earl Mitchell to his family, n.d., Letters of Earl Mitchell, 118th Infantry Regiment, Miscellaneous World War I Manuscripts, Tennessee State Library and Archives. (Hereafter Mitchell Letters.)

4. Denfield, "World War I Mobilization Camps."

5. Sutliffe, *Seventy-First New York in the World War*,49–50; O'Ryan, *The Story of the 27th Division*, 1:99–115.

6. Harris, *Harlem's Hell Fighters*, 120–132.

7. Stewart, *The History of Company "K,"* 6–7.

8. Murphy and Thomas, *The Thirtieth Division in the World War*, 33.

9. Ibid., 20.

10. Ibid., 49.

11. East Tennessee Historical Society, *First Families of Tennessee*, 25–26.

12. Walker, *Official History of the 120th Infantry "3rd North Carolina" 30th Division*, 7.

13. Ibid.

14. The War College Division was one of the sections of the General Staff. See Bethel, *Preliminary Checklist of the Records of the War Department General Staff: Record Group 165.*

15. Smythe, *Pershing: General of the Armies*, 37.

16. Sheffield, *Forgotten Victory*, 102.

17. Murphy and Thomas, *The Thirtieth Division in the World War*, 22–23.

18. Cooper, *The Rise of the National Guard*, 169.

19. Ibid.

20. Earl Mitchell to his family, n.d., Mitchell Letters.

21. Joe Willoughby Thompson, response to 30th Division Army Service Experience Questionnaires, United States Army Military History Institute, Carlisle Barracks, Pennsylvania.

22. "Testimony of Maj. Gen. John F. O'Ryan," in United States Senate, *Reorganization of the Army*, 511–544.

23. Ibid., 512.

24. Peter Simkins to author, 10 March 2006.

25. Peter Simkins to author, 8 November 2004.

26. See the entry for "William Warlick" at "The Old North State and 'Kaiser Bill': North Carolinians in World War I," available at http://www.ah.dcr.state.nc.us/Archives/wwI/OldNorthState/SoldierStories.htm.

27. Hostess houses were built and run by the YWCA near the entrance to military camps as a place where families could stay while visiting soldiers. O'Ryan, *The Story of the 27th Division*, 111.

28. Murphy and Thomas, *The Thirtieth Division in the World War*, 42–43.

29. 30th Division Historical Records, "Training History," n.d., File #54.9, Entry 1241, RG 120, NARA.

30. "Correspondence regarding the Payment of Foreign Instructors," 31 October 1917, War College Division, File #10071-35, Entry 296, RG 165, NARA.

31. Sutliffe, *Seventy-First New York in the World War*, 42–43.

32. Ibid.

33. Long, "The Legacy of the Army of 1918," 21.

34. Jacobson, *History of the 107th Infantry, U.S.A.,* 13–15; Gow, *Letters of a Soldier,* 142–143; and O'Ryan, *The Story of the 27th Division,* 1:117–128.

35. "Memorandum of British Instructors in Training Camps," 12 November 1917, War College Division, File #11071-55, Entry 296, RG 165, NARA.

36. Lt. Col. Murray, Military Attaché, "Information on the American Army," n.d., WO 106/474, Public Record Office, National Archives, Kew, England.

37. Gow, *Letters of a Soldier,* 237.

38. 19 September 1917, 30th Division Historical Files, File #474.1, Entry 1241, RG 120, NARA.

39. Canfield, *U.S. Infantry Weapons of the First Word War,* 64–69.

40. Pershing, *My Experiences in the Great War,* 1:153.

41. Odom, "The Spirit of the Bayonet: Offensive Doctrine in the U.S. Army, 1917–1941." For a larger discussion of this issue, see Odom, *After the Trenches;* and Rainey, "Ambivalent Warfare: The Tactical Doctrine of the AEF in World War I."

42. Smythe, "The Wisdom of a Separate Army," 263.

43. Nenninger, "Tactical Dysfunction in the AEF, 1917–1918," 177.

44. O'Ryan, *The Story of the 27th Division,* 1:134.

45. Ibid.

46. Report on Maj. Gen. John F. O'Ryan, in "Officers' Reports—Reports by British on American Officers Visiting British Front," 2 February 1918, Pershing Papers, Entry 23, RG 200, NARA.

47. Maj. Gen. John F. O'Ryan to the Chief of Staff, AEF, 31 October 1917, "Report of Observations," File #7396-C, Entry 9, RG120, NARA.

48. Berry, *Make the Kaiser Dance: Living Memories of the Doughboys* (New York: Arbor House, 1978), 205.

49. Clarke, *Over There with O'Ryan's Roughnecks,* 22–23.

50. Letters of Mack Slagle, 2 December 1917, *Spartanburg Herald,* 9 August 1917. Shared with me by Edward Slagle, Falls Church, Virginia.

51. Weigley, *History of the United States Army,* 366.

52. Ada Clark to Governor Thomas Rye, 22 November 1917, Governor Thomas Rye Papers, Tennessee State Library and Archives.

53. "Medical History of Camp Wadsworth," n.d., File #314.7, Entry 25, RG 112, NARA.

54. "Medical History of Camp Sevier, South Carolina," n.d., File #314.7, Entry 25, RG 112, NARA.

55. "General O'Ryan Appeals for Sobriety in Army," *Spartanburg Herald,* 9 August 1917.

56. Ibid., 9 August 1917.

57. "Much Interest in Military Police," *Spartanburg Herald,* 8 September 1917.

58. Ferrell, *Woodrow Wilson & World War I,* 189–190.

CHAPTER 5. ORGANIZING II CORPS

1. Center of Military History, *Order of Battle of the United States Land Forces in the World War*, vol. 1, *American Expeditionary Forces: General Headquarters, Army Corps, Services of Supply, Separate Forces* (Washington, D.C.: Government Printing Office, 1937), 223. This general order also established I, III, and IV Corps, which eventually served under the AEF First Army.

2. Col. Chauncey B. Baker of the Quartermaster Corps was ordered to Britain, France, and Belgium to visit camps and other establishments to observe Allied training, transportation, operations, supply, and administration. Several officers from the various army branches accompanied him. This was known as the Baker mission.

3. George S. Simonds, "General Correspondence," File # 205667, Entry 25, RG 94, NARA.

4. Davis, *Generals in Khaki*.

5. Shrader, "'Maconochie's Stew,'" 107.

6. George S. Simonds, "Confidential Stenographic Notes of a Talk by Brig. Gen. George S. Simonds on Operations of II Corps, AEF, Given at Historical Section, AWC, 14 October 1931," File #5436, Entry 310C, RG 165.

7. Pershing, *My Experiences in the Great War*, 1:23.

8. Simonds, "Confidential Stenographic Notes of a Talk by Brig. Gen. George S. Simonds on Operations of II Corps.

9. Ibid.

10. Ibid.

11. Ibid.

12. Ibid.

13. Lt. Gen. Sir Charles Bonham-Carter, "Diary 9 April–21 May 1918," Papers of Gen. Sir Charles Bonham-Carter, Churchill Archive Centre, Churchill College, Cambridge. (Hereafter Bonham-Carter Papers.)

14. John Bourne to Mitchell Yockelson, 17 May 2005.

15. Robbins, *British Generalship on the Western Front, 1914–18*, 136–137.

16. Brig. Gen. James McAndrew and Lt. Col. Alfred W. Bjornstad, "The Plan for the General Staff College," 1 November 1917, Entry 567, RG 120, NARA; and Cooke, *Pershing and His Generals*, 34–35.

17. Maj. Gen. Sir A. H. Russell, New Zealand Division, "Attachment of Officers of the United States Army," February 1918, WA 22-6/23, National Archives of New Zealand.

18. "The Last German Offensive," *The Army Quarterly* XLI, no. 2 (January 1941): 263.

19. Middlebrook, *The Kaiser's Battle*, 151.

20. Zabecki, *Steel Wind: Colonel George Bruchmuller and the Birth of Modern Artillery*, 53–56 and 72–76. Historians do not agree about which army invented the creeping barrage; we do know that the Germans used a variation in the east in 1915 and that the Allies did the same in 1916.

21. Lupfer, *The Dynamics of Doctrine*, 49.

22. H. G. Taylor, *The Mob That Shot the Camel*, 137, AWM 8863, Australian War Memorial, Canberra.

23. Kitchen, *The German Offensives of 1918*, 53–55. Also see Zabecki, *The German 1918 Offensives*.

24. Kitchen, *The German Offensives of 1918*, 60.

25. Becker, *The Great War and the French People*, 312–313.

26. George S. Simonds to G-5, AEF, "Bulletins 3 and 7," 28 March 1918 and 1 April 1918, File #1511-1 and File #1511-2, Entry 7, RG 120, NARA.

27. Ibid.

28. Simonds, "Confidential Stenographic Notes of a Talk by Brig. Gen. George S. Simonds on Operations of II Corps.

29. Ibid.

30. Ibid.

31. As generalissimo, Foch was given the power to coordinate the movements of all Allied armies on the Western Front. National commanders, however, were given full tactical control over their own troops. See French, *The Strategy of the Lloyd George Coalition*, 226–227.

32. Kitchen, *The German Offensives of 1918*, 103; and Blake, *The Private Papers of Douglas Haig*, 302.

33. Kitchen, *The German Offensives of 1918*, 103.

34. Terraine, *Ordeal of Victory*, 432–433.

35. Ibid., 106–108; and Simkins, *The First World War*, 3:54.

CHAPTER 6. GOODBYE, SOUTH CAROLINA: THE FINAL WEEKS OF TRAINING

1. Morale Reports, 1917–1918, 30th Division, Entry 368, Record Group 165; and Adjutant General of the Army to the Commanding General, 30th Division, Camp Sevier, 14 March 1918, Misc. File, Entry 1241, RG 120, NARA.

2. Adjutant General of the Army to Commanding General, 30th Division, Camp Sevier, 14 March 1918, 30th Division Correspondence, File #370.E.E., Entry 124, RG 120, NARA.

3. Stewart, *The History of Company "K,"* 10.

4. War Department, Office of the Chief of Staff, "Memorandum for the Director, War Plans Division," files of the Brigade and Field Officers School, for Sam Houston, Entry 310, RG 165, NARA.

5. Pvt. Fred Elston Pierce, Letters, 4–17 March 1918, available at http://www.oryansroughnecks.org/letters.html.

6. Stewart, *The History of Company "K,"* 10.

7. Marshall, *Memories of World War I*, 19.

8. Entry for 13 February 1918, in Gow, *Letters of a Soldier*, 231.

9. Sutliffe, *Seventy-First New York in the World War*, 53.

10. Report of the Adjutant General, 27th Division, 7 March 1918, File #333.1, Entry 1241, RG 120, NARA.

11. "When the Soldiers Came to Town," *Spartanburg Herald*, 8 January 1918; and General Orders 4, 6 January 1918, Entry 452, RG 120, NARA.

12. *Brooklyn Daily Eagle*, 6 February 1918, Section 8-E, page 3.

13. O'Ryan, *The Story of the 27th Division*, 1:411–412.

14. Acting Secretary of War to the Honorable J. W. Wadsworth, Jr., 12 March 1918, File #10766-25, Entry 296, RG 165, NARA.

15. Adjutant General to Commanding General, 27th Division, Camp Wadsworth, 15–17 April 1918, War Department Cables, RG 407, NARA.

16. Whitehorne, *The Inspector General of the United States Army*, 165.

17. Brig. Gen. Eli A. Helmick, N. A. Inspector, to Adjutant General of the Army, "Report of Inspection, 30th Division," File #97-8-64, Entry 296, RG 165, NARA.

18. Sgt. Judson W. Dennis, Company L, 119th Infantry, American Expeditionary Forces, to his mother, 28 April 1918, available at http://www.pastvoices.com/usa/jud19180428.shtml.

19. Ibid.

20. Entry for 18–19 May 1918, Willard Newton Diary, published as "Over There for Uncle Sam," *Charlotte Observer*, 22 August 1920, available at http://www.cmstory.org/ww1/diary.asp.

21. Ibid.

22. Dennis to his mother, 28 April 1918.

23. Burial file for Judson W. Dennis, Entry 1942, RG 92, NARA.

24. Roberts, *Encyclopedia of Historic Forts*, 512.

25. Center of Military History, *Order of Battle of the United States Land Forces in the World War*, vol. 3, part 1, *Zone of the Interior* (Washington, D.C.: Government Printing Office, 1949), 516–518, 748.

26. American Expeditionary Forces, General Order #30, 15 February 1918, Entry 452, RG 120, NARA.

27. Baldwin, "The American Enlisted Man in World War I," 146–150.

28. Ibid.

29. Roper, "Paul Green's War Songs," 38.

30. O'Ryan, *The Story of the 27th Division*, 1:147.

31. Stewart, *The History of Company "K,"* 14–18.

32. Adjutant General's Office, "Vessel File," *Tuscania*, A.G.O. General Correspondence, 1917–1925, RG 407, NARA.

33. Edward Graham Melvin, "One Man's War: World War I From the Memories of a Tennessee Farm Boy," unpublished manuscript at the United States Army Military History Institute, Carlisle Barracks, Pennsylvania. Published as Edward Graham Melvin, Sr., *One Man's War* (Kingston, Tenn.: Ella M. Winsboro, 1996).

34. Ibid.

35. Jacobson, *History of the 107th Infantry, U.S. A.*, 18.

36. Berry, *Make the Kaiser Dance*, 209.

37. O'Ryan, *The Story of the 27th Division*, 1:147.

38. Ibid., 148–149.

39. War Veterans' Association, *History of Company "E,"* 74.

CHAPTER 7. ARRIVAL

1. Entry for 13 June 1918, in Joseph Pratt, "War Diary of Col. Joseph Pratt," *North Carolina Historical Review* 1:1–2:2 (January 1924 and April 1925): 35–71, 269–299. (Hereafter Pratt Diary.)

2. Entry for 8–9 June 1918, Willard Newton Diary, published as "Over There for Uncle Sam," *Charlotte Observer*, 29 August 1920, available at available at http://www.cmstory.org/ww1/diary.asp.

3. Entry for 9 May 1918, Sgt.-Maj. Albert Breunig Diary, 30th Division Veterans Questionnaires, United States Army Military History Institute, Carlisle Barracks, Pennsylvania.

4. Entry for 14–15 June 1918, Pratt Diary.

5. AEF Base Section 4, "Reports, Studies, Monographs, and other Records Relating to the Activities of Base Section No. 4," 131, Entry 2532, RG 120, NARA.

6. *Souvenir Booklet of Brest*, 3–5.

7. Jacobson, *History of the 107th Infantry U.S.A.*, 22–23. A *poilu* is a French soldier.

8. Ellis, *Eye-Deep in Hell*, 153–154.

9. Young was brought to France by Pershing to deal with the problem of venereal disease among the French population so there would be less chance that the American troops would be infected. In 1918, 6,000 men in the British army reportedly had a venereal disease. McCarthy, "Not All Beer and Skittles,"162.

10. Smythe, "Venereal Disease: The AEF's Experience."

11. AEF General Orders #6, 2 July 1917; AEF General Orders #34, September 9, 1917; and AEF General Orders #77, 18 December 1917, all in Entry 452, RG 120, NARA.

12. Simkins, "Soldiers and Civilians: Billeting in Britain and France," 186.

13. AEF Surgeon General Weekly Reports of Sick and Wounded, 5–29 June 1918, Entry UD, RG 120, NARA.

14. Berry, *Make the Kaiser Dance*, 209.

15. O'Ryan, *The Story of the 27th Division*, 1:152.

16. 27th Division Bulletin #39, 9 June 1918, 27th Division Historical Files, Entry 1241, RG 120, NARA.

17. "British Officers," 8 June 1918, File #336.4 (British Officers), Entry 1241, 30th Division Historical Files, RG 120, NARA. Sergeant Major Tector and Major Sharp, who spent most of their time at Camp Wadsworth, were not among this group.

18. Entry for 29 May 1918, Sgt.-Maj. Albert Breunig Diary, 30th Division Veterans Questionnaires, United States Army Military History Institute, Carlisle Barracks, Pennsylvania.

19. Rutherford Ireland, "History of the Twenty-Third N.G.S.N.Y.," unpublished monograph, 1937, 272, New York State Military Museum, Saratoga.

20. Commander-in-Chief to Chief of the British Mission, 17 March 1918, "British Publications," File #15091, Entry 9, RG 120, NARA.

21. George S. Simonds to G.H.Q., I, BEF, "Postal Censorship Arrangements," 1 April 1918, Entry 1241, RG 120, NARA.

22. W. G. Busby, "History of A.P.O. No. 790," File #182-26.5, Entry 1023, RG 120, NARA.

23. Headquarters, II Corps, American E.F., to Commanding Officer, 412th Telegraph Battalion, American E.F. "Disciplinary Action," 8 November 1918, File #182-26.5, Entry 1023, RG 120, NARA.

24. Lt. Col. H. S. Sternberger, 27th Division quartermaster, "History of the Quartermaster Corps Attached to 27th Division, U.S. A."; and Col. H. B. Springs, Inf., U.S.A., "Operations of Quartermaster Department, 30th Division, with British Expeditionary Force, 24 May 1918 to 20 November 1918," both in Entry 1915, RG 92, NARA.

25. Lt. J. M. L. Grover, "Experiences of a Platoon Commander from 1914–1918," #28, Reel 04, page 28, Department of Sound Records, Imperial War Museum, London.

26. O'Ryan, *The Story of the 27th Division*, 1:180.

CHAPTER 8. TRAINING OVERSEAS COMMENCES

1. "Program of Training for American Divisions Training with British," G-3 Library Files, File #13-1320, Entry 264, RG 120, NARA.

2. Ibid.

3. Chief of Staff, II Corps, to Commanding Generals of Divisions, "Training," 9 June 1918, Commander-in-Chief Training Correspondence, File #15721-7, Entry 9, RG 120, NARA.

4. George S. Simonds, "Confidential Stenographic Notes of a Talk by Brig. Gen. George S. Simonds on Operations of II Corps, AEF, Given at Historical Section, AWC, 14 October 1931," File #5436, Entry 310C, RG 165.

5. Entry for 29 April 1918, Gen. Sir Charles Bonham-Carter Diaries; and Correspondence Book, 1918, 16–17, both in Bonham-Carter Papers.

6. Clarke, *Over There with O'Ryan's Roughnecks*, 35.

7. Memoir of Gen. Sir Philip Christison, 10 June 1918, IWM 82/15/1, Imperial War Museum, London.

8. Ibid.

9. Griffith, *Battle Tactics of the Western Front*, 79.

10. Maj. Paul H. Clark to Commander-in-Chief, 14 June 1918, "Military Situation," Pershing Papers, NARA.

11. Sheffield, "The Performance of British Troops in 1918," 75.

12. Sheffield, *Leadership in the Trenches*, 183; and Sheffield, "The Morale of the British Army," in Jensen and Wiest, *War in the Age of Technology*, 105–139.

13. Bond and Robbins, eds., *Staff Officer: The Diaries of Walter Guinness*, 215–219.

14. Ibid.

15. Ibid.

16. Ibid.

17. Whitehorne, *The Inspector General of the United States Army*, 168–172; and Maj. Gen. A. W. Brewster, "Report of Inspections," Entry 22, File #400, RG 120, NARA.

18. Entry for 18 June 1918, Diary of Capt. L. G. Pinnell, IWM 83/17/1, Imperial War Museum, London.

19. Warren, "Buffalo Bill Meets Dracula," 1124–1125.

20. Hutchinson, *The Thirty-Third Division in France and Flanders*, 117–118.

21. Members of the Battalion, *History and Memoirs of the 33rd Battalion Machine Gun Corps*, 74.

22. Ibid., 73.

23. 39th Division, "Notes on American Divisions Compiled by 39th Division, BEF," PRO 95/2597, National Archives, Public Record Office, Kew, England.

24. Hiscock, *The Bells of Hell Go Ting-a-Ling-a-Ling*, 95.

25. Jacobson, *History of the 107th Infantry U.S.A.*, 29–30.

26. Fleming, *The Illusion of Victory*, 62–66.

27. Ibid.

28. Gow, *Letters of a Soldier*, 299.

29. G. D. Sheffield to author, February 2004.

30. Maj. Gen. John F. O'Ryan to G-3, AEF, "Confidential Report," 19 December 1918, Entry 267, RG 120, NARA.

31. Hancock, *Smuts*, 1:483.

32. Entry for 8 June 1918, Pershing Diary, Pershing Papers, LOC.

33. Ibid.

34. Pershing, *My Experiences in the Great War*, 2:315.

35. Comment on Col. Robert H. Bacon, entry for 12 June 1918, Diary of Lord Derby, MSS 920DER, Liverpool Record Office. Provided to author by Jim Beach.

CHAPTER 9. DIVISION TRAINING

1. Entry for 9 June 1918, Diary of George A. Morrice, United States Army Military History Institute, Carlisle Barracks, Pennsylvania.

2. Ibid.

3. Jacobson, *History of the 107th Infantry U.S.A.*, 27–28.

4. Canfield, *U.S. Infantry Weapons of the First World War*, 98.

5. Entry for 12 June 1918, Willard Newton Diary, published as "Over There for Uncle Sam," *Charlotte Observer*, 29 August 1920, available at available at http://www.cmstory.org/ww1/diary.asp.

6. Jacobson, *History of the 107th Infantry U.S.A.*, 22.

7. Ibid., 23.

8. Stewart, *The History of Company "K,"* 21.

9. Ibid., 24.

10. O'Ryan, *The Story of the 27th Division*, 1:180.

11. Howard, "The Sweetheart of the AEF," 7.

12. Brig. Gen. W. W. Harts to Maj. Gen. James W. McAndrews, 14–19 July 1918, File #86980, Entry 6, RG 120, NARA.

13. O'Ryan, *The Story of the 27th Division*, 1:212.

14. Janis, *So Far, So Good!* 219–223.

15. Blake, *The Private Papers of Douglas Haig*, 313.

16. The 35th Division collapsed on the first day of the offensive, while the 77th became famous for its "Lost Battalion." The 82nd Division included America's hero of the war, Alvin York.

17. Correspondence Book, 1918, 22–23, Bonham-Carter Papers.

18. Millett, *The General*, 378.

19. Coffman, *The War to End All Wars*, 285.

20. "Officer Evaluation," George W. Read, 8 October 1884, Appointments, Commissions and Personnel File, 1159, Entry 297, RG 94, NARA.

21. United States Military Academy, *Sixty-Sixth Annual Report of the Association of Graduates of the United States Military Academy at West Point*, 124.

22. Sir Douglas Haig to General Pershing, 30 June 1918, Haig Correspondence, Field Marshal Sir Douglas Haig Papers, National Library of Scotland, Edinburgh. (Hereafter Haig Papers.)

23. Entry for 6 July 1918, Rawlinson Diary, National Army Museum. I wish to thank Peter Simkins for pointing out this quote.

24. "My War Experience," manuscript among the Papers of George Sherwin Simonds, 1918–1932, Box 14, Correspondence, 1917–1920, Manuscript Division, Library of Congress, Washington, D.C. (Hereafter Simonds Papers.)

25. The authoritative study on Belleau Wood is Asprey, *At Belleau Wood*. The 3rd Brigade was part of the 2nd Division. Harbord had left Pershing's staff and taken command of the 4th Marine Brigade (5th and 6th Regiments), then he was promoted to 2nd Division commander.

26. "Officer Evaluation," Edward M. Lewis, 14 November 1886, Appointments, Commissions and Personnel File, 3790, Entry 297, RG 94, NARA.

27. Tyson to Matthew Steele, 22 January 1919, Lawrence D. Tyson Papers, East Tennessee Historical Society, Knoxville.

28. Maj. Gen. E. M. Lewis's rating of Lawrence D. Tyson and Faison and Lt. Gen. Hunter Liggett's rating of Tyson are found in "AEF Officer's Ratings," Entry 31, AGO General Correspondence, 1917–1925, File #210.01, RG 407, NARA.

29. Entry for 1 July 1918, Pershing Diary, Pershing Papers, LOC.

30. The fact that Faison was not permanently chosen as division commander would haunt Pershing well after the war. In 1922, Tyson wrote to Pershing in an attempt "to do justice to General Faison." Brigadier General Tyson to General Pershing, 14 January 1922, Pershing Papers, LOC. The War Department, according to Tyson, was trying to force Faison to retire at his prewar rank of colonel; the rank of brigadier general was only temporary during the war. Tyson maintained his argument that Faison had actually trained the division the longest and that others (Read and Lewis) had benefited from his hard work. Pershing, who no longer wanted to get involved

in War Department matters regarding promotion, politely declined Tyson's request to intervene.

31 Field Marshal Sir Douglas Haig to the Secretary, War Office, 16 June 1918, C.B./2255. Copy of letter among the papers of Sir Ivor Maxse, IWM.

32. Charles Bonham-Carter to Joan Bonham-Carter, 8 July 1918, Bonham-Carter Papers.

33. Sheffield, *Forgotten Victory*, 70.

34. Maj. Lloyd C. Griscom to Commander-in-Chief, G.H.Q., AEF, "Canadians to Help Train American Troops," 22 June 1918, Pershing Papers, LOC.

35. The title of Shane Schreiber's book, *The Shock Army of the British Empire*.

36. Griscom to Commander-in-Chief, 8 July 1918.

37. "Sammy: Australian Soldiers' Relations with Americans," available at http://www.awm.gov.au/1918/soldier/sammy.htm.

38. Welborn, *Bush Heroes*, 149.

39. Ward, *Between the Big Parades*, 45.

40. Andrews, *The Story of A Machine Gun Company*, 43.

41. Brown, *Imperial Museum Book of 1918*, 162.

42. Andrews, *The ANZAC Illusion*, 60–62.

43. Ibid., 62.

44. MacVeagh and Brown, *The Yankee in the British Zone*, 193.

45. Terraine, *To Win a War*, 67.

CHAPTER 10. WE HAVE FOUND EACH OTHER AT LAST

1. Chief of Operations, G.H.Q., BEF, to Chief of Staff, II Corps, 9 June 1918, "Training of American Troops with British," File #182-56.5, Entry 874, RG 120, NARA.

2. Ibid.

3. Commanding General-in-Chief, British Armies in France, to Commander-in-Chief, American Expeditionary Forces, 14 June 1918, File #658-B, Entry 267, RG 120, NARA.

4. Ibid.

5. Andrews, *The Story of a Machine Gun Company*, 30.

6. Center of Military History, *Order of Battle of the United States Land Forces in the World War, American Expeditionary Forces, Divisions* (Washington, D.C.: Government Printing Office, 1931), 3: 135, 165.

7. Dunn, *The War the Infantry Knew, 1914–1919*, 476.

8. Holmes, *The Oxford Companion to Military History*, 1013–1015.

9. Walker, *Official History of the 120th Infantry*, 14.

10. Lawrence, *Fighting Soldier*, 16–17.

11. O'Ryan, *The Story of the 27th Division*, 1:197–201; and Murphy and Thomas, *The Thirtieth Division in the World War*, 71–72.

12. Entry for 20 August 1918, Pratt Diary.

13. Burial File for Robert P. Friedman, Entry 1941, RG 92, NARA. Friedman, a member of Company A, 105th Engineers, died on 13 July 1918.

14. Levinger, *A Jewish Chaplain in France*, 127–128.

15. "These Men: For Conspicuous Bravery Above and Beyond the Call of Duty," unpublished manuscript at United States Army Military History Institute, Carlisle Barracks, Pennsylvania.

16. Entry for 24 July 1918, Pratt Diary.

17. *New York Sun*, 7 March 1919, 1.

18. Ibid.

19. Capt. Henry Maslin, Company D, 105th Infantry, to GHQ (through 27th Division, AEF), "Report of Tour of Duty in British Trenches," 25 June 1918, File #16427-R, Entry 9, RG 120, NARA.

20. Capt. George P. Nichols, 107th U.S. Inf., to C.O., 107th U.S. Inf., "Report on Visit to Front Line Trenches," 16 July 1918, File #16427-P, Entry 6, RG 120, NARA.

21. Strength Returns, 30th Division, July 1918, RG 407, NARA.

22. Murphy and Thomas, *The Thirtieth Division in the World War*, 73.

23. Commanding General, 59th Infantry Brigade, to Assistant Chief of Staff, General Headquarters, A.E.F., "Report on Relations under British 2nd Corps," 15 December 1918, Entry 267, RG 120, NARA.

24. Lt. Col. D. K. Leonard, General Headquarters, BEF, 12 June 1918, "State of Training," British File, 33rd Division, Folder 1, Entry 318, RG 165, NARA.

25. O'Ryan, *The Story of the 27th Division*, 1:141.

26. Commanding General, 30th Division, to Commanding General, II Corps, AEF, 9 July 1918, "Status of Training of 30th Division," File #353, Folder 36, Entry 267, RG 120, NARA.

27. John K. Herr, "My Personal Experiences and Observations in Connection with the Great War" unpublished manuscript, John K. Herr Papers, United States Military Academy Archives, West Point, New York.

CHAPTER 11. VISITORS AND INSPECTORS

1. Ward, *Between the Big Parades*, 51.

2. O'Ryan, *The Story of the 27th Division*, 1:169.

3. Carl Boyd, A.D.C., to Maj. Gen. John F. O'Ryan, 12 July 1918, Pershing Papers, LOC.

4. Holmes, *Acts of War*, 136.

5. Lt. John Jerome Callahan, 105th Infantry, to C.O., 1st BN, 105th Inf., "Report on Working Detail," 3 August 1918, File #333.1, Entry 1241, RG 120, NARA.

6. Jacobson, *History of the 107th Infantry U.S.A.*, 44.

7. Berry, *Make the Kaiser Dance*, 212.

8. Entry for 6 July 1918, War Diary, 9th (Glasgow Highlanders) Battalion, Highland Light Infantry. Thanks to Alec Weir for bringing this to my attention.

9. Entry for 24–25 September 1918, Diary of Robert Cude (55th Infantry Brigade), Imperial War Museum, London.

10. F. A. J. Taylor, "The Bottom of the Barrel: 1918," 90–91, unpublished manuscript, United States Army Military History Institute, Carlisle Barracks, Pennsylvania.

11. Entry for 4 August 1918, General Philip Diary, Imperial War Museum, London.

12. Commanding General, II Corps, to C-in-C (G-5) G.H.Q., AEF, "Inspection of Divisions of the II Corps," 14 August 1918, File #13599-A-93, Entry 9, RG 120, NARA.

13. Brig. Gen. C. H. MacMillan, "Resume of Points Brought to Notice during Attachment of American 27th Division," 16 August 1918, File #333.1, Entry 1241, RG 120, NARA.

14. Inspector General, II Corps, AEF, to Inspector General, G.H.Q., AEF, "Monthly Report on Discipline," 7 July 1918, File #56.2, Entry 1023, RG 120, NARA.

15. Walker, *Official History of the 120th Infantry*, 13.

16. John K. Herr, "My Personal Experiences and Observations in Connection with the Great War," 15, unpublished manuscript, John K. Herr Papers, United States Military Academy Archives, West Point, New York.

17. Read to G-3, 23 August 1918, WO 166/466, National Archives, Public Record Office, Kew, England.

18. Palazzo, *Seeking Victory on the Western Front*, 60–61.

19. Griffith, *Battle Tactics of the Western Front*, 116–117.

20. Palazzo, *Seeking Victory on the Western Front*, 29.

21. Herr, "My Personal Experiences and Observations in Connection with the Great War," 15.

22. 30th Division Gas Officer to Commanding General, 30th Division, "Report of Gas Attack, 24 August 1918," 105th Engineers Historical Files, File #230-12.3, Entry 1241, RG 120, NARA.

23. Distinguished Service Cross citation for Sgt. Guy R. Hinson, in Murphy and Thomas, *The Thirtieth Division in the World War*, Appendix J, 251.

24. Report of the Chief of Chemical Warfare Service, AEF, to the Chief Gas Officer, II Corps, 30 June 1918, United States War Department, *U. S. Army in the World War*, 3:161. For a comprehensive study of the training of American troops in gas warfare, see Heller, *Chemical Warfare in World War I*.

CHAPTER 12. ALONE WITH THE BRITISH

1. Entry for 12 August 1918, Pershing Diary, Pershing Papers, LOC.

2. O'Ryan, *The Story of the 27th Division*, 1:177.

3. Entry for 12 August 1918, Pershing Diary.

4. Entry for 15 August 1918, Pershing Diary.

5. Entry for 12 August 1918, Diary of Field Marshall Sir Douglas Haig, National Library of Scotland, Edinburgh.

6. Ibid., 25 August 1918.

7. Sir William Robertson to Gen. John J. Pershing, 18 July 1918, Correspondence Files, Pershing Papers, LOC.

8. Entry for 27 August 1918, Pershing Diary.

9. Pershing to Haig, 20 August 1918, Haig Papers.

10. Ibid.

11. Pershing to Haig, 14 August 1918, Haig Papers.

12. Ibid.

13. Harbord was promoted to major general in July 1918 when he took over the Services of Supply.

14. When Pershing's *My Experiences in the World War* was published in 1931, the main criticism it elicited was Pershing's lack of appreciation for the work of other AEF staff officers and the War Department's chief of staff, Peyton March. In response, March wrote his own narrative of the war that downplayed Pershing's role. Harbord responded on Pershing's behalf with his own work (see note 15).

15. Harbord, *The American Army in France, 1917–1919*; and Pershing, *My Experiences in the Great War*, 2:217.

16. Entry for 27 August 1918, Diary of Field Marshall Sir Douglas Haig.

17. Haig to Pershing, 18 July 1918, Haig Papers.

18. George S. Simonds to Fox Connor, G-3, G.H.Q., AEF, 23 August 1918, II Corps General File, Folder 302, Entry 267, RG 120, NARA.

CHAPTER 13. YPRES

1. American Battle Monuments Commission, *27th Division Summary of Operations in the World War*, 7–8; and American Battle Monuments Commission, *30th Division Summary of Operations in the World War*, 7.

2. Entry for 18 August 1918, Willard Newton Diary, published as "Over There for Uncle Sam," *Charlotte Observer*, 26 September 1920, available at http://www.cmstory.org/ww1/diary.asp.

3. War Veterans' Association, *History of Company "E,"* 87.

4. Headquarters, 30th Division, 5 October 1918, "Report of Operations in Ypres Sector," File #4, Entry 270, RG 120, NARA.

5. Murphy and Thomas, *The Thirtieth Division in the World War*, 70.

6. Headquarters, 105th Infantry, U.S.A., "Memorandum from Maj. Gen. John F. O'Ryan," 6 September 1918, 105th Infantry Regiment Historical Files, File #227-22.3, Entry 1241, RG 120, NARA.

7. Capt. D. T. Dunbar, Acting 53rd Brigade Adjutant, "Orders No. 3," 31 August 1918, File #227-32.13, Entry 1241, RG 120, NARA.

8. Powell, *Plumer: The Soldiers' General*, 271.

9. Maj. Gen. John F. O'Ryan, "Operations Report, 27th Division, AEF, 29 May–22 September 1918," File #5, Entry 270, RG 120, NARA.

10. Dunbar, "Orders No. 3," 31 August 1918.

11. Lt. Col. James G. Taylor, "Extract from Personal Narrative No. 979," Entry 1260, RG 120, NARA.

12. 2nd Lt. John R. Boston, "The Position of the Front Line in the Ypres Sector," 30th Division Officer Questionnaires, Entry 22, RG 117, NARA.

13. Commander, 115th Machine Gun Battalion, to Commanding Officer, 30th Division, "Report of Death of 1st Lt. Robert E. Turner," 26 July 1918; and Headquarters, 60th Infantry Brigade, to Commanding General, 30th Division, 15 August 1918, both in File #210.8, 30th Division Correspondence, Entry 1241, RG 120, NARA.

14. "Report of Death of 1st Lt. Robert E. Turner."

15. W. H. Cavannah, "Location of Front Lines of 30th Division South of Ypres, 17 August–3 September," Entry 22, RG 117, NARA.

16. Distinguished Service Cross citation for Burt T. Forbes, in Murphy and Thomas, *The Thirtieth Division in the World War*, Appendix J, 248 and 276.

17. Taylor, Taylor, "Extract from Personal Narrative No. 979," 2.

18. Entry for 3 September 1918, Pratt Diary.

19. Maj. Gen. Edward M. Lewis, "Report of Operations for the 30th Division," Entry 270, RG 120, NARA.

20. 106th Infantry, AEF, Headquarters, "Field Order #15," 31 August 1918, 106th Infantry Regiment Historical Files, File #227-32.1, Entry 1241, RG 120, NARA.

21. Commanding General, 53rd Infantry Brigade, to Commanding General, 27th Division, "Report of Operations," 10 September 1918, 53rd Infantry Brigade Historical Files, File #227-33.6, Entry 1241, RG 120, NARA.

22. Office of the Chief Signal Officer, 27th Division, to Assistant Chief of Staff, 20 December 1918, "Activities of the Signal Corps in Recent Operations," Entry 1290, RG 120, NARA.

23. Field Message, 31 August 1918, 1st Battalion, 105th Infantry Regiment, File #227-32.16, Entry 1241, RG 120, NARA.

24. Distinguished Service Cross citation for Kenneth M. McMann, in O'Ryan, *The Story of the 27th Division*, 2:910.

25. Commanding General, 53rd Infantry Brigade, to Commanding General, 27th Division, "Report on Recent Operations," 10 September 1918, 27th Division Historical Files, File #227-33.6, Entry 1241, RG 120, NARA.

26. Ibid.

27. Unfortunately, Blanding's report is the only evidence we have on Hildreth's removal, as O'Ryan ignores the entire incident in *The Story of the 27th Division*. For a through discussion of the AEF relief system, see Nenninger, "John J. Pershing and Relief for Cause in the American Expeditionary Forces."

28. Sidney G. DeKay, "Comments on Fighting of 31 August to 2 September, 1918," 21 February 1927, 27th Division Files, Entry 22, RG 117, NARA.

29. O'Ryan, "Operations Report, 27th Division, AEF."

CHAPTER 14. AFTERMATH OF BATTLE

1. The Hall of Remembrance was originally intended to be part of proposed National War Museum. Although the hall was never built, the

Imperial War Museum in London serves the same purpose and some of Sargent's paintings are among its collections.

2. Mary Crawford Volk, "Catalogue," in Kilmurray and Ormond, *John Singer Sargent*, 263–270.

3. Ibid.; and O'Ryan, *The Story of the 27th Division*, 1:239–240. The impact of the Western Front was captured in one of Sargent's best-known paintings. It shows a field full of gassed and blindfolded men that stands as a lasting symbol of the horrors of war.

4. O'Ryan, *The Story of the 27th Division*, 1:524.

5. Entry for 7 September 1918, Pratt Diary.

6. Conway and Shutford, *History of the 119th Infantry, 60th Brigade, 30th Division, U.S.A.*, 35.

7. Although O'Ryan mentions the reports in his own reports of the 27th Division operations from August to October, they were somehow lost before the division left France, and he was not able to print them in *Story of the 27th Division*. For the published 30th Division version, see Murphy and Thomas, *The Thirtieth Division in the World War*.

8. Commanding Officer, Co. E, 119th Inf., to Commanding Officer, 119th Inf., 8 September 1918, Entry 1241, RG 120, NARA; and Murphy and Thomas, *The Thirtieth Division in the World War*, 191.

9. Memorandum of 1st Lt. A. H. Cox, 8 September 1918, Entry 1241, RG 120, NARA.

10. 1st Lt. F. J. Dieterle, attached to B Company, 3rd Platoon, "Report of Recent Operations," Entry 1241, RG 120, NARA.

11. Headquarters, 30th Division, AEF, France, "Program of Training—June 17–24, 1918," 15 June 1918, 30th Division Historical Files, File #57.1, Entry 1241, RG 120, NARA.

12. Hamann, "Depreciation of American Tactics and German Defensive Organization," German File, 8th Inf. Div., File #689-33.5, Folder 1, War Diary, Entry 322, Record Group 165, NARA. Also published in United States War Department, *U.S. Army in the World War*, 4:320.

13. Ibid.

14. 41st British Division, "Order #267," 31 August 1918, File #904-32.9, Entry 318, RG 165, NARA.

15. O'Ryan, *The Story of the 27th Division*, 1:242.

16. Gow, *Letters of a Soldier*, 343.

17. Pvt. Marvin Islen, Company L, 117th Infantry Regiment, to his family, n.d., Miscellaneous World War I Manuscripts, Tennessee State Library and Archives, Nashville.

18. Cates, *Company E, 117th Infantry, 30th Division in the World War I*, 38.

19. Stewart, *The History of Company "K,"* 29.

20. Ibid., 31.

21. O'Ryan, *The Story of the 27th Division*, 1:240.

22. John K. Herr, "My Personal Experiences and Observations in Connection with the Great War," 16, unpublished manuscript, John K. Herr Papers,

United States Military Academy Archives, West Point, New York; and Harry T. Mitchell, *Company L, 107th Infantry: 54th Brigade, 27th Division, American Expeditionary Forces: 1917–1919* (New York: War Veterans Association, 1920), 26.

23. Commanding General, Headquarters, II Corps, to Asst. Chief of Staff, G-5, G.H.Q., AEF, "Training Divisions," 9 August 1918; and Adjutant General to Commanding General, II Corps, 13 August 1918, both in File #16914-3, Entry 9, RG 120, NARA.

24. Walker, *Official History of the 120th Infantry*, 18.

25. Entry for 8–15 September 1918, Willard Newton Diary, published as "Over There for Uncle Sam," *Charlotte Observer*, 3 October 1920, available at available at http://www.cmstory.org/ww1/diary.asp.

26. Entry for 7 September 1918, Pratt Diary.

27. O'Ryan, *The Story of the 27th Division*, 1:243.

28. Harris, "The Rise of Armor," 131.

29. O'Ryan, *The Story of the 27th Division*, 243.

30. The 301st was originally designated the 41st Heavy Tank Battalion but changed on 8 June to comply with the new unit designation system inaugurated by the War Department. See Wilson, *Treat 'Em Rough*, 56–57.

31. Conway and Shutford, *History of the 119th Infantry, 60th Brigade, 30th Division, U.S.A.*, 35.

32. Oldham, *Battleground Europe: The Hindenburg Line*, 16–28.

33. Joseph Hyde Pratt, "The St. Quentin-Cambrai Canal Tunnel," *Military Engineer* XIX, no. 106 (July–August 1927): 324–329.

34. Passingham, *All the Kaiser's Men*, 138.

35. Blake, *The Private Papers of Douglas Haig*, 326.

36. Ibid., 326–327.

37. Harris and Barr, *Amiens to the Armistice*, 131.

38. Ibid., 170–171; Beach, "British Intelligence and the German Army."

39. United States War Department, *Histories of Two Hundred and Fifty-One Divisions of the German Army which Participated in the War, 1914–1918*; Edmonds and Maxwell-Hyslop, *Military Operations in France and Belgium, 1918*, 5:97.

40. Montgomery, *The Story of the Fourth Army in the Battles of the Hundred Days*, 121.

41. Hughes, "The Battle for the Hindenburg Line," 44.

42. Edmonds and Maxwell-Hyslop, *Military Operations in France and Belgium*, 96; and Report of H.Q. Fourth Army, 7 September 1918, "Action to be Taken on the Captured German Defence Scheme," copy available in Haig Papers.

CHAPTER 15. PRELUDE TO THE BIG BATTLE

1. Monash, *The Australian Victories in France in 1918*, 235–236.

2. Bean, *The Official History of Australia in the War, 1914–1918*, 6:945.

3. Adam-Smith, *The Anzacs*, 418–422.

4. For an extensive discussion of the mutiny and its repercussions, see Blair, *Dinkum Diggers*, 159–164; and "Mutinies in the 1st AIF," available at http://www.diggerhistory.info/pages-asstd/mutiny.htm.

5. Maj. Gen. John F. O'Ryan to Brig. Gen. George S. Simonds, 14 February 1921, Simonds Papers. By this time, Simonds had been promoted to brigadier general and was in command of the Panama Department.

6. Jones, *The War in the Air*, 4:513.

7. Potette, *Promenades Autor de St. Quentin*, 105–109.

8. *Operations of the 2nd American Corps*, 15.

9. Ibid., 15; and Burdett, "A Critical Analysis of the Operations of the American II Corps," 11–12.

10. Maj. Gen. Edward M. Lewis, "Report of Operations for the 30th Division," 3–4, Entry 270, RG 120, NARA; and John K. Herr, "My Personal Experiences and Observations in Connection with the Great War," 21, unpublished manuscript, John K. Herr Papers, United States Military Academy Archives, West Point, New York.

11. Monash, *The Australian Victories in France in 1918*, 237–239.

12. Travers, "The Allied Victories, 1918," 287; Harris and Barr, *Amiens to the Armistice*, 211; Monash, *The Australian Victories in France in 1918*, 241; and Pedersen, *Monash as Military Commander*, 282.

13. Prior and Wilson, *Command on the Western Front*, 62; and Harris and Barr, *Amiens to the Armistice*, 211–212.

14. Terraine, *To Win a War*, 121.

15. Blake, *The Private Papers of Douglas Haig*, 326.

16. Maurice, *The Life of General Lord Rawlinson of Trent*, 237.

17. Oldham, *Battleground Europe: The Hindenburg Line*, 160.

18. Montgomery, *The Story of the Fourth Army in the Battles of the Hundred Days*, 137.

19. Thanks to Thérèse Martin for providing information on her grandmother.

20. For the Commission for Relief in Belgium, see Nash, *The Life of Herbert Hoover*, chapters 13–14.

21. Document provided by Thérèse Martin.

CHAPTER 16. THE AMERICANS MOVE FORWARD

1. Entries for 18–21 September 1918, Rawlinson Diary, National Army Museum, Chelsea, London.

2. Montgomery, *The Story of the Fourth Army in the Battles of the Hundred Days*, 140.

3. Ward, *The 74th (Yeomanry) Division in Syria and France*, 228–234; and III Corps Operation Report for 18–21 September 1918, Papers of Maj. Gen. Sir Richard Butler, Imperial War Museum, London.

4. Simkins, "The War Experience of a Typical Kitchener Division," 309.

5. Nichols, *The 18th Division in the Great War*, 410.

6. Montgomery, *The Story of the Fourth Army in the Battles of the Hundred Days*, 141–142.

7. Entries for 16–21 September 1918, Rawlinson Diary.

8. Prior and Wilson, *Command on the Western Front*, 354; and Holmes, *Tommy: The British Soldier on the Western Front, 1914–1918*, 221–222.

9. Entry for 16 September 1918, Rawlinson Diary.

10. Ibid.; and Prior and Wilson, *Command on the Western Front*, 354–355.

11. Field order, 25 September 1918, in United States War Department, *Records of the World War: Field Orders, 2nd Army Corps.*

12. *History of Company F, 118th Infantry (Hampton Guards), 30th Division*, 19.

13. Stewart, *Seventy-First New York in the World War*, 136.

14. Mitchell, *Company L, 107th Infantry*, 27.

15. Chief Surgeon, AEF, Statistical Reports, Week Ending September 26, 1918, Entry UD, RG 120, NARA.

16. For an exhaustive study of the influenza outbreak and its effect on the U.S. Army in World War I, see Byerly, "The Politics of Disease and War."

17. Special Order 263, 21 September 1918, 27th Division Historical Files, File #210.63; and Adjutant General, AEF, to Commanding General, 30th Division, "Investigation; Duties and Assignment of Officers," 12 September 1918, File #220.7, both in Entry 1241, RG 120, NARA.

18. During the latter half of 1918, a British division had no more than 7,000 officers and men and the German army had divisions between 3,000 and 4,000 strong. Prior and Wilson, *Command on the Western Front*, 316.

19. Monash, *The Australian Victories in France in 1918*, 243.

20. United States War Department, *Operations of the 2nd American Corps in the Somme Offensive*.

21. O'Ryan, *The Story of the 27th Division*, 1:246.

22. Ibid., 254.

23. Ibid.

24. Simkins, *The First World War*, 3:69–70; and Coffman, *The War to End All Wars*, 283.

25. Entry for 22 September 1918, Diary of Field Marshall Sir Douglas Haig, National Library of Scotland, Edinburgh.

26. General Lewis to Tyson, 14 September 1918, Lawrence S. Tyson Papers, East Tennessee Historical Society.

27. Ibid.

28. Dennis and Grey et al., *The Oxford Encyclopedia of Australian Military History*, 548–549.

29. Bean, *Official History of Australia in the War*, 6:947. See also Pedersen, *Monash as Military Commander*, 286–287; and Essame, *The Battle for Europe, 1918*, 183–184.

30. Monash, *The Australian Victories in France in 1918*, 245.

31. "Beaurevoir Offensive Plan," Gen. Sir John Monash Papers, 3DRL/2316, Australian War Museum, Canberra.

32. Pedersen, *Monash as Military Commander*, 285.

33. John K. Herr, "My Personal Experiences and Observations in Connection with the Great War," 20, unpublished manuscript, John K. Herr Papers, United States Military Academy Archives, West Point, New York.

34. Monash, *The Australian Victories in France in 1918*, 247–248.

35. O'Ryan, *The Story of the 27th Division*, 1:256.

36. Ibid., 256–257.

37. Ibid., 257.

38. George S. Simonds, "Confidential Stenographic Notes of a Talk by Brig. Gen. George S. Simonds on Operations of II Corps, AEF, Given at Historical Section, AWC, 14 October 1931," File #5436, Entry 310C, RG 165.

CHAPTER 17. THE AMERICANS ENTER THE LINE

1. Brig. Gen. Lawrence D. Tyson to Maj. Matthew F. Steele, 22 January 1919, Lawrence D. Tyson Papers, East Tennessee Historical Society.

2. *History of Company F, 118th Infantry (Hampton Guards), 30th Division*, 19; and Nichols, *The 18th Division in the Great War*, 407. Thanks to Dale Blair for providing the strength of British and Australian units for this period of the war.

3. "30th Division Summary of Operations," 14–15, Entry 326, RG 165, NARA.

4. 1st Lt. F. M. Mack, Intelligence Officer, 118th Inf., "Intelligence Summary No. 8," 24–25 September 1918, File #230-20.1, Entry 1241, RG 120, NARA.

5. Col. Wolfe, Commanding 118th Infantry Regiment, Field Message to 59th Infantry Brigade, 27 September 1918, File #230-32.16, Entry 1241, RG 120, NARA.

6. "Summary of Events and Information," Historical Section British File, Folder 8-10, War Diary, Entry 316, RG 165, NARA.

7. Cutlack, *The Australian Flying Corps in the Western and Eastern Theatres of War*, 329.

8. 30th Division Field Messages, 24 September 1913, File #230-32.16, Entry 1241, RG 120, NARA.

9. Maj. Gen. John F. O'Ryan, "Operations Report, 27th Division, AEF, 29 May–22 September 1918," File #5, Entry 270, RG 120, NARA.

10. Letter of E. G. Graham, 3 October 1918, 118th Infantry Regiment. Private collection of Ed Slagle; thanks to him for bringing this source to my attention.

11. United States War Department, *Operations of the 2nd American Corps in the Somme Offensive*.

12. Palazzo, *Seeking Victory on the Western Front*, 185.

13. United States War Department, *Operations of the 2nd American Corps in the Somme Offensive*, 36–39 and Appendix I. The field hospitals with 27th Division were reinforced by the 11th Australian Field Ambulance and the British Field Ambulance No. 133, as well as ten Red Cross ambulances. British Field Ambulance 134, which established a temporary

advance dressing station, assisted the 30th Division, and British Field Ambulance No. 132 cared for gas victims and the walking wounded.

14. This included the 2nd, 3rd, 4th and 5th Australian Divisional Artillery; the 6th and 12th Army Brigades; the Australian Field Artillery; and eight brigades and four batteries of the Royal Garrison Artillery. See United States War Department, *Operations of the 2d American Corps in the Somme Offensive*, 36–39.

15. Office of the Provost Marshal, Headquarters II Corps, AEF, "History of the II Army Corps Military Police Company," File #182-35, Entry 1023, RG 120, NARA.

16. "Much Interest in Military Police," *Spartanburg Herald*, 8 September 1917.

17. Monash, *The Australian Victories in France in 1918*, 250.

18. Pedersen, *Monash as Military Commander*, 287.

19. Terraine, *Ordeal of Victory*, 469–470; and O'Ryan, *The Story of the 27th Division*, 1:258. Haig referred to the attack on the 26 September, the start of the Meuse-Argonne Offensive to the east.

20. American II Corps, Field Orders, ca. September 1918, File #22.16, Entry 821, RG 120, NARA.

21. American II Corps, "Field Order #16," ca. September 1918, File #22.16, Entry 821, RG 120, NARA.

22. American Battle Monuments Commission, *30th Division Summary of Operations*, 14.

23. Maj. Gen. John F. O'Ryan, "Operations Report, 27th Division, AEF, 29 May–22 September 1918," Folder #5, Entry 270, RG 120, NARA.

24. Ibid.

25. Ibid.

26. Four tanks supported each of the three battalions.

27. Commanding General, 53rd Infantry Brigade, to Commanding General, 27th Division, "Report of Recent Operations," 7 October 1918, File #227-33.6, Entry 1241, RG 120, NARA.

28. "History of Company M, 105th Infantry," 105th Infantry Regiment Historical Files, File #11.4, Entry 1241, RG 120, NARA.

29. O'Ryan, "Operations Report, 27th Division, AEF."

30. Ibid.

31. Ibid.

32. Ibid.

33. Col. Wolfe, "Operations from 12:00–12:00 26–27 September 1918," File #230-33.1, Entry 1241, RG 120, NARA; "Summary of Operations of the 30th Division, Near Le Catelet," 24–29 September 1918, Entry 326, RG 165, NARA; and Strength Returns, 118th Infantry, September 1918, Entry 327, RG 407, NARA.

34. Headquarters, 106th Inf., to 118th Inf., 27 September 1918, File #230-32.16, Entry 1241, RG 120, NARA.

35. Headquarters, 106th Inf., to 118th Inf., 25 September 1918, File #230-32.16, Entry 1241, RG 120, NARA.

36. O'Ryan, "Operations Report, 27th Division, AEF."

37. Frederick Palmer, *Our Greatest Battle* (New York: Dodd, Meade, and Company, 1919), 240.

38. "Group of Armies Boehn," Historical Section, German File, File #810-33.5, Folder II, "Report of Operations," Entry 320, RG 165, NARA.

39. Second German Army Order, "Enemy Attacks Repulsed," 27 September 1918, File #811-33.5, Folder I, Entry 320, RG 165, NARA.

40. Brigadier General Blanding to Commander, 27th Division, "Operation Report," September–October 1918, Entry 1241, RG 120, NARA.

41. Maj. Gen. Edward M. Lewis, "Operations Report of 28 September 1918," 30th Division Historical Files, File #33.2, Entry 241, RG 120, NARA.

42. Name File of Dead and of Severely Wounded Casualties of Infantry Divisions in the A.E.F., 1918, Entry 588, RG 120, NARA; and World War I Organization Records, Office File: Casualties of the AEF by Division, Entry 11, RG 407, NARA.

43. Cutlack, *The Australian Flying Corps in the Western and Eastern Theatres of War*, 330.

44. Knapp was the general officer commanding, Royal Artillery (GOCRA) of British VII Corps. The GOCRA was in charge of artillery planning under the corps commander and assigned units (brigades) on an as-needed basis. Rawlinson directed him to assist the American II Corps in coordinating the infantry with the artillery barrage. Thanks to Sanders Marble for his insight into this subject. Letter to author, 6 July 2004.

45. MacVeagh and Brown, *The Yankee in the British Zone*, 365.

46. Pedersen, *Monash as Military Commander*, 287.

47. Montgomery, *The Story of the Fourth Army in the Battles of the Hundred Days*, 157.

48. O'Ryan, *Story of the 27th Division*, 1:300.

49. Blake, *The Private Papers of Douglas Haig*, 328.

50. Rawlinson Diary, 28 September 1918, Papers of Field Marshal Sir Henry Rawlinson, RWLN 1/11, Churchill Archive Centre, Churchill College, Cambridge. See also Maurice, *The Life of General Lord Rawlinson of Trent*, 238.

51. Entry for 28 September 1918, C. E. W. Bean Diary, 3DRL/606, Australian War Memorial, Canberra.

CHAPTER 18. MAIN OPERATION: 29 SEPTEMBER 1918

1. Entry for 27 September 1918, Pratt Diary.

2. Entry for 30 September 1918, Pratt Diary.

3. Murphy and Thomas, *The Thirtieth Division in the World War*, 100.

4. Berry, *Make the Kaiser Dance*, 216. Pershing strictly forbade his troops from drinking rum and specifically noted this in the training agreement of 12 February 1918. Also, Shrader, "'Maconochie's Stew,'" 130n87.

5. Maze, *A Frenchman in Khaki*, 347.

6. Edward Graham Melvin, Sr., "One Man's War: World War I from the Memories of Tennessee Farm Boy," unpublished manuscript, United States Army Military History Institute, Carlisle, Pennsylvania.

7. Toole, *From Auburn's Own.* Toole was killed eighteen days later at St. Souplet.

8. Murphy and Thomas, *The Thirtieth Division in the World War,* 98.

9. Maj. Gen. Edward M. Lewis, "Report of Operations for the 30th Division," Entry 270, RG 120, NARA.

10. Weather forecast for 29 September 1918, File #321.91, 30th Division Historical Files, Entry 1241, RG 120, NARA.

11. Commanding General, 27th Division, to Chief of Staff, U.S. Army [O'Ryan], "Report of Observations, Battlefields, 27th Division," 16 August 1920, MID #242-30, Entry 65, RG 165, NARA. O'Ryan was asked to submit this report by the Chief of Staff, Maj. Gen. Peyton March.

12. Maj. R. I. Sasse, Tank Corps, "Report: 2nd Tank Brigade, 27 September–1 October, 1918," Folder 397, Entry 267, RG 120, NARA.

13. Montgomery, *The Story of the Fourth Army in the Battles of the Hundred Days,* 163.

14. Toole, *From Auburn's Own,* 23. Next to artillery shelling, no other killing mechanism is more associated with the First World War than the machine gun. It "became a decisive battlefield weapon," according to John Ellis in *The Social History of the Machine Gun* (London: Pimlico, 1976), "capable of mowing down troops by the hundreds," 167.

15. Maj. Gen. John F. O'Ryan, "Operations Report, 27th Division, AEF, 29 May–22 September 1918," Folder #5, Entry 270, RG 120, NARA.

16. Berry, *Make the Kaiser Dance,* 217.

17. Order No. 1038, 29 September 1918, Historical Section, German File, Second Army, File #811-33.5, Folder I, Entry 320, RG 165, NARA.

18. Peter S. Sadler, *The Paladin: A Life of Major-General Sir John Gellibrand* (Victoria: Oxford University Press, 2000), 172.

19. O'Ryan, "Operations Report, 27th Division, AEF."

20. Franki and Slatyer, *Mad Harry: Australia's Most Decorated Soldier,* 142–144. For his heroism in World War I, Murray was awarded six decorations; among them was the Victoria Cross.

21. O'Ryan, "Operations Report, 27th Division, AEF."

22. Toole, *From Auburn's Own,* 21.

23. James M. Andrews, "Operations," 25–29 September 1918, 27th Division, 105th Infantry Regiment, Entry 21, RG 117, NARA.

24. "3rd Division Messages, 29 September 1918, 2:20 P.M.," Maj. Gen. Sir John Gellibrand Papers, 3DRL 1473/103, AWM.

25. "3rd Division Messages, 29 September 1918, 4:30 P.M.," Papers of Sir John Gellibrand, 3DRL 1473/103, AWM.

26. O'Ryan, "Operations Report, 27th Division, AEF."

27. Commanding General, 27th Division, to Commanding Generals, 53rd and 54th Infantry Brigades, "Defensive Line of Support," 29 September 1918, 5 PM Entry 1241, RG 120, NARA.

28. O'Ryan, "Operations Report, 27th Division, AEF."

29. Harris, *Duty, Honor, Privilege*, 294.

30. Burial File for Cpl. Alexander A. Kim, Entry 1942, RG 92, NARA; and Commanding Officer, Company I, 107th Infantry, to Roger H. Williams, Correspondence Files of the 107th Infantry Regiment, Entry 2133, RG 391, NARA.

31. John Bowman to his family, 2 October 1918, John Bowman Letters, United States Army Military History Institute, Carlisle Barracks, Pennsylvania.

32. Lt. Col. Murray, Commander, 4th Australian Machine Gun Battalion, to Commanding General, 27th Division, 30 September 1918, Simonds Papers.

33. Maj. Gen. John F. O'Ryan to G-3, AEF, "Confidential Report," 19 December 1918, Entry 267, RG 120, NARA.

34. "Walker from 106th Survives German Prison Camps, and Diet of Raw Turnips," in Newspaper Clipping Scrapbook, New York National Guard Papers, New York State Military Museum, Saratoga Springs.

35. Pfc. Charles L. Campbell, 102nd Military Police, "History of the 102nd Military Police," available at http://www.oryansroughnecks.org/campbell.html.

CHAPTER 19. ATTACK BY 30TH DIVISION

1. Murphy and Thomas, *The Thirtieth Division in the World War*, 102.

2. Maj. Gen. Edward M. Lewis, "Report of Operations for the 30th Division," Entry 270, RG 120, NARA.

3. Melvin, "One Man's War: World War I from the Memories of Tennessee Farm Boy," 3, unpublished manuscript, United States Army Military History Institute, Carlisle, Pennsylvania.

4. Lewis, "Report of Operations for the 30th Division."

5. 30th Division, Field Messages, October 1918, File #230-32.16, Entry 1241, RG 120, NARA.

6. Ibid.

7. Harris and Barr, *Amiens to the Armistice*, 223–224.

8. "Report of Operations," 29 September 1918, Papers of Brig. Gen. H. A. Goodard, 9th Infantry Brigade, AIF, 3DRL/2379, AWM.

9. Murphy and Thomas, *The Thirtieth Division in the World War*, 104.

10. Ibid.

11. Maj. Gen. Edward M. Lewis, 30th Division, to Commanding General, 60th Brigade (Brig. Gen. Lawrence D. Tyson) and Commanding General, 59th Brigade (Brig. Gen. Samson L. Faison), "Reorganization of 30th Division," 30 September 1918, File #230-32, 16 Field Messages, 30th Division Historical Files, Entry 1241, RG 120, NARA.

12. Entry for 30 September 1918, Diaries of Lt. Gen. Sir Iven MacKay, 3DRL/6850/6, Australian War Museum, Canberra.

13. Lewis, "Report of Operations for the 30th Division."

14. Letter of Pvt. Edgar G. Blanchard, 5 October 1918, Company G, 120th Infantry Regiment, available at "Wildcats Never Quit: North Carolina in World War One," online at http://www.ah.dcr.state.nc.us/archives/wwi/.

15. Major Hobbs to his family, 26 October 1918. Thanks to Henry Mintz for locating this unarchived letter and making a copy.

16. Maj. Gen. Edward M. Lewis, "Operations Report of 30 September 1918," 30th Division Historical Files, File #33.2, Entry 1241, RG 120, NARA.

CHAPTER 20. ASSESSING THE BATTLE PERFORMANCE OF THE AMERICANS

1. For biographical information on Gibbs, see Farrar, *News from the Front.*

2. Brown, *Robert Bacon: Life and Letters*, 402–403.

3. Entry for 29–30 September 1918, Charles H. Brent Diary, Papers of Charles Henry Brent, 1860–1991, Library of Congress, Washington, D.C. The Episcopal missionary bishop's acquaintance with Pershing went back to 1913, when the latter was governor of the Moro Province in the Philippines. For his loyalty, Pershing had Bishop Brent commissioned a major in the National Army. Pershing, *My Experiences in the Great War*, 2:129, 132.

4. Entry for 29 September 1918, Rawlinson Diary, National Army Museum, Chelsea, London.

5. Maurice, *The Life of General Lord Rawlinson of Trent*, 239.

6. Monash, *The Australian Victories in France in 1918*, 248–249.

7. Ibid.

8. Dennis, Grey, et al, *The Oxford Companion to Australian Military History*, 406.

9. Ibid.

10. C. E. W. Bean, "Relations of the A.I.F. with the Americans in France, 1918," 22 August 1940, Papers of C. E. W. Bean, 3DRL/606, AWM. Thanks to Peter Pedersen for telling me about this document.

11. Holmes, *The Western Front*, 210.

12. Brig. Gen. Brand, 4th Australian Brigade, 4th Australian Division, to General O'Ryan, 27th American Division, "Few Notes on Eight Days' Tour of Duty with 27th American Division," Operations Files, 1914–18, AWM 26, Australian War Museum, Canberra.

13. O'Ryan, *The Story of the 27th Division*, 1:313.

14. Ibid.

15. John F. O'Ryan to Maj. X. H. Price, 6 January 1918, Entry 28, RG 117, NARA.

16. 1st Lt. W. O. Pasfield, "Notes on Report of 1st Lt. W. O. Pasfield, 11th Australian Field Artillery Brigade, in Regard to the Operations of the 27th Division, 29 September 1918," copy among Simonds Papers.

17. "Enemy Line of Defense," II Corps Historical Files, File #22.21, Entry 1023, RG 120, NARA.

18. Maj. Gen. C. E. D. Budworth, "Fourth Army Artillery in the Attack on the Hindenburg Line, September 29, 1918," 23 October 1918, Files of the British Army, Entry 32, RG 165, NARA.

19. Schwensen, *The History of the 102nd M. P.*, 56.

20. Entry for 5 October 1918, Rawlinson Diary, National Army Museum, Chelsea, London.

21. "History of the AEF Signal Corps," 218–239, Entry 1521, RG 120, NARA.

22. Ibid.

23. "Engineer Traps and Mines," File #182-42.21, Entry 1023, RG 120, NARA.

24. 1st Lt. Carelton Reynell, U.S. Tank Corps, H.O. 2nd Tank Brigade, "2nd Tank Brigade, American E.F., Report on Operations, 27 September to 1 October 1918," 5 October 1918, 13, Papers of George S. Patton, 1807–1938, Library of Congress, Washington, D.C.

25. "History of the AEF Signal Corps," 204–205.

26. Fletcher, ed., *Tanks and Trenches*, 183.

27. W. F. L. Hartigan, "Observations of the Battlefield of September 29th of Troops of 30th Division," File #230-33.9, RG 120, NARA; and Fletcher, *Tanks and Trenches*, 95–103.

28. Nichols, *The 18th Division in the Great War*, 427.

29. Commanding General, II Corps, Report to the Assistant Chief of Staff, G-3, G.H.Q.A.E.F., 18 December 1918, Entry 270, RG 120, NARA.

CHAPTER 21. BACK TO THE FRONT

1. On 30 September, the 27th Division reported its strength at 18,055, while the 30th Division reported 23,380. See American Battle Monuments Commission, *27th Division Summary of Operations in the World War*, 38; and American Battle Monuments Commission, *30th Division Summary of Operations in the World War*, 38.

2. Harris and Barr, *Amiens to the Armistice*, 232–235; and Montgomery, *The Story of the Fourth Army in the Battles of the Hundred Days*, 173–174.

3. Montgomery, *The Story of the Fourth Army in the Battles of the Hundred Days*, 184–186.

4. Butler, *Official History of the Australian Medical Services*, iii. The exact casualty figures for Montbrehain are unavailable.

5. Pedersen, *Monash as Military Commander*, 291.

6. Ibid., 291–292.

7. Montgomery, *The Story of the Fourth Army in the Battles of the Hundred Days*, 189–190.

8. Andrews, *The Story of a Machine Gun Company*, 34.

9. "Rations," File #430.2, Entry 1241, RG 120, NARA.

10. United States War Department, *Operations of the 2d American Corps in the Somme Offensive*, 22; and "Operations of II Corps," File #182-33.3, Entry 1241, RG 120, NARA.

11. II Corps to General Headquarters, AEF, 4 October 1918, Telegram, File #182.10.2, Entry 1023, RG 120, NARA.

12. Murphy and Thomas, *The Thirtieth Division in the World War*, 108.

13. Report of Operations, Company L, 117th Infantry Regiment, 30th Division Historical Files, File #230-33.2, Entry 1241, RG 120, NARA.

14. Entry for 10 October 1918, Pratt Diary.

15. Ibid.

16. G-1, American II Corps, to Commanding General, 30th Division, AEF, "Danger of Rumors," 7 October 1918, File #182-10.2, RG 120, NARA.

17. American Battle Monuments Commission, *American Armies and Battlefields in Europe*, 393.

18. Conway and Shutford, *History of the 119th Infantry, 60th Brigade, 30th Division, U.S.A.*, 50.

19. The problems associated with relaying the attack order of 9 October in the 59th Brigade sector became a discussion point after the war for officers at the U.S. Army Infantry School when it was published in *Infantry in Battle*. Officers concluded that the commander of the 1st Battalion made the correct decision but that both battalions were essentially lucky that they had the right amount of troops in the right place at the right time. Infantry, Journal, *Infantry in Battle*, 131–133.

20. Ibid., 51.

21. Brown, *Robert Bacon: Life and Letters*, 405.

22. Edmonds and Maxwell-Hyslop, *Military Operations in France and Belgium, 1918* (1947), 5: 238.

23. Montgomery, *The Story of the Fourth Army in the Battles of the Hundred Days*, 231.

CHAPTER 22. A CHANGE IN THE LINE

1. American Battle Monuments Commission, *30th Division Summary of Operations*, 35.

2. Clarke, *Over There with O'Ryan's Roughnecks*, 92.

3. Field Order #56, 8 October 1918, File #182-33.3, Entry 1241, RG 120, NARA.

4. O'Ryan, *The Story of the 27th Division*, 1:347.

5. Montgomery, *The Story of the Fourth Army in the Battles of the Hundred Days*, 204.

6. Ibid., 347–348.

7. 27th Division, AEF, Field Orders No. 63 (extract), 15 October 1918, in United States War Department, *U. S. Army in the World War*, 7:584–587; O'Ryan, "Operations Report, 27th Division AEF, 29 May–22 September 1918," File #5, Entry 270, RG 120, NARA.50–52; American Battle Monuments Commission, *27th Division Summary of Operations in the World War*, 30–31; Headquarters 106th Infantry, AEF, Field Orders No. 28, 16 October 1918; Headquarters, 107th Infantry, AEF, Field Orders No. 37, 16 October 1918; Headquarters, 108th Infantry, AEF, Field Orders No.49, 16 October 1918, all in RG 120, Entry 1241, NARA. I also wish to thank Mark Whisler, author of "'Der Tommy Kommt': British Expeditionary Force Campaign Orchestration and Fourth Army Operational Executions at the Battle of the Selle

River, October 1918: A Case Study in 1918 British Offensive Operations against the Imperial German Army." (M.A. thesis, United States Marine Corps Command and Staff College, 2001). This is the definitive study of the Selle River Operation, and Whisler's advice on this chapter was invaluable.

8. Battle Instructions, Series D, 30th Division, 15 October 1918, 30th Division Historical Files, Entry 1241, RG 120, NARA.

9. Maj. Ralph I. Sasse, "Report of Operations, 301st Tank Battalion, 27 September–1 October 1918," Folder 112, RG120, NARA. See also Wilson, *Treat 'Em Rough*, 205.

10. G-3, American II Corps, AEF, 16 October 1918, "Operations Instructions Series B, No. 7 Aircraft," in United States War Department, *U. S. Army in the World War*, 7:612.

11. Ibid.

12. The company lost ten dead and forty-five wounded in the shelling. Also, see O'Ryan quoted in in Sutliffe, *Seventy-First New York in the World War*, 365.

13. O'Ryan, *The Story of the 27th Division*, 1:370–371.

14. Headquarters 107th Infantry, Field Orders No. 37, 16 October 1918, File #227-32-1, 27th Division Historical Files, Entry 1241, RG 120, NARA.

15. "Effective Fighting Strength of Machine-Gun Company, 107th Infantry," File #227-10-5, 27th Division Historical Files, Entry 1241, RG 120, NARA. When the unit arrived in France at the end of May 1918, it reported strength of five officers and 158 men.

16. Jacobson, *History of the 107th Infantry U.S.A.*, 427; and Burial File for Lt. Kenneth Gow, Entry 1941, RG 92, NARA.

17. Gow, *Letters of a Soldier*, entry for 21 September 1918, 343-344.

18. Oakleaf, *Notes on the Operations of the 108th Infantry Overseas*, 18; O'Ryan, "27th Division Operations Report," 53–54; American Battle Monuments Commission, *27th Division Summary of Operations*, 32; O'Ryan, *The Story of the 27th Division*, 1:8; Headquarters, 3rd Battalion, 108th Infantry AEF, 1 November 1918, Subject: Report on Operations from 11–20 October, 108th Infantry Operation Reports, Entry 1241, RG 120, NARA.

19. Dunn, *The War the Infantry Knew*, 558.

20. O'Ryan quoted in Sutliffe, *Seventy-First New York in the World War*, 372.

21. O'Ryan to the U.S. Army Chief of Staff, 16 August 1920, MID File #224, Entry 65, RG 165, NARA.

22. John K. Herr, "My Personal Experiences and Observations in Connection with the Great War," unpublished manuscript, John K. Herr Papers, United States Military Academy Library, West Point, New York.

23. Edmonds and Maxwell-Hyslop, *Military Operations in France and Belgium, 1918*, 5:300–303.

24. Murphy and Thomas, *The Thirtieth Division in the World War*, 112.

25. Judson W. Dennis to his brother, 4 October 1918, available at http://pastvoices.com/usa/judletters.shtml; and Burial File for Judson W. Dennis, Entry 1941, RG 92, NARA.

26. Hedgecock and Waite, *Images of London: Haringy at War*, 38.
27. Entry for 10 October 10, Pratt Diary.
28. Entry for 18 October 1918, ibid.

CHAPTER 23. REFLECTIONS ON THE SELLE OPERATION

1. Whisler, "'De Tommy Kommt,'" 40.
2. Harrison, "Famous Charges Told of the U.S. Tank Brigade," 15.
3. United States War Department, *Operations of the 2d American Corps in the Somme Offensive*, 38.
4. Harris and Barr, *Amiens to the Armistice*, 262.
5. Pershing, *My Experiences in the Great War*, 1:352–353.
6. Acting Inspector General, II Corps, to Inspector General, G.H.Q. AEF, "Notes on Training and Discipline," 19 October 1918, II Corps Historical Files, File #326/24, Entry 586, RG 120, NARA.
7. Entry for 2 November 1918, Sgt.-Maj. Albert Breunig Diary, 30th Division Veterans Questionnaires, United States Military History Institute, Carlisle Barracks, Pennsylvania.
8. Gen. John J. Pershing to Maj. Gen. John F. O'Ryan, Commanding 27th Division, AEF, 24 October 1918, Pershing Papers, LOC.
9. Ibid.
10. Brig. Gen. W. J. Dugan, C.M.G., D.S.O., "Notes on Visit to II American Corps," 10 November 1918, Gen. Sir Ivor Maxse Papers, Imperial War Museum, London.
11. Ibid.
12. O'Ryan, *The Story of the 27th Division*, 1:397.
13. Clarke, *Over There with O'Ryan's Roughnecks*, 117.
14. MacVeagh and Brown, *The Yankee in the British Zone*, 343.

CHAPTER 24. BROTHERS IN ARMS

1. Hamburger, *Learning Lessons in the American Expeditionary Forces*, 15.
2. Ibid., 14.
3. Ibid., 26.
4. Sir Douglas Haig to the 27th Division, 12 February 1919, British Files, Entry 315, RG 165, NARA.
5. Pershing, *My Experiences in the Great War*, 2:114.
6. Lloyd C. Griscom, "Liaison," lecture presented to the Army War College in 1940, copy among War Plans Course No. 5, 1939–1940, Entry 299, RG 165, NARA.
7. Jacob took command of British II Corps in May 1916 and remained there throughout the war. His command style was noted for thorough planning and preparation, and a willingness to stand up to his superiors. See Bourne, *Who's Who in World War One*, 143.
8. Entry for 22 November 1918, Pershing Diary, Pershing Papers, LOC.

9. Lt. Col. Calvin C. Goddard, "Relations between the American Expeditionary Forces and the British Expeditionary Force, 1917–1920," June 1942, Historical Section Files, Army War College, Entry 310, RG 165, NARA.

10. Assistant Chief of Staff, G-3, to Commanding Generals (27th and 30th Divisions), "Report," 10 December 1918, Entry 267, RG 120, NARA. Fox Conner directed "by order from Pershing," that each general submit "a detailed report of each operation with your division engaged in while serving as a unit of the British" (ibid.)"

11. Ibid.

12. Maj. Gen. John F. O'Ryan to G-3, AEF, "Confidential Report," 19 December 1918, Entry 267, RG 120, NARA.

13. Brig. Gen. Samson L. Faison to Maj. Gen. E. M. Lewis, "Notes on Confidential Report," 14 December 1918, Entry 267, RG 120, NARA.

14. Brig. Gen. Lawrence D. Tyson to Mathew Steele, 22 January 1919, Lawrence D. Tyson Papers, East Tennessee Historical Society.

15. "Report to AEF, G-3 from Commander, American II Corps," 19 December 1918, Entry 270, RG 120, NARA.

16. George S. Simonds, "Confidential Stenographic Notes of a Talk by Brig. Gen. George S. Simonds on Operations of II Corps, AEF, Given at Historical Section, AWC, 14 October 1931," File #5436, Entry 310C, RG 165.

17. Maj. George S. Simonds to the Acting Chief of Staff, G-2, G.H.Q., AEF, "Estimate of General Officers of the English Army,"16 September 1919, File #1017, Entry 268, RG 120, NARA.

18. Ibid.

19. Shrader, "'Maconochie's Stew,'" 121; and Walton, "Looked after by John Bull," 26.

20. Lt. Col. Calvin C. Goddard, "Relations between the American Expeditionary Forces and the British Expeditionary Force, 1917–1920," June 1942, Historical Section Files, Army War College, Entry 310, RG 165, NARA.

21. Ibid.

CHAPTER 25. BORROWED SOLDIERS

1. George W. Read, "My Personal Experience in the World War," 3, unpublished monograph, Simonds Papers.

2. For a larger study of this issue, see Grotelueschen, "The AEF Way of War."

3. Pugsley, The ANZAC Experience, 276–277.

EPILOGUE

1. New York Times, 5 February 1928, 38.

2. Robin Prior and Trevor Wilson, "Haig, Douglas, first Earl Haig (1861–1928), army officer" in Oxford Dictionary of National Biography (Oxford: Oxford University Press, 2004–2005).

3. Asheville Times, 28 September 1928, 77.

4. Thanks to Lisa Budreau for sharing the information about this pilgrimage. For more information, see Budreau, "The Politics of American Commemoration in the Aftermath of the First World War."

5. The American Battle Monuments Commission, *Somme American Cemetery and Memorial*.

6. Thanks to historian Ben Byrnes for providing me access to the various papers relating to Sarah Harris and the death of Ezra Harris.

7. Thanks to Thérèse Martin for her research into the municipal archives of Bony and the surrounding villages.

APPENDIX C. ORDER OF BATTLE, ALLIED ARMY, 29 SEPTEMBER 1918

1. See "Fourth Army Order of Battle at Zero" for a more exhaustive listing of all units designated for the attack on 29 September 1918. Reproduced in United States War Department, *U.S. Army in the World War*, 7:95.

APPENDIX E. COMPARATIVE STRENGTH OF AMERICAN AND BRITISH DIVISIONS, 1918

1. American Battle Monuments Commission, *American Armies and Battlefields in Europe*, 529–530.

2. Travers, *How the War Was Won*, 183.

BIBLIOGRAPHY

ARCHIVES AND MANUSCRIPT COLLECTIONS

Australian War Memorial, Canberra
    Operations Files, 1914–1918 War, AWM26
    Private Papers Collection, AWM30
    Official History of the AIF, 1914–1918 War, AWM44
    Confidential and Security Classified Records Originally Maintained by
        the Australian War Memorial, AWM51
    Papers of Field Marshal Sir William Birdwood, 3DRL/3376
    Papers of C. E. W. Bean, 3DRL/606
    Papers of Brig. Gen. H. E. Elliot, 3DRL/3297
    Papers of Maj. Gen. Sir John Gellibrand, 3DRL 1473/103
    Papers of Gen. Sir John Monash, 3DRL/2316

Bodleian Library, Oxford University
    Library Collections

Bony Municipal Archives
    Library Collections

Churchill Archive Centre, Churchill College, Cambridge
    Papers of Gen. Sir Charles Bonham-Carter
    Papers of Field Marshal Sir Henry Rawlinson

Columbia University, New York, New York
    John F. O'Ryan, Oral History Interview, 1957

East Carolina University, Greensboro, North Carolina
    World War I Manuscript Collection

East Tennessee History Museum, Knoxville, Tennessee
    Lawrence D. Tyson Papers

Houghton Library, Harvard University, Cambridge
    Oswald Garrison Villard Papers

Imperial War Museum, London
    Department of Documents
        Letters of 2nd Lt. H. C. Blagrove
        Papers of Maj. Gen. Sir Richard Butler
        Letters of Col. Sir Geoffrey Christine-Miller
        Memoir of Gen. Sir Philip Christison, IWM 82/15/1
        Diary of Robert Cude
        Letters of Maj. C. H. Dudley Ward
        Letters of Capt. K. Earle
        Fourth Army Papers
        Letters of Capt. A. Gibbs
        Letters of Maj. Gen. J. M. Gower
        Papers of Gen. Sir Ivor Maxse
        Misc 2073 Letters
        Diary of General Philip
        Diary of Capt. L. G. Pinnell, IWM 83/17/1
    Department of Sound Archives
        Experiences of Maj. Gen. J. M. L. Grover

Library of Congress, Washington, D.C.
    Manuscript Division
        Papers of Newton Diehl Baker, circa 1898–1962
        Papers of Charles Henry Brent, 1860–1991
        Papers of James G. Harbord, 1886–1938
        Papers of George S. Patton, 1807–1979
        Papers of John J. Pershing, 1882–1971
        Papers of George Sherwin Simonds, 1918–1932
    Newspaper and Periodical Research Room
        Albany Evening Journal (New York)
        Asheville Times (North Carolina)
        Brooklyn Daily Eagle (New York)
        Charleston Courier (South Carolina)
        Nashville Tennessean
        New York Times

Knoxville News-Sentinel (Tennessee)
Raleigh News and Observer (North Carolina)
Spartanburg Herald-Journal (South Carolina)
Post-Standard (Syracuse, New York)

The Liddell Hart Centre for Military Archives, King's College London
    Papers of Field Marshal Sir Archibald Montgomery-Massingberd

National Archives of New Zealand, Wellington
    WA 22-6/3

National Archives and Records Administration, Washington, D.C., and College
        Park, Maryland
    Records of the Office of the Quartermaster General, Record Group 92
    Records of the Adjutant General's Office, 1780s–1917, RG 94
    Records of the Surgeon General's Office, RG 112
    Records of the American Battle Monuments Commission, Record Group
        117
    Records of the American Expeditionary Forces (World War I), Record
        Group 120
    Records of the Office of the Chief of Ordnance, Record Group 156
    Records of the War Department General and Special Staffs, Record Group
        165
    National Archives Gift Collection, Record Group 200
    U.S. Army Mobile Commands, RG 391.
    Records of the Adjutant General's Office, Record Group 407

The National Archives, Public Record Office, Kew, England
    Documents relating to British Air Power, AIR 1
    War Diaries and Narratives of Operations, WO 95
    Western Front Operations, WO 158

The National Army Museum, Chelsea, London
    General Sir Henry Rawlinson Papers

National Library of Scotland, Edinburgh
    Field Marshal Sir Douglas Haig Diaries and Papers

New York State Military Museum, Saratoga
    New York National Guard Papers

North Carolina Division of Archives and History, Raleigh
    World War I Papers, Private Collections

Prince's Consort Library, Aldershot
    Library Collection

Royal Military Academy, Sandhurst
    Library Collections

South Carolina Department of Archives and History, Columbia
    Military Department, Record Group 192000

Tennessee State Library and Archives, Nashville
    Theodore Oswald Avery Papers
    Robert Edward Barclay Papers
    Ray Wallace Billington Papers
    Boyd Family Papers
    Ellsworth Brown Papers
    John A. Catlett Papers
    James Franklin Corn Papers
    Francis S. Harmon Papers
    David F. McGinnis Papers
    Men in the Great War World War, 1914–1918 from Hawkins County,
        Tennessee
    Governor Thomas Rye Papers
    Tipton County World War I Letters
    Miscellaneous World War I Manuscripts

United States Army Military History Institute, Carlisle Barracks, Pennsylvania
    Broadus Bailey Papers
    John Bowman Letters
    Timberman-Fiske Family Papers
    American II Corps Soldiers Questionnaires
    27th Division Soldiers Questionnaires
    30th Division Soldiers Questionnaires

University of North Carolina, Southern History Collection, Chapel Hill
    Lawrence D. Tyson Papers
    Joseph Hyde Pratt Papers

PRIMARY SOURCES

Andrews, Walter G. *The Story of a Machine Gun Company, 1918–1919.*
    Buffalo, N.Y.: Matthews-Northrup Works, 1924.
Blake, Robert, ed. *The Private Papers of Douglas Haig, 1914–1919.* London:
    Eyre & Spottiswoode, 1952.
Butler, A. G. *Official History of the Australian Army Medical Services.*
    Canberra: Australian War Memorial, 1943.
Bean, C. E. W. *The Official History of Australia in the War, 1914–1918.*
    Vol. 6, *The Australian Imperil Force in France during the Allied
    Offensive, 1918.* Sydney: Angus and Robertson, 1942.

Bond, Brian, and Simon Robbins, eds. *Staff Officer: The Diaries of Walter Guinness (First Lord Moyne), 1914–1918.* London: Leo Cooper, 1987.

Center of Military History. *Order of Battle of the United States Land Forces in the World War, 1917–1919.* 5 Parts in 3 Volumes. Washington, D.C.: Government Printing Office, 1931–1949.

Conway, Coleman Berkley, and George A. Shutford. *History of the 119th Infantry, 60th Brigade, 30th Division, U.S.A.: Operations in Belgium and France, 1917–1919.* [Wilmington, N.C.]: Wilmington Chamber of Commerce, 1920.

Dunn, Captain J. C. *The War the Infantry Knew, 1914–1919.* London: Abacus, 2001.

Edmonds, Brigadier General James E. *Military Operations: Belgium and France, 1918.* Vols. 4–6. London: His Majesty's Stationery Office, 1947.

Eggers, John H. *The 27th Division: The Story of Its Sacrifices and Achievements.* New York: J. H. Eggers, 1919.

Ferrell, Robert H., ed. *A Soldier in World War I: The Diary of Elmer H. Sherwood.* Indianapolis: Indiana Historical Society, 2004.

"From a National Guardsman." *Outlook* 113 (August 2, 1916): 773.

Gow, Kenneth. *Letters of a Soldier.* New York: Herbert B. Cover, 1920.

Harrison, Maj. Roger B. "Famous Charges Told of the U.S. Tank Brigade." *The Army* 1, no. 1 (1919).

History of Company F, 118th Infantry (Hampton Guards), 30th Division: Belgium, Somme Offensive, Bellicourt, Montbrehain, Brancourt, and St. Martin's Reviere. Spartanburg, S.C.: Band & White Printers, 1919.

Hutchinson, Lt. Col. Graham Seton. *The Thirty-Third Division in France and Flanders, 1915–1919.* London: Waterlow & Sons Limited, 1921.

Infantry Journal. *Infantry in Battle.* Washington, D.C.: The Infantry Journal, 1939.

Jones, H. A. *Statistics of the Military Effort of the British Empire during the Great War.* London: War Office, 1922.

——. *The War in the Air.* Vol. 6. Oxford: Clarendon Press, 1937.

——. *The War in the Air: Appendices.* Oxford: Clarendon Press, 1937.

Link, Arthur, ed. *The Papers of Woodrow Wilson.* Vol. 44. Princeton, N.J.: Princeton University Press, 1983.

Ludendorff, General Erich von. *My War Memories, 1914–1918.* London: Hutchinson, 1919.

Members of the Battalion. *History and Memoirs of the 33rd Battalion Machine Gun Corps and of the 19th, 98th, 100th, and 248th M.G. Companies.* London: Waterlow Brothers & Layton, 1919.

Nichols, Capt. G. H. F. *The 18th Division in the Great War.* London: William Blackwood and Sons, 1922.

Nicholson, Colonel G. W. L. *Official History of the Canadian Army in the First World War: Canadian Expeditionary Force, 1914–1919.* Ottawa: Queen's Printer and Controller of Stationery, 1962.

Pershing, John J. *My Experiences in the Great War.* 2 vols. New York: Frederick A. Stokes, 1931.

Potette, C. *Promenades Autor de St. Quentin*. St. Quentin: Privately Published, 1899.

Pratt, Joseph Hyde. "The St. Quentin-Cambrai Canal Tunnel." *Military Engineer* XIX, no. 106 (July–August 1927): 324–329.

Sheffield, Gary, and John Bourne, eds. *Douglas Haig: War Diaries and Letters, 1914–1918*. London: Weidenfeld and Nicholson, 2005.

Stewart, Worth P. *The History of Company "K" 117th Infantry in the Great War: With Anecdotes by Other Members of the Company*. N.p.: n.p., 1919.

Toole, Corp. James. *From Auburn's Own: In Their Own Words*. Memoirs compiled by Raymond E. Keefe, Jr. N.p.: Raymond E. Keefe, Jr., 2002.

United States Military Academy. *Sixty-Sixth Annual Report of the Association of Graduates of the United States Military Academy at West Point, New York: June 11, 1935*. Newburgh, N.Y.: Moore Printing Company, 1935.

United States Senate. *Reorganization of the Army: Hearings before the United States Senate Committee on Military Affairs, First Session, and Sixty-Sixth Congress, Second Session*. Washington, D.C.: U.S. Government Printing Office, 1919.

United States War Department. *British Tactical Notes*. Washington, D.C.: Government Printing Office, 1918.

———. *Histories of Two Hundred and Fifty-One Divisions of the German Army which Participated in the Great War, 1914–1918*. Washington, D.C.: Government Printing Office, 1919.

———. *The Medical Department of the United States Army in the World War*. Vol. 8, *Field Operations*. Washington, D.C.: Government Printing Office, 1925.

———. *Operations of the 2nd American Corps in the Somme Offensive: 8 August to November 11, 1918*. Monograph No. 10. Washington, D.C.: Historical Branch, War Plans Division, 1920.

———. *Records of the World War: Field Orders, 2nd Army Corps*. Washington, D.C.: Government Printing Office, 1921.

———. *A Survey of German Tactics*. Washington, D.C.: War Department, Historical Section, 1918.

———. *U.S. Army in the World War*. 19 vols. Washington, D.C.: Government Printing Office, 1947.

von Hindenburg, Field Marshal Paul. *Out of My Life*. 2 vols. London: Cassell, 1920.

Walker, John Otey. *Official History of the 120th Infantry "3rd North Carolina" 30th Division from August 5, 1917, to April 17, 1919, Canal Sector, Ypres-Lys Offensive, Somme Offensive*. Lynchburg, Tenn.: J. P. Bell Company, 1919.

Walton, Col. E. S. "Looked after by John Bull." *Quartermaster Review* 1, no. 2 (September–October 1921).

War Office. *The Quarterly Army List for the Quarter Ending 30th June 1919*. London: His Majesty's Stationery Office, 1919.

War Veterans' Association. *History of Company "E," 107th Infantry, 54th Brigade 27th Division, U.S.A. (National Guard: New York), 1917–1919.* New York: Veteran's Association, 1920.

Whitehorne, Joseph W. A. *The Inspector General of the United States Army: 1903–1939.* Washington, D.C.: United States Army Office of the Inspector General and Center of Military History, 1998.

Wise, Sydney F. *Canadian Airmen and the First World War: The Official History of the Royal Canadian Air Force.* Vol. 1. Toronto: University of Toronto Press, 1980.

SECONDARY SOURCES

A Company. *History of the 301st Tank Battalion.* Philadelphia: E. G. Wright Company, 1919.

Adam, R. J. Q. *The Great War, 1914–1918: Essays on the Military, Political, and Social History of the First World War.* College Station: Texas A&M University Press, 1990.

Adam-Smith, Patsy. *The Anzacs.* Melbourne: Sphere Books, 1981.

American Battle Monuments Commission. *American Armies and Battlefields in Europe.* Washington, D.C.: American Battle Monuments Commission, 1938.

———. *Somme American Battlefield and Memorial.* Washington, D.C.: American Battle Monuments Commission, n.d.

———. *30th Division Summary of Operations in the World War.* Washington, D.C.: American Battle Monuments Commission, 1944.

———. *27th Division Summary of Operations in the World War.* Washington, D.C.: American Battle Monuments Commission, 1944.

Andrews, Eric M. *The ANZAC Illusion.* Cambridge: Cambridge University Press, 1993.

Arthur, Max. *Forgotten Voices of the Great War: A New History of World War I in the Words of the Men and Women Who Were There.* London: Elbury Press, 2003.

Ashworth, Tony. *Trench Warfare, 1914–1918: The Live and Let Live System.* London: MacMillan Press, 1980.

Asprey, Robert B. *At Belleau Wood.* New York: G. P. Putnam and Sons, 1965.

Babcock, Conrad S. "The Australian-American Tank Action at Hamel, July 4, 1918." *Infantry Journal* 20 (April 1922): 394–400.

Baldwin, Fred D. "The American Enlisted Man in World War I." Ph. D. diss., Princeton University, 1964.

Baynes, John. *Far from a Donkey: The Life of Sir Ivor Maxse.* London: Brassey's, 1995.

Beach, Jim. "British Intelligence and the German Army, 1914–1918." Ph.D. diss., University College, London, 2004.

Becke, Major A. F. *Order of Battle.* Part 4. *The Army Council, G.H.Q.s, Armies, and Corps, 1914–1918.* London: His Majesty's Stationary Office, 1945.

Becker, Jean-Jacques. *The Great War and the French People*. Dover: Berg Publishers, 1985.

Beckett, Ian F. W. Beckett. *The Great War: 1914–1918*. New York: Longman, 1999.

———. *The Victorians at War*. London: Hambledon and London, 2003.

Berry, Henry. *Make the Kaiser Dance: Living Memories of the Doughboys*. New York: Arbor House, 1978.

Bethel, Elizabeth. *Preliminary Checklist of the Records of the War Department General Staff: Record Group 165*. Washington, D.C.: National Archives, 1965.

Bidwell, Shelford, and Dominic Graham. *Fire-Power: Army Weapons and Theories at War, 1904–1945*. London: George Allen and Unwin, 1982.

Birtle, Andrew J. *U.S. Army Counterinsurgency and Contingency Operations Doctrine, 1860–1941*. Washington, D.C.: U.S. Army Center of Military History, 1998.

Blake, Robert, ed. *The Private Papers of Douglas Haig, 1914–1919*. London: Eyre and Spottiswoode, 1952.

Blair, Dale James. "Diggers and Doughboys: Australian and American Troop Relations on the Western Front." Unpublished paper, 2001. In author's possession.

———. *Dinkum Diggers*. Melbourne: Melbourne University Press, 2001.

Bonasso, Russell Peter. "The Evolution of the Supreme War Council: The Unified Command and the First American Army in World War I." M.A. thesis, Georgetown University, 1951.

Bond, Brian. *The Unquiet Western Front: Britain's Role in Literature and History*. Cambridge: Cambridge University Press, 2002.

———, ed. *The First World War and British Military History*. Oxford: Oxford University Press, 1991.

———, and Nigel Cave, *Haig: A Reappraisal 70 Years On*. South Yorkshire: Leo Cooper and Pen & Sword Books, 1999.

Bourke, Joanna. *An Intimate History of Killing: Face-to-Face Killing in 20th Century Warfare*. New York: Basic Books, 1999.

Bourne, John. *Who's Who in World War One*. London: Routledge, 2001.

Braim, Paul F. *The Test of Battle: The American Expeditionary Forces in the Meuse-Argonne Campaign*. Newark: University of Delaware Press, 1987.

Bridges, Tom. *Alarms and Excursions*. New York: Longmans, Green & Co., 1939.

Brown, Malcolm. *Imperial War Museum Book of 1918: Year of Victory*. London: Pan Books, 1998.

Bruce, Robert B. *A Fraternity of Arms: America and France in the Great War*. Lawrence: University Press of Kansas, 2003.

Budreau, Lisa. "The Politics of American Commemoration in the Aftermath of the First World War." Ph.D. diss., Oxford University, 2006.

Bullard, Robert L. *Fighting Generals: Illustrated Biographical Sketches of Seven Major Generals in World War I*. Ann Arbor, Mich.: J. W. Edwards, 1944.

————. *Personalities and Reminiscences of the War.* Garden City, N.Y.: Doubleday, Page, 1925.

Burdett, Allen M. "A Critical Analysis of the Operations of the American II Corps from September 20 to October 2, 1918." Paper prepared at the Command and General Staff School, Fort Leavenworth, Kansas, 1934.

Byerly, Carol R. "The Politics of Disease and War: Infectious Disease in the United States Army during World War I." Ph. D. diss., University of Colorado, 2001.

Canfield, Bruce N. *U.S. Infantry Weapons of the First World War.* Lincoln, R.I.: Andrew Mowbray Publishers, 2000.

Cates, John H. *Company E, 117th Infantry, 30th Division in the World War I.* Johnson City: East Tennessee State University Press, 1964.

Cecil, Hugh, and Peter H. Liddle, eds. *Facing Armageddon: The First World War Experienced.* South Yorkshire: Leo Cooper and Pen & Sword Books, 1996.

Clarke, William F. *Over There with O'Ryan's Roughnecks.* Seattle, Wash.: Superior Publishing Company, 1966.

Clendenen, Clarence C. *Blood on the Border: The United States Army and the Mexican Irregulars.* Toronto: MacMillan, 1969.

Coffman, Edward M. *The War to End All Wars: The American Military Experience in World War I.* New York: Oxford University Press, 1968.

Committee of Officers Who Served with the Battalion. *The War History of the Sixth Battalion, The South Staffordshire Regiment T. F.* London: William Heinemann, 1924.

Conway, Coleman Berkley. *History of 119th Infantry, 60th Brigade, 30th Division, U.S.A.: Operations in Belgium and France, 1917–1919.* [Wilmington, N.C.]: Wilmington Chamber of Commerce, 1920.

Cooke, James. "The American Soldier in France, 1917–1919." In *Facing Armageddon: The First World War Experienced,* ed. Hugh Cecil and Peter H. Liddle. London: Leo Cooper, 1996.

————. *Pershing and His Generals: Command and Staff in the AEF.* Westport, Conn.: Praeger, 1997.

Cooper, Duff. *Haig.* Garden City, N.Y.: Doubleday Doran, 1936.

Cooper, Jerry. "The National Guard Mobilizations of 1916 and 1917: The Historical Importance." In *Cantigny at Seventy-Five,* ed. John Votoaw. Wheaton, Ill.: First Division Museum, 1995.

————. *The Rise of the National Guard: The Evolution of the American Militia, 1865–1920.* Lincoln: University of Nebraska Press, 1997.

Cron, Hermann. *Imperial German Army, 1914–1918: Organisation, Structure, Orders of Battle.* Translated by C. F. Colton. Solihull, West Midlands, England: Helion & Company, 2002.

Cutlack, F. M. *The Australian Flying Corps in the Western and Eastern Theatres of War, 1914–1918.* Queensland: University of Queensland Press, 1984.

————, ed. *War Letters of General Monash.* Sydney: Angus and Robertson, 1935.

Dallas, Gregor. *1918: War and Peace.* Woodstock, N.Y.: Overlook Press, 2001.

Davis, Henry Blaine, Jr. *Generals in Khaki*. Raleigh, N.C.: Pentland Press, 1998.

Defrancisco, Joseph E. "Amalgamation: A Critical Issue in British-American Command Relations, 1917–1918." M.A. thesis, Rice University, 1973.

DeGroot, Gerard J. *Douglas Haig, 1861–1928*. London: Unwin Hyman, 1988.

Denfeld, D. Colt. "World War I Mobilization Camps." *Journal of America's Military Past* 29 (Fall/Winter 2002): 28–54.

Dennis, Peter, and Jeffrey Grey, eds. *1918: Defining Victory*. Canberra, Australia: Army History Unit, Department of Defence, 1998.

—— et al. *The Oxford Companion to Australian Military History*. New York: Oxford University Press, 1995.

DeWeerd, Harvey A. *President Wilson Fights His War: World War I and the American Intervention*. New York: Macmillan Company, 1968.

Dimbleby, David, and David Reynolds. *An Ocean Apart: The Relationship between Britain and America in the Twentieth Century*. New York: Vintage Books, 1988.

Doubler, Michael D. *I Am the Guard: A History of the Army National Guard, 1636–2000*. Washington, D.C.: Department of the Army, 2001.

Doyle, Sir Arthur Conan. *The British Campaign in France and Flanders: July to November 1918*. Vol. 6. London: Hodder and Stoughton, 1919.

Doyle, Peter. *Geology of the Western Front, 1914–1918*. [London]: Geologist's Association, 1998.

——. "Military Geography: Terrain Evaluation and the British Western Front, 1914–1918." *Geographic Journal* 163, no. 1 (March 1997): 1–24.

Dunn, Capt. J. C. *The War the Infantry Knew, 1914–1919: A Chronicle of Service in France and Belgium*. Ed. Keith Simpson. London: Abacus, 1999.

East Tennessee Historical Society. *First Families of Tennessee: A Register of Early Settlers and Their Present-Day Descendants*. Knoxville: East Tennessee Historical Society, 2000.

Edmonds, Brig. Gen. James E., and Lt. Col. R. Maxwell-Hyslop, eds. *Military Operations in France and Belgium, 1918*. Vol. 5. London: His Majesty's Stationary Office, 1947.

Ellis, Captain A. D. *The Story of the Fifth Australian Division: Being an Authoritative Account of the Division's Doings in Egypt, France, and Belgium*. London: Hodder and Stoughton, n.d.

Ellis, John. *Eye Deep in Hell: Trench Warfare in World War I*. Baltimore, Md.: Johns Hopkins University Press, 1976.

——. *The Social History of the Machine Gun*. London: Pimlico, 1976.

Esposito, David M. "Woodrow Wilson and the Origins of the AEF." *Presidential Quarterly* 19, no. 1 (Winter 1989): 127–129.

Essame, Hubert. *The Battle for Europe, 1918*. London: Batsford, 1972.

Evans, Martin Marix. *American Voices of World War I: Primary Source Documents, 1917–1920*. Chicago: Fitzroy Dearborn, 2001.

——. *1918: The Year of Victories*. London: Arcturus Publishing Limited, 2002.

————. *Retreat Hell! We Just Got Here: The American Expeditionary Force in France, 1917–1918.* Oxford: Osprey Books, 1998.

Falls, Cyril. *The Great War, 1914–1918.* New York: Capricorn Books, 1959.

Farrar, Martin J. *News from the Front: War Correspondents on the Western Front, 1914–1918.* London: Sutton Publishing, 2002.

Ferrell, Robert H. *Woodrow Wilson & World War I: 1917–1921.* New York: Harper and Row, 1985.

Fleming, Thomas. *The Illusion of Victory: America in World War I.* New York: Basic Books, 2003.

Fletcher, David. "Hot, Noisy, and Dark, World War One: Tank Battle at Hamel, July 1918." *Military Illustrated* 122 (July 1998): 44–47.

————, ed. *Tanks and Trenches: First Hand Accounts of Tank Warfare in the First World War.* Phoenix Mill, Gloucestershire: Sutton, 1994.

Fohlen, Yves. *With Guts and Bayonets: Diggers and Doughboys on the Hindenburg Line, 1918.* Loftus, Australia: Publishing Services, 2001.

Fowler, William B. *British-American Relations, 1917–1918: The Role of Sir William Wiseman.* Princeton, N.J.: Princeton University Press, 1969.

Franki, George, and Clyde Slatyer. *Mad Harry: Australia's Most Decorated Soldier.* East Roseville: Kangaroo Press, 2003.

Frankl, George, and Clyde Slatyer. *Mad Harry: Australia's Most Decorated Soldier.* East Roseville, New South Wales: Kangaroo Press, 2003.

Franks, Norman. *Dog-Fight Tactics: Aerial Tactics of the Aces of World War I.* London: Greenhill Books, 2003.

————, Russell Guest, and Frank Bailey. *Bloody April . . . Black September: An Exciting and Detailed Analysis of the Two Deadliest Months in the Air in World War One.* London: Grub Street Press, 1995.

French, David. *The Strategy of the Lloyd George Coalition, 1916–1918.* Oxford: Clarendon Press, 1995.

Frothingham, Thomas. *The American Reinforcement in the World War.* Garden City, N.Y.: Doubleday, 1927.

Gibbs, Philip. *The Way to Victory.* Vol. 2, *The Repulse.* New York: George H. Doran Company, 1919.

Gilbert, Martin. *The First World War: A Complete History.* New York: Henry Holt and Company, 1994.

Gow, Lt. Kenneth. *Letters of a Soldier.* New York: Herbert B. Covert, 1920.

Graham, Dominick, and Shelford Bidwell. *Coalitions, Politicians & Generals: Some Aspects of Command in Two World Wars.* London: Brassey's, 1993.

Griffith, Paddy. *Battle Tactics of the Western Front: The British Army's Art of Attack, 1916–1918.* New Haven, Conn.: Yale University Press, 1994.

————. *Fortifications of the Western Front, 1914–1918.* Oxford: Osprey Books, 2004.

————, ed. *British Fighting Methods in the Great War.* London: Frank Cass, 1996.

Grotelueschen, Mark E. "The AEF Way of War: The American Army and Combat in the First World War." Ph.D. diss., Texas A&M University, 2003.

Gudmundsson, Bruce I. *Stormtroop Tactics: Innovation in the German Army, 1914–1918*. New York: Praeger, 1989.

Halsey, Francis Whiting. *The Literary Digest History of the World War*. New York: Funk & Wagnalls, 1920.

Hall, James Norman. *Kitchener's Mob: The Adventures of an American in the British Army*. Toronto: Thomas Allen, 1916.

Hamburger, Kenneth E. *Learning Lessons in the American Expeditionary Forces*. Washington, D.C: U.S. Army Center of Military History, 1997.

Hancock, W. K. *Smuts*. Vol. 1, *The Sanguine Years, 1870–1919*. Cambridge: Cambridge University Press, 1962.

Harbord, James G. *The American Army in France, 1917–1919*. Boston: Little, Brown and Company, 1936.

Harries, Mierion, and Susie Harries. *The Last Days of Innocence*. New York: Random House, 1997.

Harris, J. P. "The Rise of Armor." In *British Fighting Methods in the Great War*, ed. Paddy Griffith. London: Frank Cass, 1996.

————, with Niall Barr. *Amiens to the Armistice: The BEF in the Hundred Days' Campaign, 8 August–November 1918*. Washington, D.C.: Brassey's, 1998.

Harris, Stephen L. *Duty, Honor, Privilege: New York's Silk Stocking Regiment and the Breaking of the Hindenburg Line*. Washington, D.C.: Brassey's, 2001.

————. *Harlem's Hell Fighters: The African-American 369th Infantry in World War I*. Washington, D.C.: Brassey's, 2003.

Haythornwaite, Philip J. *The World War One Source Book*. London: Arms and Armour Press, 1991.

Hedgecock, Deborah, and Robert Waite. *Images of London: Haringy at War*. Stroud, Gloustershire: Tempus Publishing, 2004.

Heller, Charles E. *Chemical Warfare in World War I: The American Experience, 1917–1918*. Fort Leavenworth, Kans.: U.S. Army Command and General Staff College, 1984.

Herwig, Holger H. *The First World War: Germany and Austria-Hungary, 1914–1918*. London: Arnold, 1997.

Hiscock, Eric. *The Bells of Hell Go Ting-a-Ling-a-Ling*. London: Corgi Books, 1976.

Holmes, Richard. *Acts of War: The Behavior of Men in Battle*. New York: The Free Press, 1985.

————. *Tommy: The British Soldier on the Western Front*. London: HarperCollins, 2004.

————. *The Western Front*. London: BBC Worldwide, 1999.

————, ed. *The Oxford Companion to Military History*. Oxford: Oxford University Press, 2001.

Howard, William F. "The Sweetheart of the A.E.F." *New York Archives* 4, no. 3 (Winter 2005): 6–9.

Hughes, Jackson. "The Battle for the Hindenburg Line." *War & Society* 17, no. 2 (October 1999): 41–57.

Jacobson, Gerald F. *History of the 107th Infantry U.S.A.* New York: Seventh Regiment Armory, 1920.

James, Lawrence. *Warrior Race: A History of the British at War.* London: Little, Brown, and Company, 2001.

Janis, Elsie. *So Far, So Good! An Autobiography by Elsie Janis.* New York: E. P. Dutton & Co., 1932.

Jensen, Geoffrey, and Andrew Wiest, eds. *War in the Age of Technology: Myriad Faces of Modern Armed Conflict.* New York: New York University Press, 2001.

Johnson, Douglas V, II. "A Few 'Squads-Left' and Off to France: Training the American Army in the United States for World War I." Ph.D. diss., Temple University, 1992.

———, and Rolfe L. Hillman, Jr. *Soissons, 1918.* College Station: Texas A&M University Press, 1999.

Johnson, Hubert C. *Breakthrough! Tactics, Technology, and the Search for Victory on the Western Front in World War I.* Novato, Calif.: Presidio Press, 1994.

Johnson, J. H. *1918: The Unexpected Victory.* London: Arms and Armour Press, 1997.

Jones, H. A. *The War in the Air: Being the Story of the Part Played in Great War by the Royal Air Force.* Vols. 4 and 6. Oxford: Clarendon Press, 1937.

Kerr, Greg. *Private Wars: Personal Records of the ANZACS in the Great War.* Victoria: Oxford University Press, 2000.

Kilmurray, Elaine, and Richard Ormond, eds. *John Singer Sargent.* Princeton, N.J.: Princeton University Press, 1998.

Kitchen, Martin. *The German Offensives of 1918.* London: Tempus Publishing, 2001.

Laffin, John. *The Battle of Hamel: The Australians' Finest Victory.* Roseville, New South Wales: Kangaroo Press, 1999.

———. *On the Western Front: Soldiers' Stories from France and Flanders, 1914–1918* Phoenix Mill, Gloucestershire: Budding Books, 1985.

Lawrence, Douglas Joseph. *Fighting Soldier: The AEF in 1918.* Ed. Robert H. Ferrell. Boulder: Colorado Associated University Press, 1985.

Leland, Claude G. *From Shell Hole to Chateau with Company I: Personal Recollections of a Line Officer of the 107th U.S. Infantry Regiment, 27th Division, in France, 1918.* New York: Society of the Ninth Company Veterans, 7th Regiment New York National Guard, 1950.

Levinger, Rabbi Lee J. *A Jewish Chaplain in France.* New York: Macmillan, 1921.

Lewis, Jon E., ed. *The Mammoth Book of Eyewitness: World War I.* New York: Carroll & Graf, 2003.

Liddle, Peter, Ian Whitehead, and Bourne, John, eds. *The Great War, 1914–45.* Vol. 1. *Lightning Strikes Twice.* London: Harper Collins Publishers, 2000.

———. *The Great War, 1914–45.* Vol. 2, *The Peoples' Experience.* London: HarperCollins Publishers, 2001.

Liddle Hart, B. H. *Through the Fog of War*. London: Faber, 1938.

Lloyd George, David. *War Memoirs of David Lloyd George*. Vol. 2, *1917 to Armistice and Reflections*. London: Oldhams Press, 1936.

Lonergan, Thomas Clement. *It Might Have Been Lost*. New York: G. P. Putnam's Sons, 1929.

Long, G. "The Legacy of the Army of 1918." *Stand To: The Journal of the Western Front Association* (January 2007).

Lupfer, Timothy T. *The Dynamics of Doctrine: The Changes in German Tactical Doctrine during the First World War*. Fort Leavenworth, Kans.: Command and General Staff College, 1981.

MacDonald, Lyn. *To the Last Man: Spring 1918*. New York: Carol and Graff, 1999.

Macintyre, Ben. *The Englishman's Daughter: A True Story of Love and Betrayal in World War I*. New York: Farrar, Straus, and Giroux, 2001.

MacVeagh, Ewen C., and Lee D. Brown. *The Yankee in the British Zone*. New York: G. P. Putnam and Sons, 1920.

Mahon, John K. *History of the Militia and the National Guard*. New York: MacMillan, 1983.

Marshall, R. Jackson, III. *Memories of World War I: North Carolina Doughboys on the Western Front*. Raleigh: North Carolina Department of Cultural Resources, 1998.

Maslowski, Peter, and Allen R. Millett. *For the Common Defense: A Military History of the United States*. New York: Free Press, 1984.

Maurice, Major-General Sir Frederick. *The Last Four Months: How the War Was Won*. Boston: Little, Brown, and Company, 1919.

———. ed. *The Life of General Lord Rawlinson of Trent: From His Journals and Letters*. London: Cassell and Company, 1928.

Maze, Paul, A. *Frenchman in Khaki*. London: William Heinemann, 1934.

McCarthy, Chris. "Not All Beer and Skittles: Everyday Life and Leisure on the Western Front." In *War in the Age of Technology: Myriad Faces of Modern Armed Conflict*, ed. Geoffrey Jensen and Andrew Wiest. New York: New York University Press, 2001.

McKenzie, F. A. *Through the Hindenburg Line: Crowning Days on the Western Front*. London: Hodder and Stoughton, 1918.

McMullin, Ross. *Pompey Elliott*. Melbourne: Scribe Publications, 2002.

McPhail, Helen. *The Long Silence: Civilian Life under the German Occupation of Northern France, 1914–1918*. New York: St. Martins Press, 2001.

Mead, Gary. *The Doughboys: America and the First World War*. London: Allen Lane, Penguin Press, 2000.

Members of the Battalion. *History and Memoir of the 33rd Battalion Machine Gun Corps and of the 19th, 98th, 100th, and 248th M.G. Companies*. London: Waterlow Brothers & Layton, 1919.

Middlebrook, Martin. *The Kaiser's Battle*. London: Allen Lane, 1978.

———, and Mary Middlebrook. *The Somme Battlefields: A Comprehensive Guide from Crecy to the Two World Wars*. London: Penguin Books, 1991.

Millman, Brock. *Pessimism and British War Policy: 1916–1918.* London: Frank Cass, 2001.

Millett, Allan R. *The General: Robert L. Bullard and Officership in the United States Army, 1881–1925.* Westport, Conn.: Greenwood Press, 1975.

———. "Over Where? The AEF and the American Strategy for Victory, 1917–1918." In *Against All Enemies: Interpretations of American Military History from Colonial Times to the Present,* ed. Kenneth J. Hagan and William R. Roberts. Westport, Conn.: Greenwood Press, 1986.

Millett, Allan R., and Williamson Murray, eds. *Military Effectiveness.* Vol. 1, *The First World War.* Boston: Allen & Unwin, 1988.

Mitchell, Harry T. *Company L, 107th Infantry, 54th Brigade, 27th Division, American Expeditionary Force, 1917–1919.* New York: War Veterans Association, 1920.

Monash, Sir John. *The Australian Victories in France in 1918.* London: Hutchinson & Company, 1920.

Montgomery, Maj. Gen. Sir Archibald. *The Story of the Fourth Army in the Battles of The Hundred Days, August 8th to November 11th, 1919.* London: Hodder and Stoughton, 1920.

Murphy, Elmer A., and Robert S. Thomas. *The Thirtieth Division in the World War.* Lepanto, Ark.: Old Hickory Publishing Company, 1936.

Nash, George H. *The Life of Herbert Hoover: The Humanitarian, 1914–1917.* New York: Norton, 1988.

Neillands, Robin. *The Great War Generals on the Western Front, 1914–1918.* London: Robinson, 1998.

Nenninger, Timothy K. "American Military Effectiveness in the First World War." In *Military Effectiveness.* Vol. 1, *The First World War.* Ed. Allan R. Millett and Williamson Murray. Boston: Allen and Unwin, 1988.

———. "John J. Pershing and Relief for Cause in the American Expeditionary Forces, 1917–1918." *Army History* 61 (Spring 2005): 20–33.

———. *The Leavenworth Schools and the Old Army: Education, Professionalism, and the Officer Corps of the United States Army, 1881–1918.* Westport, Conn.: Greenwood Press, 1978.

———. "Tactical Dysfunction in the AEF, 1917–1918." *Military Affairs* 51, no. 4 (October 1987): 177–181.

Nichols, Captain G. H. F. *The 18th Division in the Great War.* Edinburgh: William Blackwood and Sons, 1922.

Nunan, Peter. "Diggers Fourth of July." *Military History* (Summer 2000): 26–32, 80.

Oakleaf, J. F. *Notes on the Operations of the 108th Overseas.* Olean, N.Y.: Olean Times Publishing Company, 1921.

Odom, William O. *After the Trenches: The Transformation of U.S. Army Doctrine, 1918–1939.* College Station: Texas A&M University Press, 1999.

———. "The Spirit of the Bayonet: Offensive Doctrine in the U.S. Army, 1917–1941." Paper presented at the meeting of the Society of Military History, Quantico, Virginia, April 2000.

Oldham, Peter. *Battleground Europe: The Hindenburg Line.* London: Leo Cooper, 1997.

O'Ryan, John F. *History of the 27th: New York's Own.* New York: Bennett and Churchill, 1919.

———. *The Story of the 27th Division.* 2 vols. New York: Wynkoop Hallenbeck Crawford, 1921.

Palmer, Frederick. *Newton D. Baker: America at War.* Vol. 1. New York: Dodd, Meade, and Company, 1931.

———. *Our Greatest Battle.* New York: Dodd, Mead, and Company, 1919.

Palazzo, Albert. *Seeking Victory on the Western Front: The British Army and Chemical Warfare in World War I.* Lincoln: University of Nebraska Press, 2000.

Paschall, Rod. *The Defeat of Imperial Germany: 1917–1918.* Chapel Hill, N.C.: Algonquin Press, 1989.

Passingham, Ian. *All the Kaiser's Men: The Life and Death of the German Army on the Western Front, 1914–1918.* Phoenix Mill, Gloucestershire: Sutton, 2003.

———. "The Kaiser's War." *Military Illustrated* 184 (September 2003): 32–39.

———. *Pillars of Fire: The Battle of Messines Ridge, June 1917.* Phoenix Mill, Gloucestershire: Sutton, 1998.

Pedersen, P. A. *Monash as Military Commander.* Melbourne: Melbourne University Press, 1985.

Pegler, Martin. *British Tommy.* Oxford: Osprey Publishing, 1996.

Perry, F. W. *Order of Battle of Divisions.* Part 5A. *The Divisions of Australia, Canada and New Zealand and Those of East Africa.* Newport, Gwent: Ray Westlake Military Books, 1992.

Pitt, Barrie. *1918: The Last Act.* New York: Ballantine Books, 1963.

Poett, C. *Promenades Autors de St. Quentin.* St. Quentin, 1899.

Potter, Captain C. H., and Captain A. S. C. Fothergill. *The History of the 2/6th Lancashire Fusiliers.* Rochdale: Observer General Printing Works, 1927.

Priestly, Raymond E. *Breaking the Hindenburg Line: The Story of the 46th North Midland Division.* London: T. Fisher Unwin, 1919.

Powell, Geoffrey. *Plumer: The Soldiers' General.* South Yorkshire: Pen & Sword Limited, 2004.

Prior, Robin, and Trevor Wilson. *Command on the Western Front: The Military Career of Sir Henry Rawlinson, 1914–1918.* Oxford: Blackwell, 1992.

———. *The First World War.* London: Cassell, 1999.

———. *Passchendaele: The Untold Story.* New Haven, Conn.: Yale University Press, 1996.

Pugsley, Christopher. *The ANZAC Experience: New Zealand, Australia and Empire in the First World War.* Birkenhead, Auckland, New Zealand: Reed, 2004.

Rainey, James W. "Ambivalent Warfare: The Tactical Doctrine of the AEF in World War I." *Parameters* 13, no. 3 (Fall 1983): 34–46.

————. "The Questionable Training of the AEF in World War I." *Parameters* 22, no. 4 (Winter 1992): 89—103.

————. "The Training of the American Expeditionary Forces in World War I." M.A. thesis, Temple University, 1981.

Ramsay, M. A. *Command and Cohesion: The Citizen Soldier and Minor Tactics in the British Army, 1870–1918.* London: Praeger, 2002.

Rawling, Bill. *Surviving Trench Warfare: Technology and the Canadian Corps, 1914–1918.* Toronto: University of Toronto Press, 1992.

Reid, Richard, Courtney Page, and Robert Rounds. *Beaucoup Australians ici: The Australian Corps in France, 1918.* [Canberra]: Commonwealth Dept. of Veterans' Affairs, 1999.

Risch, Erna. *Quartermaster Support of the Army: 1775–1939.* Washington, D.C.: Center of Military History, U.S. Army, 1989.

Robbins, Simon. *British Generalship on the Western Front, 1914–1918: Defeat into Victory.* London: Frank Cass, 2005.

Roberts, Robert B. *Encyclopedia of Historic Forts.* New York: MacMillan, 1988.

Roper, John Herbert. "Paul Green's War Songs." *North Carolina Literary Review* 2, no. 1 (1994).

Schoen, Elliott. *History of the 107th U.S. Infantry, AEF, in the Battle of the Hindenburg Line, September 29, 1918 during World War I.* New York: American Legion, New York Post 107, 1968.

Shrader, Charles R. "'Maconochie's Stew': Logistical Support of American Forces with the BEF, 1917–1918." In *The Great War, 1914–1918: Essays on the Military, Political, and Social History of the First World War*, ed. R. J. Q. Adams. College Station: Texas A&M University Press, 1990.

Schreiber, Shane B. *Shock Army of the British Empire: The Canadian Corps in the Last 100 Days of the Great War.* Westport, Conn.: Praeger, 1997.

Schwensen, Kai. *The History of the 102nd M.P.* N.p.: Kai Schwensen, 1919.

Scott, Maj.-Gen. Sir Arthur B., and P. Middleton Brumwell. *History of the 12th Eastern Division in the Great War.* London: Nisbet & Co., 1923.

Scott, James Brown. *Robert Bacon: Life and Letters.* New York: Doubleday, Page & Company, 1923.

Seidule, James Tyrus. "Morale in the American Expeditionary Forces during World War I." Ph.D. diss., Ohio State University, 1997.

Serle, Geoffrey. *John Monash: A Biography.* Melbourne: Melbourne University Press, 1985.

Sheffield, Gary. *Forgotten Victory: The First World War Myths and Realties.* London: Headline Book Publishing, 2001.

————. *Leadership in the Trenches: Officer-Man Relations, Morale, and Discipline in the British Army in the Era of the First World War.* London: MacMillan, 2000.

————. "The Performance of British Troops in 1918." In *1918: Defining Victory*, ed. Peter Dennis and Jeffrey Grey. Canberra: Army History Unit, Department of Defense, 1999.

————. *The Somme.* London: Cassell, 2003.

————, and Dan Todman, eds. *Command and Control on the Western Front: The British Army's Experience, 1914–18.* Kent: Spellmount Limited, 2004.

A Short History of the 105th Infantry, United States Army. Philadelphia, Pa.: Press of Edward Stern & Co. 1918.

A Short History of the 106th Infantry, United States Army. Philadelphia, Pa.: Press of Edward Stern & Co., 1918.

A Short History of the 108th Infantry, United States Army. Philadelphia, Pa.: Press of Edward Stern & Co., 1918.

Simkins, Peter. *The First World War.* Vol. 3, *The Western Front, 1917–1918.* Oxford: Osprey Publishing, 2002.

————. *Kitchener's Army: The Raising of New Armies, 1914–1916.* Manchester: Manchester University Press, 1988.

————. "Soldiers and Civilians: Billeting in Britain and France." In *A Nation in Arms: A Social Study of the British Army in the First World War,* ed. Ian F. Beckett and Keith Simpson. Manchester: Manchester University Press, 1985.

————. "The War Experience of a Typical Kitchener Division: The 18th Division, 1914–1918." In *Facing Armageddon: The First World War Experienced,* ed. Hugh Cecil and Peter H. Liddle. South Yorkshire: Leo Cooper and Pen & Sword Books, 1996.

Simpson, Andy. *The Evolution of Victory: British Battles on the Western Front, 1914–1918.* London: Tom Donovan Publishing, 1995.

Sixsmith, E. K. G. *Douglas Haig.* London: Weidenfeld and Nicholson, 1976.

Smith, Gene. *Until the Last Trumpet Sounds: The Life of General of the Armies John J. Pershing.* New York: John Wiley and Sons, 1998.

Smith, Leonard V. Stephane Audoin-Rouzeau, and Annette Becker. *France and the Great War, 1914–1918.* Cambridge: Cambridge University Press, 2003.

Smythe, Donald. "The Battle of the Books." *Army* (September 1972): 30–32.

————. *Guerrilla Warrior: The Early Life of John J. Pershing.* New York: Charles Scribner and Sons, 1973.

————. *Pershing, General of the Armies.* Bloomington: Indiana University Press, 1986.

————. "Venereal Disease: The AEF's Experience." *Prologue: Quarterly of the National Archives* (Summer 1977): 64–74.

————. "The Wisdom of a Separate Army." In *Major Problems in American Military History,* ed. John Whiteclay Chambers II and G. Kurt Phieler. New York: Houghton Mifflin Company, 1999.

Societe Academique de St. Quentin. *L'Invasion de 1914 dans le canton due Catelet.* St. Quentin: Imprimente Generale Du "Guetteur," 1933.

Souvenir Booklet of Brest: Giving Brief History of Brest and Brittany. Paris: Imprimerie A. Davy, 1919.

Spagnoly, Tony. *Cameos of the Western Front, Ypres Sector, 1914–1918.* London: Leo Cooper, 1995.

Stallings, Laurence. *The Doughboys.* New York: Harper and Row, 1963.

Starlight, Alexander, comp. *The Pictorial Record of the 27th Division.* New York: Harper and Brothers, 1919.

Strachan, Hew. *The First World War.* New York: The Penguin Group, 2004.

———, ed. *World War I: A History.* Oxford: Oxford University Press, 1998.

Stubbs, Kevin D. *Race to the Front: The Materiel Foundations of Coalition Strategy in the Great War.* Westport, Conn.: Praeger, 2002.

Swetland, Maurice J., and Lilli Swetland. *"These Men": For Conspicuous Bravery Above and Beyond the Call of Duty.* Harrisburg, Pa.: Military Service Publishing Company, 1940.

Sutliffe, Robert Stewart. *Seventy-First New York in the World War.* New York: Robert S. Sutliffe, 1922.

Syk, Andrew. "The Learning Curve: The 46th North Midland Division on the Western Front.'" *History Today* 54 (11 November 2004): 12–18.

Terraine, John. *Douglas Haig: The Educated Soldier.* London: Hutchinson, 1963.

———. *Ordeal of Victory.* New York: J. B. Lippincott Company, 1963.

———. *The Smoke and the Fire: Myths & Anti-Myths of War, 1861–1945.* London: Leo Cooper, 1992.

———. *To Win a War: 1918, the Year of Victory.* London: Sidgewick and Jackson, 1978.

"The Last German Offensive." *The Army Quarterly* XLI, no. 2 (January 1941).

Thomas, Shipley. *The History of the A.E.F.* New York: George H. Moran, 1920.

Thompson, Hugh. *Trench Knives and Mustard Gas: With the 42nd Rainbow Division in France.* Edited with and introduction by Robert H. Ferrell. College Station: Texas A&M University Press, 2004.

Toland, John. *No Man's Land: 1918, the Last Year of the Great War.* New York: Konecky & Konecky, 1980.

Trannois, Pierre Paul. *Avant Avec Apres Hindenburg: Vie de populations civiles du Vermandois Est en 14/18.* St. Quentin: Production Littaire, 1998.

Trask, David. *The AEF and Coalition War Making: 1917–1918.* Lawrence: University Press of Kansas, 1973.

———. *The United States in the Supreme War Council.* Middleton, Conn.: Wesleyan University Press, 1961.

Travers, Timothy. *How the War Was Won: Command and Technology in the British Army on the Western Front, 1917–1918.* London: Routledge, 2000.

———. "The Allied Victories, 1918." In *World War I: A History,* ed. Hew Strachan. Oxford: Oxford University Press, 1998.

———. "The Evolution of British Strategy and Tactics on the Western Front, 1918: GHQ, Manpower, and Technology." *Journal of Military History* 54 (April 1990): 173–200.

———. *The Killing Ground.* London: Routledge, 1990.

Triplet, William S. *A Youth in the Meuse-Argonne: A Memoir, 1917–1918.* Edited by and introduction by Robert H. Ferrell. Columbia: University of Missouri Press, 2000.

Turpin, Susan, Carolyn Creal, Ron Crawley, and James Crocker, eds. *When the Soldiers Came to Town: Spartanburg's Camp Wadsworth (1917–19) & Camp Croft (1941–45)*. Spartanburg, S.C.: Hub City Writers Project, 2004.

Urwin, Gregory J. W. *The United States Infantry: An Illustrated History, 1775–1918.* New York: Sterling Publishing Company, 1991.

Vale, Colonel W. L. *History of the South Staffordshire Regiment.* Aldershot: Gale & Polden, 1969.

Vandiver, Frank E. *Black Jack: The Life and Times of John J. Pershing.* 2 vols. College Station: Texas A&M University Press, 1977.

Various Authorities. *Canada in the Great World War: An Authentic Account of the Military History of Canada from the Earliest Days to the Close of the War of the Nations.* Vol. 5, *The Triumph of the Allies.* Toronto: United Publishers of Canada, 1920.

Votaw, John. *The American Expeditionary Forces in World War I.* Oxford: Osprey Books, 2005.

Wallach, Jehuda L. *Uneasy Coalition: The Entente Experience in World War I.* Westport, Conn.: Greenwood Press, 1993.

Ward, Major C. H. Dudley. *The 74th Yeomanry Division in Syria and France.* London: John Murray, 1922.

Ward, Franklin Wilmer. *Between the Big Parades.* New York: Frederick M. Waterbury, 1952.

Warren, Louis S. "Buffalo Bill Meets Dracula: William F. Cody, Bram Stoker, and the Frontiers of Racial Decay." *American Historical Review* 107, no. 4 (October 2002):

Weigley, Russell F. *History of the United States Army.* New York: Macmillan, 1967.

Welborn, Suzanne. *Bush Heroes: A People, a Place, a Legend.* Freemantle, W.A.: Freemantle Arts Centre Press, 2002.

Whisler, Mark. "'De Tommy Kommt': British Expeditionary Force Campaign Orchestration and Fourth Army Operational Executions at the Battle of the Selle River, October 1918: A Case Study in 1918 British Offensive Operations against the Imperial German Army." M.A. thesis, United States Marine Corps Command and Staff College, 2001.

William, John Francis, II. *Experiences in the Great War.* North Carolina: John Francis Williams, II, 1975.

Wilson, Dale E. *Treat 'Em Rough: The Birth of American Armor, 1917–20.* Novato, Calif.: Presidio Press, 1989.

Winter, Denis. *Haig's Command: A Reassessment.* London: Penguin Books, 1991.

Winter, J. M. *The Great War and the British People.* Cambridge, Mass.: Harvard University Press, 1986.

Wolff, Leon. *In Flanders Field: The 1917 Campaign.* London: Penguin Books, 1979.

Woodward, David R. *Field Marshal Sir William Robertson: Chief of the Imperial General Staff in the Great War.* Westport, Conn.: Praeger, 1998.

———. *Lloyd George and the Generals*. Newark: University of Delaware Press, 1983.

———. *Trial by Friendship: Anglo-American Relations, 1917–1918*. Lexington: University Press of Kentucky, 1993.

———, ed. *The Military Correspondence of Field Marshal Sir William Robertson CIGS, December 29–25 February 1918*. London: Bodley Head/Army Records Society, 1989.

Wright, Patrick. *Tank: The Progress of a Monstrous War Machine*. New York: Viking, 2002.

Zabecki, David T. *The German 1918 Offensives*. Abingdon: Taylor and Francis, 2005.

———. "Operational Art and the German Offensives." Ph.D. diss., Royal Military College of Science, 2003.

———. *Steel Wind: Colonel Georg Bruchmuller and the Birth of Modern Artillery*. Westport, Conn.: Praeger, 1994.

INDEX

American 108th Infantry Regiment, 98, 119, 131, 166, 169, 171, 172, 173, 176, 185, 186, 200, 201, 202, 204
American 117th Infantry Regiment, 54, 98, 110, 119, 126, 169, 180, 181, 193, 194, 195, 196, 197
American 118th Infantry Regiment, 118, 119, 159, 160, 162, 165, 166, 169, 193, 194, 195, 196, 198, 207
American 119th Infantry Regiment, 24, 25, 49, 52, 63, 81, 82, 88, 90, 98, 102, 104, 108, 112, 117, 169, 180, 181, 196, 197, 198, 206, 207
American 120th Infantry Regiment, 24, 81, 87, 88, 89, 90, 98, 102, 104, 117, 119, 169, 179, 181, 182, 196, 197, 198, 207
American 369th Infantry Regiment, 20, 22
American 104th Machine-Gun Battalion, 31, 53, 199
American 105th Machine-Gun Battalion, 53, 63, 164
American 106th Machine-Gun Battalion, 46, 164
American 113th Machine-Gun Battalion, 205
American 115th Machine-Gun Battalion, 26, 102, 206
American 6th New York Division, 6
American warfare doctrine: British refusal to teach elements of, 37–38; on open-warfare, 29–30, 171
Amiens, 112, 210
Andrews, Col. James M., 174
Area and subarea system, 70
Armistice, 211–12
Armstrong huts, 81–82
Artillery: in Hindenburg Line offensive, 160–61, 167, 182, 188; II Army Corps' lack of, 89–90
Attack in Position Warfare, The (German publication), 39
Australian Army Corps: allegations of looting of dead by, 177, 223; on American battle performance, 185; American impression of, 223; in Hindenburg Line offensive, 119, 126, 173; near-mutiny in, 116; training of Americans by, 77; undisciplined reputation of, 77–78
Australian Flying Corps, 202
Australian mission, in Hindenburg Line offensive, 129–30
Aviation elements: air reconnaissance in Selle River Campaign, 200; in Hindenburg Line offensive, 117, 166; training on German use of, 59

Bacon, Col. Robert, 36, 69, 86, 116, *150*, 183, 197
Baker, Col. Chauncey B., 247n2
Baker, Newton D., 10, 16, 25, 69
Balfour, Sir Arthur, 10
Bean, C.E.W., 78, 116, 168, 185
Beaurevoir Line, 191
Belgium: civilian hardship in, 82; royal family of, 89
Bellamy, 2nd Lt. (120th Infantry), 87
Belleau Wood, 86
Bellicourt, France, 121–22, 123, *139*, 228
Bellicourt monument, 226
Bissett, 1st Lt. Wily O., 82
Biziaux, Emile, 228
Blanchard, Pvt. Edgar, 182
Blanding, Brig. Gen. Albert H., 105, 106, 166
Bliss, Maj. Gen Tasker, 16, 18, 19
Bonaparte, Napoleon, 117
Bonham-Carter, Lt. Gen. Sir Charles: on American enlisted men, 63, 76; early career of, 38; as primary source, xv; in transfer of American units to French front, 73
Bony, France: American donations in reconstruction of, 228; resistance in, and evacuation of, 121–23
Booby traps, 207
Borden, Sir Robert, 76–77

Conion, Pvt. Curtis, 60
Connor, Fox, 11
Conscription, 65
Creeping barrage, 39, 125, 160, 164, 204, 247n20
Crowell, Benedict, 47–48
Currie, Lt. Gen. Sir Arthur, 76

DeBevoise, Col. Charles I., 84
Defense in-depth, 209
Dennis, Sgt. Judson W., 49–50, 207
Deployment criteria, 48
Depot brigades, 45
Dick, Charles W., 5
Dick Act (1903), 5
Dietrele, Lt. F.J., 109
Discipline: of Australian troops, 77–78, 223; of British infantry units, 64–65; of II Army Corps, 88–89, 222; inspections revealing lack of, 46, 48–49, 85; O'Ryan on British, 30; O'Ryan on need for during training, 58–59; of 27th Division, 210
Division of Militia Affairs, 5
Dobbie, Col. W.G.S., 116
Dog messengers, 105
Dog tags, 51
"Doughboy," 241n4
Drum, Hugh, 11
Duckboards, 30
Dugan, Brig. Gen. W.J., 211

Eastern Front, 11, 15, 123
East Poperinghe line, 80
Eisenhower, Gen. Dwight D., 219
Elisabeth of Bavaria, 89
Embarkation procedures, 50–51
Entertainers, 71–72, 111
Equipment shortages: infantry rifles, 29, 84; winter uniforms, 31–32

Faison, Brig. Gen. Sampson L., 24, 84, 88; on amalgamation, 217; on American relationship with allies, 217; qualifications of, for 30th Division commander,

74–75; support for promotion of, 253n30
Field hospitals, 161, 263n13
5th Australian Division, 181
Fisk, Col. Willard C., 84
Fit to Fight (film), 32
Foch, Gen. Ferdinand, 42, 72, 94, 112
Forbes, Cpl. Burt T., 104
Ford, Col. Stanley, *155*
Foster, Sgt. Gary Evans, 196
Foulkes, Maj. Gen. C.H., 90
4th Australian Division, 129
France: American donations for rebuilding of, 227–28; brothels in, 55–57; German offensive in, 40–41; training of American troops by, 20; uneasy coalition with Britain, 10–11
French Army: discipline of, 64; relief of British positions by, 42
French First Army, 116
French front, 86; need for American troops on, 94–95
French Sixth Army, 72
French 38th Division, 30–31
French training instructors, 27, 38, 222
Friedman, Pvt. Robert P., 82
Front lines: British criticism of American performance on, 87; II Army Corps' training on, 79–84, 86–87; O'Ryan's pre-deployment observation of, 30–31; women visitors to, 72. *See also specific actions*

Gallipoli, 78
Gas warfare: allied use of mustard gas in Hindenburg Line offensive, 161; friendly attack losses, 90–91; training drills in, 28, 45–46; transportation of material for, 90
Gellibrand, Maj. Gen. Sir John, 174
General Staff College, Langres, 38
George V (England), 89, *138*
German American soldiers, 68
German Army: machine gun use by, 41; storm trooper tactics of, 39

Weapons and weapons training:
  delays in weapons issue, 84;
  machine guns, 28, 45, 46, 62;
  SMLE rifle, 71; Springlfield 03, 29
Wilson, Sir Henry, 77, 113, 120
Wilson, Woodrow, 15; on British
  offer to transport American
  troops, 18; resistance to
  amalgamation by, xi, 10
Wood, Leonard, 6
World War II, 219
Wytschaete-Messines Ridge, 13

Young, Col. Hugh H., 56
Ypres, First Battle of, 81
Ypres, Second Battle of, 161
Ypres, Third Battle of, 13, 57, 129

Ypres-Lys offensive, 98–106, *103*;
  after-action reports on, 108–10,
  128–29; battle of Vierstraat
  Ridge, 105–6; communication
  failures in, 109; enlisted men's
  impression of, 110; friendly fire
  incidents during, 102, 104;
  German assessment of American
  inexperience in, 99, 101, 109–10;
  medical units at, 161
Ypres sector, 80–81, 83
YWCA, New York City, 50, 51
YWCA hostess houses, 245n27

Zillebeke Lake, 81
Zone of advance system, 70